I0755758

Stones from Other Mountains

Published and Forthcoming by New Academia Publishing

Visual Culture, Popular Culture, Cinema

VISUAL CULTURE IN SHANGHAI, 1850s-1930s, edited by Jason C. Kuo

PERSPECTIVES ON CONNOISSEURSHIP OF CHINESE PAINTING, edited by Jason C. Kuo

SUPER HEROES: From Hercules to Superman, edited by Wendy Haslem, Angela Ndalianis, and Chris Mackie.

SHOPPING FOR JESUS: Visual Culture and the Marketing of Christianity, edited by Dominic Janes.

RUSSIAN FUTURISM: A History, by Vladimir Markov

WORDS IN REVOLUTION: Russian Futurist Manifestoes 1912-1928, A. Lawton and H. Eagle, eds., trs.

EVERY STEP A STRUGGLE: Interviews with Seven Who Shaped the African-American Image in Movies, by Frank Manchel.

HERETICAL EMPIRICISM, by Pier Paolo Pasolini.
Ben Lawton and Louise K. Barnett, trs., eds., with Ben Lawton's Introduction and the first approved English-language translation of Pasolini's essay, "The Repudiation of the 'Trilogy of Life'."

PIER PAOLO PASOLINI: In Living Memory, edited by Ben Lawton and Maura Bergonzoni

IMAGING RUSSIA 2000: Film and Facts, by Anna Lawton.

BEFORE THE FALL: Soviet Cinema in the Gorbachev Years, by Anna Lawton.

Art History

THE COMMUNITY ARTS COUNCIL MOVEMENT: History, Opinions, Issues, second edition, by Nina Freedlander Gibans

To read an excerpt, visit: www.newacademia.com

Stones from Other Mountains

Chinese Painting Studies in Postwar America

Edited with an Introduction by

Jason C. Kuo

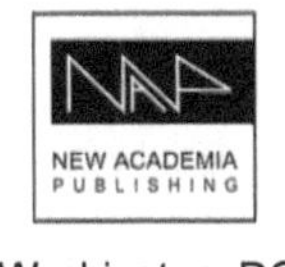

Washington, DC

New Academia Publishing, 2009

Printed in the United States of America

Library of Congress Control Number: 2009921178
ISBN 978-0-9818654-8-5 hardcover (alk. paper)

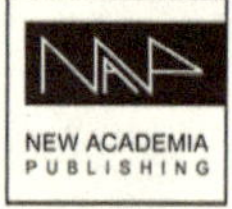

New Academia Publishing, LLC
P.O. Box 27420, Washington, DC 20038-7420
www.newacademia.com - info@newacademia.com

In gratitude
to
Richard Edwards
and
in memory of
Rudolph Arnheim

The crane cries in the ninth pool of the marsh,
And her voice is heard in the [distant] wilds.
The fish lies in the deep,
And now is by the islet.
Pleasant is that garden,
In which are the sandal trees;
But beneath them are only withered leaves.
The stones of those hills,
May be made into grind-stones.

The crane cries in the ninth pool of the marsh,
And her voice is heard in the sky.
The fish is by the islet,
And now it lies hid in the deep.
Pleasant is that garden,
In which are the sandal trees;
But beneath them is the paper-mulberry tree.
The stones of those hills,
May be used to polish gems.

Shijing or *The Book of Poetry*,
Part II, Book III, Ode X, trans. Legge

Contents

Acknowledgments

This volume was inspired by a conference I organized at the University of Maryland in November of 2005. Most of the essays are revised versions of papers presented at the conference. A few essays pertinent to the theme of the book have been added. I am most grateful to all the participants in the conference and the contributors to the book for sharing their insights. The conference and this volume were generously supported by the Department of Art History and Archaeology. My colleagues in the department have been generously supportive in all stages of the project. In particular, I would like to thank Sally Promey and Bill Pressly for their administrative and intellectual support. I am grateful to Quint Gregory and Lauree Sails of the department's Visual Resources Center for preparing the illustrations. I am also most grateful to James Harris, Dean, College of Arts and Humanities at the University of Maryland, for his support. I would like to thank all the cosponsors of the conference, such as the Center for East Asian Studies (directed by Robert Ramsey), the Institute for Global Chinese Affairs (directed by Chuan Sheng Liu), and the Center for Historical Studies, all at the University of Maryland, for hosting the event. Once again, I am grateful to Joel Kalvesmaki for his patient copyediting.

Jason C. Kuo

Note on Transcription

In general, the pinyin system of transcribing Chinese names and terms is used in this book. Exceptions include self-chosen names of modern Chinese scholars and artists (such as Chang Dai-chien, Wen C. Fong, Wai-kam Ho, C. C. Wang, Ju-hsi Chou, and Shen C. Y. Fu), names and terms in titles of publications using different systems of transcription (such as the Wade-Giles system), and a few names in Southern Chinese dialects. Japanese names and terms are transcribed according to the modified Hepburn system.

Introduction

Jason C. Kuo

The aim of this book is, through reflections on the writings of leading art historians of Chinese painting in Postwar America, to examine critically the historiography of the field of Chinese painting, to assess what achievements have been made, and to understand what and how personal backgrounds of scholars and institutional constraints (universities and museums, for example) may have affected various practices in the field. As the field of Chinese art history moves into postcolonial studies, institutional critique, and economic and social contextualization, it is especially important that questions of canon, value, historiographical interest, and large-scale historical structures not be left behind.

Starting with the Greek myth of the luxury and decadence of Asia, through Marco Polo's account of the gorgeous "East," to the influence of Japanese art on Manet, Whistler, and Van Gogh, to the French writer Victor Segalen's literary encounter with and "re-creation" of Chinese art, the story of Westerners' changing images, perceptions, impressions, and constructions of Asian art is a history of mutual misunderstanding and understanding between "East" and "West." In the writings on Chinese painting by some of the most well-known Western art historians and critics—for example, Roger Fry, Clement Greenberg, Ernest Gombrich, and Arthur Danto—the trope of "difference," however, is unmistakable.[1]

There is no doubt that the study of Chinese painting has, over the past five decades, made tremendous progress in the

United States, where Chinese, Japanese, Korean, and European expatriate scholars in Chinese painting have come to study and work. Many important, world-class collections of Chinese paintings have been formed and many exhibitions of previously unpublished paintings have been held in the United States. Furthermore, in American graduate programs painting has been the most popular subject for people working on their doctorates in Chinese art. For example, among the doctoral dissertations on Chinese art completed in the United States and Canada between 1939 and 1974, six were on general archaeological topics, five on ceramics, four on sculpture, and twenty-seven on painting.[2] The development of the field of Chinese painting in the United States has been shaped by a number of historical, cultural, and institutional factors. We must know what these factors were and how they have shaped the study of Chinese painting as an academic discipline if the field is to maintain its momentum.

Chapter 1 ("Is Art History a Global Discipline?") by James Elkins, who takes "globalism" to denote the sharing of interpretive methods, publishing protocols, and institutional structures (and not necessarily the sharing of subject matter), considers five reasons why art history around the world (art history in general) might be considered to be several disciplines instead of one; and then five reasons why it might be best to continue thinking of art history as a single enterprise. The decision affects how art history might be taught in different parts of the world, and it impinges on current ideas of multiculturalism. Elkins believes that imperfection is the order of the day—we have no choice but to balance Western and Chinese interests and ideas. He might not be as firmly committed to the idea of taking non-Western art on its own terms as it appears from the project called *Is Art History Global?* (edited by Elkins, with contributions by more than thirty scholars worldwide),[3] but he is very concerned about the unnoticed importation of Western ideas under the twin guises of (a) modernism, with its interest in visuality and intrinsic visual properties, and (b) institutional protocols, by which he means the apparatus of disciplinary art history—conferences, departments, publications, and the kinds of knowledge they admit or prefer.

In the first half of his "Visual, Verbal, and Global (?): Some Observations on Chinese Painting Studies" (Chapter 2), James Cahill discusses the ways in which Chinese painting studies in the United States and Europe since around 1950 have been especially strong in visual approaches, and not neglectful of the verbal or documentary. Reasons include the prominence of museums and their growing collections as centers for this study, and exhibitions and associated symposia. Specialists have come from diverse backgrounds and traditions, bringing their special strengths to form a richly multicultural and pluralistic practice. Proposals that we might "go in search of indigenous critical concepts" and "avoid Western interpretive strategies" (by Elkins in Chapter 1 of this volume) so as to embrace instead an indigenous Chinese tradition of studying painting raise serious difficulties that render them, he believes, unwise. The extant literature on which such a project would necessarily be based can provide only a very partial account of its supposed subject, and limiting ourselves to it would, among other things, cut short investigations increasingly pursued in areas of Chinese painting not treated in that literature.

The second half of Cahill's essay argues that adopting either of Elkins's more radical proposals for replacing our critical concepts and methods with those from the Chinese tradition as it is preserved in their literature on painting, moves that would be in keeping with Elkins's urgings toward the creation of a "global art history," would deeply impoverish our studies and not bring many benefits. Cahill attempts to define as a fundamental function of art history a process of sensitizing our students and readers to visual properties of the paintings, distinctions between them, and criteria of quality within them. In doing this, Cahill maintains, we should try to avoid imposing preexisting patterns and interpretations onto the Chinese materials, while realizing that we can do this only imperfectly.

In Chapter 3 ("Chinese Landscape Painting as Western Art History") James Elkins attempts to see how Chinese landscape painting appears through the lens of art history, a discipline that, he claims, is partly, but finally and decisively, Western. His subject is Chinese landscape painting, and he would like to understand it as well as he is able to, but he is equally interested in how the history of any non-Western art can be represented. This essay grew out of his inextinguishable interest in Chinese art, an interest that refused to shrink from a possible "minor field" into an avocation or pastime, an interest that slowly grew until it became, illogically, an emblem for art historical understanding in general. Although he is very much aware that he is not a specialist in Chinese art, he finds himself intrigued and often confused by the ways art historians present Chinese painting, and also by the very conditions of such understanding and representation.

That, at least, is Elkins's excuse for writing about Chinese landscape painting as if it could also be an inquiry into art-historical representation of any sort. The two problems have become entangled in his mind: the "general" philosophic question of representing other visual practices, and the "specific" example of Chinese landscape painting. At one moment Chinese landscape painting is just one art among many, and in the next it is the exemplary moment in which Western art-historical understanding encounters another tradition very much the West's equal in duration and complexity. At such times it becomes especially difficult to understand what it means that the major Western art historians, from Panofsky to Gombrich, from Schapiro to Belting—the historians who had the interest and means to look beyond Western practices—

remained centered on Western art. Can Chinese landscape painting ever appear as the *central* instance of painting? If it can, then it remains to be said why it does not. And if it cannot, then we need to come to terms with an inherently Western structure of historical understanding that prevents Chinese painting from being more than the most important, complex, fascinating example of non-Western painting.

Elkins argues that despite our best efforts at enlightened multiculturalism, *all* attempts to write the art history of non-Western cultures result in Western narratives that serve Western purposes and are supported by Western ideas. His position implies several critiques of the effects of postcolonial theory. It seems to him, for example, that postcolonial theory disguises hopeless interpretive situations as occasions for learning and analysis; that it fosters the illusion that we have a grasp of the art of non-Western countries; that it makes it seem as if a history of world art might someday again be possible, as it was thought in the nineteenth century; and that it implies art history is diverse and malleable enough to refashion itself in all sorts of new contexts. Chapter 4 ("The Cahill–Elkins Exchange") expands on their essays in Chapters 1, 2, and 3.

In Chapter 5 ("Narrative and Metanarrative in Chinese Painting"), Richard Vinograd focuses on James Cahill's *Chinese Painting,*[4] a major signpost in Chinese painting studies in Postwar America. While making the subject accessible to a broad audience, this book also shaped the agenda of the field for other and future scholars—identifying major artists and monuments, offering a scheme for understanding art-historical developments, and exemplifying ongoing projects of connoisseurship, attribution, stylistic analysis, and interpretation. *Chinese Painting,* like all books (or works of art), is a product of its time, editorial circumstances, and discursive environment. It might be easily contrasted with Cahill's own later writings and approaches, evolving even up to the present day, to offer an overview of the changing protocols and projects of Chinese painting studies over the past half century. A more pointed contrast is presented by Craig Clunas, who is now at Oxford University after a short tenure as the Percival David Professor of Chinese and East Asian Art at the School for Oriental and African Studies, University of London, in his *Pictures and Visuality in Early Modern China,*[5] useful in part because it is so self-conscious and explicit about its methods and intellectual orientations. Even a brief comparison of the two books reveals horizons of interest and approach so divergent as to suggest radically changed, if not fundamentally different, scholarly enterprises. This essay seeks to illumine those differences by looking at their constitutive narratives—not only their explicit subjects, storylines, and expositions, but their unspoken, overarching, and underlying metanarrative structures. These structures can be embedded narratives intertextually shared with other writings (for example painting-school categories, or the world system of early modernity), established theoretical positions (e.g., humanism, reception and consumption theory), or pervasive guiding assumptions (e.g., the significance of style, the ascertainability of quality and authenticity, taste as a marker of social distinction). Finally, this paper examines the role of visual narratives in Cahill's writing about Chinese painting, in comparison to Clunas's concern with visuality in Chinese culture.

Chapter 6 ("Authenticity, Style, and Art History: Wen C. Fong and Studies of Chinese Art History") by Harold Mok is a sympathetic assessment of the scholarship on Chinese painting by Wen C. Fong, one of the most eminent scholars of Chinese painting in Postwar America. Fong is currently the Douglas Dillon Curator Emeritus of Asian Art at The Metropolitan Museum of Art and Professor Emeritus of Art and Archaeology at Princeton. Fong's students have occupied important positions in universities and museums both in the United States and abroad.[6] When he retired, The Metropolitan's press release said, "In a career at the Metropolitan that spanned nearly thirty years, Fong played a major leadership role in building the Museum's vast Asian Art collection, expanding and renovating its Asian Art galleries, modernizing the department's conservation program, organizing dozens of acclaimed special exhibitions, and supporting both publishing and educational programs. Today the Asian Art collection at the Metropolitan is the largest and most comprehensive in the West, with each of the many civilizations of Asia represented by outstanding works that provide—in both quality and breadth—an unrivaled experience of the artistic traditions of nearly half the world." Mok's essay places Fong's scholarship in the historiography of Chinese painting studies in both China and Postwar America.

In Chapter 7 ("A Tale of Two Scholars: Cahill and Fong on Chinese Painting") I compare the writings of Wen C. Fong and James Cahill, two of the most distinguished scholars of Chinese painting in Postwar America, taking into account their backgrounds and their different strategies to establish the field of Chinese painting studies as an academic discipline within the larger field of art history. In his Afterword ("Chinese Art, European Art, Art") David Carrier reflects on the issues raised in the book from the viewpoint of recent scholarly interest in constructing a "world art history" that goes beyond the Eurocentric tradition of art historical narrative.

In the section on the "changing past" toward the end of one of Gombrich's most read books, *The Story of Art*, we read:

> Our knowledge of history is always incomplete. There are always new facts to be discovered which may change our image of the past. *The Story of Art* which is in the reader's hands was never meant to be anything other than selective, but as I originally said in my note on art books, "even a simple book like this may be described as a report on the work of a large team of

> historians, living and dead, who have helped to clarify the outlines of periods, styles and personalities.[7]

The present volume should perhaps be regarded similarly as such a report.

Notes

1 See, for example, Alice Yang, "Modernism and the Chinese Other in Twentieth-Century Art Criticism," in *Why Asia? Contemporary Asian and Asian American Art*, ed. Jonathan Hay and Mimi Young (New York: New York University Press, 1992), 129–46. E. H. Gombrich squeezed, into one short chapter, art in China with that from the Islamic world and Japan: "Looking Eastwards: Islam, China, Second to Thirteenth Century," in *The Story of Art*, 13th ed. (London: Phaidon Press, 1978), 102–12; there are twenty-seven chapters in the whole book. About Gombrich, see also James Elkins, *Stories of Art* (New York: Routledge, 2002), xi, xii, xv, 57–65, 129, 149, 151. For a more extensive discussion, see Martin Powers, "Art and History: Exploring the Counterchange Condition," *The Art Bulletin* 77, no. 3 (September 1995): 382–85.

2 *Communication and the Arts*, Comprehensive Dissertation Index, 1861–1972, vol. 31 (Ann Arbor: Xerox University Microfilms, 1973) and supplements for 1973 and 1974 (Ann Arbor: Xerox University Microfilms, 1975); *Dissertation Abstracts International* (Ann Arbor: Xerox University Microfilms, 1975).

3 (New York and London: Routledge, 2007).

4 (Geneva: Editions d'Art Albert Skira, 1960).

5 (Princeton: Princeton University Press, 1997).

6 See Jerome Silbergeld and Dora Ching, eds., *Bridges to Heaven: Essays on East Asian Art in Honor of Wen C. Fong* (Princeton: Tang Center for East Asian Art and Princeton University Press, forthcoming).

7 Ernst Gombrich, *The Story of Art*, 16th ed. (Upper Saddle River, N.J.: Prentice-Hall, 1995), 626.

1
Is Art History a Global Discipline?

James Elkins

What is the shape, or what are the shapes, of art history across the world? What kind of a discipline is it becoming?

I think the single most interesting question facing art history today concerns the possibility that the discipline may become global—that is, it may become a discipline that keeps a recognizable shape wherever it is practiced. "Globalism" (for lack of a better term) raises some especially thorny questions. Can the methods, concepts, and purposes of Western art history be suitable for art outside Europe and North America? And if not, are there alternatives that are compatible with existing modes of art history? A few years ago I found out that the basics of Western art history, such as formal analysis, periodization, and iconography, along with Wölfflin, Panofsky, and Gombrich, are currently being taught in art academies in Hangzhou and Nanjing, where they are applied to both Chinese and non-Chinese art. Is that a sensible development? And if not, what are the alternatives?

Here I consider these problems from two vantage points: first, I give five reasons why art history might be considered to already comprise several different practices, which vary from one place to another. If that is the case, then what happens to art historical practices in one place will not necessarily have any interest for scholars elsewhere. (I should note I am talking not about the subject matter of a monograph written in one country being of immediate interest elsewhere but about the methods, the form of the text, the questions it raises.)

Then I give five more reasons why art history can be considered a single, fairly cohesive enterprise: certainly not one that is homogeneous, and not one that is distributed evenly around the world, but a field that shares some basic concepts and purposes. In this way of thinking art history would be a little bit like a science. A science like physics can be said to share a rigorously defined set of assumptions no matter where it is practiced. The field of art history would be a looser, less quantitative version of that kind of coherence: its interests would be compatible wherever they are taught. (I'm trying to echo the language of the Bologna Accord here, since I think their models of globalism are good for thinking about world art.)

My notion is that by and large, for better or worse, art history is becoming a global enterprise. And to the extent to which that is true, what happens in art history in Austria, say, or in Slovakia, can in fact have consequences for art history here.

After my ten reasons I end with a brief conclusion.

Five arguments against the idea that art history is, or could become, a single enterprise throughout the world.

1. In smaller and developing countries, art criticism serves as art history, because newspaper reviews and exhibition brochures constitute the written self-description of the country's art.

In Paraguay there is a brilliant critic, Ticio Escobar, but he writes cultural criticism and art theory, somewhat along the lines of Homi Bhabha or Nestór Canclini. When I visited Paraguay in 2003, the only newspaper art criticism was being written by Olga Blinder, a painter at the Instituto del Arte Superior in Asunción. Her essays range over the history of Paraguayan modernism, and so they collectively form an ad hoc history, but one focused mainly on personal appreciations of painters. There is also a book on Paraguayan modernism, but it is mainly a collection of biographical facts and critical descriptions. There is no developed field of art historical research. The available texts could be said, justly, to be either biographical appreciations or postcolonial cultural criticism, which does not focus primarily on the history of fine art.

A few years ago the Getty Research Institute funded a project intended to produce English translations of major art historical texts from around the world. I was at one of the preliminary meetings, and one of the issues that became apparent right at the outset concerned the issue of what might count as art history. Several of us at the meeting said that when it came to art of the past two centuries, the project should really concentrate on newspaper art criticism and on the essays that appear in exhibition brochures. We wondered how many countries don't have art history as a discipline at all—Paraguay is one—and how many countries would understand art criticism to be art history.

2. Art history, as a named discipline and a department in universities, is principally known in North America and Western Europe.

One way to measure the presence or absence of art history in different parts of the world is to look at the number of universities that have departments of art history. There is no definitive list, and even if there were, the results would be blurred by the existence of art schools and art academies, which often have art historians on staff, although it can be impossible to determine who have degrees in art history and who are artists or critics. A country may have one or more universities that have departments in the history of art, and as many universities that offer a few courses in art history in other departments, so there is no clear cut-off point. In Colombia, for instance, Andrés Gratán of the Pontifica Universidad Javeriana informs me that six other universities in Bogotá have art history courses, and also two in Cali, two in Medellín, and one each in Santa Marta, Cartagena, and Bucaramanga. That list includes only a couple of art academies, and most of the universities do not have art history departments; instead they have departments of communication or design with art historians on staff. A visit would be necessary to determine how many of the instructors are trained in art history.

At the University College Cork we have assembled a database of nearly eight hundred institutions worldwide that have art history departments. Institutions included in our database must have art history departments, and even though that criterion is subject to discussion, we have some indications that the list is nearly complete. Art historians from Finland, Jordan, Singapore, Germany, and Denmark have written giving us definitive lists of institutions in their countries, and their lists have corresponded well with ours. So on that admittedly insecure ground I can draw some tentative conclusions about how widespread art history is as a named discipline. So far our list is drawn mainly from universities and colleges, and not yet from art schools and academies; and so these numbers should be taken as a sample and not in absolute terms.

The approximate number of institutions with departments of art history in Ireland and the U.K. is 97. The number for Continental Europe, including Turkey (which has 10 universities with art history departments), is 193. I have been told that Horst Bredekamp, who teaches at the Humboldt-Universität in Berlin, has said that the sum total of German-language publications on art history is the same as for English-language publications. (I have heard similar things from other German art historians, and it's true that English-speaking scholars tend to ignore the German literature.) Our database would indicate that Bredekamp's claim might not be true, because even without counting North America, German-speaking countries have fifty institutions and the U.K. and Ireland roughly double that. Eastern Europe and Southeastern Europe have relatively few institutions with art history departments: our database has two in Slovakia (one, the Slovak Academy of Sciences, is very active), two in Romania, and two in Bulgaria.

The number for the United States and Canada is 226, so it appears there is more art history being taught in the States than in all of Europe. Another caveat here is that smaller colleges in America are likely to incorporate art departments, so that what would in Europe be art colleges and academies are counted disproportionately. For South and Central America the number is forty-eight, although here as in Africa and parts of Asia the numbers are low largely because of the sporadic web presence of institutions. The actual number might be more on the order of eighty. For Africa our database has seventy-nine institutions, a number that is raised by a recent poll undertaken by the University of Maryland, which gives addresses for sub-Saharan countries, but is lowered by the very uneven web presence of African institutions. I was amazed to discover that the Ahmadu Bello University in Nigeria, the country's largest, with thirty-two thousand students, had no official web page until sometime in 2005. Our database has seventeen universities with art history departments in Australia and New Zealand; sixty-five in China, Japan, and Korea; thirty-six in Southeast Asia; and another half-dozen in Central Asia, where the low numbers reflect partly the Islamic tradition, and partly the influence of the Soviet system, which placed art academies and art history outside of universities.

This survey is incomplete in the ways I have mentioned, and also in that it has no entries for countries that I assume may have universities with art history departments, such as Belarus, Moldova, and Andorra in Europe; or Guinea, Liberia, Togo, Burundi, the Democratic Republic of the Congo, and Somalia in Africa. But the survey is fairly accurate and reasonably exhaustive, and the conclusion it suggests is that as a discipline and as a unit within universities, art history is very much a North American and Western European phenomenon.

3. Another reason to conclude that art history is not potentially global is its close affiliation to senses of national and regional identity.

It is a not-so-harmless truism that art historians' interests have traditionally been driven by their senses of what visual art in their own cultures seem most important. Hans Belting's wonderful little book *The Germans and Their Art: A Troublesome Relationship* chronicles, mercilessly, the dependence of generations of German art historians on changing ideas of Germany.[1] In the decades immediately after the Second World War, for example, the question of the nature of German art could hardly be raised, he says, because of the partitioning of the country. At other times, German art history was driven by notions of the essential Germanness of certain centuries, especially the late middle ages, or the supposed Germanness of artists such as Dürer or Holbein. (Oskar Bätschmann has also written some excellent papers on this.) Belting's book is a salutary read for anyone who assumes that art historians are driven by purely personal passions, unconnected to politics, or by a disinterested sense of historical veracity. Nationalism or ethnicity has been the sometimes explicit impetus behind art historical research from its origins in Vasari and Winckelmann. The current interest in transnationality and postcolonial theory has not altered that basic impetus but only obscured it by making it appear that art historians are now free to consider themes that embrace various cultures or all cultures in general.

A few years ago, I was working on a book called *Stories of Art*,[2] a response to E. H. Gombrich's ubiquitous, and very Eurocentric, *Story of Art*.[3] In the course of researching it, I looked up as many introductory surveys of art history as I could find. In the last half of the twentieth century, Gombrich's book was the world's best seller, followed by Helen Gardner's and—at a distant third—by Horst Janson's. (In some countries, including India and China, pirated and sometimes lightly rewritten editions are as common as the copyrighted originals.) Many countries have produced their own introductory art history textbooks, and I have seen examples printed in the last quarter century in Paraguay (as I mentioned), Egypt, Romania, Iran, Japan, India, Cambodia, the Czech Republic, Australia, and Turkey. Those books tend to be deeply nationalistic in motivation, and their nationalism can strongly affect their content. Burhan Toprak's *Sanat Tarihi* (1960), a Turkish textbook, tells the history of art from prehistory to gothic architecture and the Mérode altarpiece. Perhaps Chartres and the Mérode altarpiece seemed too Christian or too European for the author, because he veers aside and ends his book with two chapters on Hindu art and Japan. That arrangement may seem imbalanced, but my argument in *Stories of Art* is that it is better understood as a contrast with texts like Gombrich's, which are just as nationalist or regionalist in their own sense.

A slippery problem lies in wait here, because it may be impossible to read a book like Toprak's as a history of art rather than as a certain excerpt from the history of art: in other words, it may be not so much habit that makes Gombrich more congenial, as much as it is the structure of art history itself, which may be based on purposes that are themselves European.

4. A fourth reason to think art history is not, or will probably not be, global, is that it seems to be dissolving into image studies or visual studies.

Given the rapid increase in the proliferation of art historical research on all subjects, it seems that art history is growing such that it will soon encompass all visual practices and lose any sense of being a coherent discipline. There was an interesting exchange recently in the *Journal of Visual Culture* on this point, in which nine scholars responded to something Mieke Bal wrote, essentially celebrating the dissolution of disciplinary boundaries. Some of the respondents, including me, were roundly criticized by Bal in her reply for allegedly trying to police the boundaries of art history. Bal is at one extreme of the spectrum of ideas about disciplinarity and de-disciplinarity, but her exhilaration at the destruction of disciplines could be in line with the majority opinion.

An increasing amount of work tries to mix art history with neighboring disciplines (for example the journals *Representations, Res, Critical Inquiry,* and *Kritische Berichte*). And a rapidly growing number of journals are associated with visual studies, for instance, the *Journal of Visual Culture, Parallax, Invisible Culture* (published on the web at Rochester), *Cultural Studies, Third Text,* and even *Screen* and *Diacritics.*

All this could be taken as a sign that art history as we recognize it is on the verge of disappearing. Certainly a number of departments worldwide are currently threatened by visual studies—including my own department of art history at the Art Institute in Chicago, which is at the moment feeling threatened by the new department of visual studies. It's another question whether that means that the study of painting, sculpture, and architecture will be edged out, first by film studies, video, and new media, and then by the study of advertising, television, and eventually such things as graffiti and tattoos. There are universities where exactly that is happening, and the question is whether that is the wave of the future, or a fad that can be resisted.

If visual studies becomes ubiquitous, then art history may get a bit lost, whether or not it is a coherent enterprise at the moment.

5. My fifth and last reason to wonder about the worldwide coherence of the discipline is that there are different kinds of publications for different art historians.

This is an especially vexed question. It's true that certain publications have less to do with what gets called "theory," for example, *The Journal of the Warburg and Courtauld Institutes, Journal of Architectural Historians, Acta historiæ artium,* the *Annual Report of the American Academy in Rome, The Burlington Magazine, Antike Kunst, Artibus Asiae, Ars Orientalis,* the *Zeitschrift des Kunsthistorisches Institut in Florenz, Hesperia, Master Drawings, Oud Holland, Studies in Iconography, Antichità viva, Antologia di belle arti, Archivo español de Arte,* the *Römisches Jahrbuch für Kunstgeschichte, Dumbarton Oaks Papers, History of European Ideas, Bollettino d'Arte,* and *Storia dell'arte.*

It's also true that some journals seem to be more invested in "theory," for instance *October, Representations, Critical Inquiry,* the French journal *Critique,* the *Journal of Aesthetics and Art Criticism,* the *Zeitschrift für Kunstgeschichte, Kritische Berichte, Qui parle, SubStance, Heresies, Diacritics, boundary 2,* or *Glyph.*

Despite a lot of effort on the part of "theorists" to claim that there is no distinction between those who use theory and those who don't, the bibliographic division is real, and it reflects a disciplinary division. (I have suggested to some intransigent theory-types that if they believe there is no difference between these kinds of journals they try publishing something in, say, *The Burlington Magazine.*)

It's also true that some theories are limited in their appeal—they become popular briefly and then they disappear. Semiotics was revived at least four different times in the past century: once by the Prague linguistic school, again by Meyer Schapiro, by Hubert Damisch in the 1970s, and then by a number of scholars in the 1990s, including Mieke Bal. Anthropological theories of liminality, derived from Victor Turner, were very popular about ten years ago. I remember Norman Bryson had a session in one of the College Art Association meetings called "What Use is Deconstruction Anyway?" The newest thing seems to be Niklas Luhmann's "systems theory," which is being written about by Tom Mitchell, the Renaissance scholar Chris Wood, and Keith Moxey.

So I wouldn't deny that the discipline is fragmented by infatuations with evanescent theories. But there is also a counterargument, and so now I turn to the second part.

Five arguments in favor of the idea that art history is, or could become, global

1. The first argument that art history can be considered as a single discipline is the other side of the coin about theory. It can be argued that some of the best scholarship in the field is done by writers who know a lot about theories, and conversely that scholars who are not conversant with theories run the risk of producing texts that are out of touch.

This is a delicate subject so I give just a few examples. T. J. Clark's *Farewell to an Idea: Episode from a History of Modernism* is, I think, one of the best books on modern art that has been produced in the last few decades.[4] It seems to engage theories in an elliptic and idiosyncratic way, but it is actually built around deeply considered responses to Hegel, to poststructuralism in general (and semiotics in particular), and especially to Paul De Man. Although it may not appear so, Michael Fried is another example: his books include encounters with phenomenology, with psychoanalysis, and most recently with German idealist philosophy, including Robert Vischer. In medieval art history there is Michael Camille; any assessments of his relation to Meyer Schapiro, for example, would have to take on board his own understanding of poststructuralism and especially Derrida.

I could go on in this vein—the claim would be that art history is potentially unified, because the writers in fullest command of relevant theories are also those who are in fullest command of the existing scholarship. There is a parallel here to a discipline like physics, although I don't want to make too much of it—in physics, a researcher who did not know the most recent theories could presumably go on working, but her results might fail to attract the attention of physicists who were working on the current issues in the field.

2. A second reason to think art history is a coherent discipline is that the distinction between art history and criticism still holds.

Depending on your point of view regarding what David Carrier calls "artwriting," you might want to argue that art history and criticism are blurred or that their boundaries cannot be drawn with any useful degree of precision. I would argue that it is both easy and useful to distinguish the two, and that they can be separated using institutional, contextual, and commercial criteria.

Institutionally, art criticism is absolutely excluded from universities. There are classes on the *history* of art criticism—on Baudelaire for example, or on the reception of the New York School—but nothing on how to write art criticism. That subject is occasionally taught in art schools, but its rigorous exclusion from universities is a sign that it differs clearly from art history.

Contextually and commercially, art history is produced for different venues. Criticism can be found, of course, in magazines and newspapers, but art history is seldom found there. (The two do mix, at a grossly adulterated level, on television.)

The differences between art history and art criticism can be used to urge that art history is as different from art criticism as historical writing is from historical novels, or as anthropology is from anthropologists' memoirs: that is, they are not mutually exclusive but also not difficult to distinguish.

3. A third reason to say that art history remains coherent is that it focuses on a specific canon of artists.

I wonder if an informal poll of art historians might not show that most of us think that there is effectively no longer a canon in art history, if only because the discipline is expanding so quickly and so unpredictably. *Canon* is an odd-sounding word in art history because we have avoided the major debates about the canon (what are called the "canon wars") that sprang up in departments of literature and languages in America in the 1980s. The issue then was basically how to make room for women writers and writers from outside the West by displacing canonical figures like Plato or Sophocles. Art history avoided the canon wars by relying on the very large survey textbooks, which were simply enlarged to include artists of color, women artists, outsider artists, and postcolonial artists, without ever really displacing any artists that had composed the canon. (The canon is a current issue in the discipline.)[5]

One way of considering this is to distinguish between *intensive* and *extensive* scholarship. If the growth of the discipline were characterized by extensive scholarship, art historians would be studying new artists, new media, and new kinds of visual practices at an increasing rate. If the discipline's growth were due more to intensive scholarship, the field would be getting larger because there are increasing numbers of studies of the major artists—that is, the canon. A few years ago I got a special printout of two decades of entries of the *Bibliography of the History of Art*, one of the two largest databases in the discipline, from Michael Rinehart, who was then its editor. The printout arranges the scholarly output of the discipline according to the artists who were being written about. I collated the list and found that art history is still quite intensive: there is a canon of artists who are still studied disproportionately more than the many artists who have been studied only recently.

Here is the top-ten list for art history. The most frequently cited artists are:

1. Picasso, 757 times
2. Dürer, 616
3. Rubens, 600
4. Michelangelo, 537
5. Leonardo, 526
6. Raphael, 460
7. Rembrandt, 442
8. Titian, 418
9. Goya, 391
10. Palladio, 377

In terms of media, note that the top ten embraces painting, sculpture, and architecture. As the list continues it is clear that painting is really the canonical medium:

11. Van Gogh, 283 times
12. Turner, 270
13. Cézanne, 267
14. Brunelleschi, 243
15. Klee, 240
16. Matisse, 224
17. Bernini, 220
18. Alberti, 218
19. Courbet, 215
20. Le Corbusier, 214
21. Schinkel, 213
22. Caravaggio, 211
23. Delacroix, 209
24. Kandinsky, 205
25. Giotto, 203
26. Poussin, 202
27. Ingres, 201

28. Manet, 200
29. Blake, 199
30. Giorgione, 191
31. Velázquez, 181
32. Piranesi, 180
33. Friedrich, 177
34. Bosch, 163
35. Rodin, 162
36. Duchamp, 161
37. Brueghel the Elder, 160
38. Ernst, 159
39. Degas, 156
40. Munch, 155
41. Cranach, 154
42. Watteau, 152
43. Monet, 151
44. Viollet-le-Duc, 151
45. Gauguin, 147
46. Donatello, 145
47. Van Eyck, 145
48. Tiepolo, 144
49. Constable, 141
50. Lotto, 141

David didn't make the list (he is number 51).

These "outliers," as they say in statistics, are evidence of intensive scholarship.

Looking at things the other way around, it is possible to count the number of artists who are cited only once, those who are cited just twice, and so forth, so for example:

No. of citations	*No. of artists*
1	ca. 10,000
2	ca. 5,000

3 ca. 1,400
4 1,105
5 715

In this count it becomes apparent that the discipline is also growing extensively, with nearly twenty-thousand different artists cited five or fewer times.

In statistical terms, there is a broad middle region between these seldom-cited artists and the "outliers" like Picasso: that is the canon of art history, and it corresponds well with the contents of the large introductory art history textbooks.

4. Reason number four why art history is a more-or-less unified field: it is guided by a stable series of narratives, such as the story of the rise of illusionism told in Gombrich's *Art and Illusion: A Study in the Psychology of Pictorial Representation,*[6] or the familiar sequences of formal elements that lead from Greece and Rome through medieval uses to Renaissance "survivals" and postmodern "appropriations." These narratives have been questioned by feminist art historians and augmented by postcolonial theory, queer theory, and disciplines such as literary theory, but they still give sense and structure to introductory texts.

It has been argued that specialized monographs in art history owe little to these large-scale narratives, but I am not so sure. The reason for studying a particular artwork or an individual artist has to do with that artist's importance in the larger scheme of things. As art historians, I think we still depend on a relatively small number of "plots." Books with titles like *Modern Cambodian Art* or *Modern Art in Tibet* will sometimes begin with promises not to be beholden to Western historiography or examples, but in my experience they soon find themselves deeply indebted not only to the inevitable Western comparisons (so-and-so Philippine painter is influenced by Bernard Buffet, and so forth) but also to the

Western storylines of naturalism or anti-naturalism, or even the Wölfflinian stories about successions of "classical" and "baroque" periods.

The grip of our accustomed narratives is best demonstrated by the few books that try to break the mold. Stan Abe's *Ordinary Images*,[7] a book about provincial Taoist bas-reliefs in China, includes anomalous examples on purpose, to upset the reader's expectations that the material will fit into neat style categories or period sequences. The result, for me, is not a sense of a new kind of historical account, but a feeling of incompletion, as if the narrative has not quite ended where it should. Another example would be Georges Didi-Huberman's recent work on Aby Warburg: it creates an alternate narrative for art history—one that is founded on the *Pathosformel* and Didi-Huberman's Lacanian interpretation of it—but I wonder if his approach will seem like a fruitful alternative for many historians.

5. And finally, the fifth reason: art history depends on Western conceptual schemata.

Perhaps the most surprising fact about worldwide practices of art history is that there may be no conceptually independent national or regional traditions of art historical writing. Chinese art history, for example, demands expertise in very different kinds of source materials and formal concepts, but the interpretive strategies remain very Western. Chinese art historians, both in China and in universities in the West, study Chinese art using the same repertoire of theoretical texts and sources—psychoanalysis, semiotics, iconography, structuralism, anthropology, and identity theory. They frame and support their arguments in the same ways Western art historians do: with abstracts, archival evidence, summaries of previous scholarship, and footnoted arguments.

I think it can be argued that there is no non-Western tradition of art history, if by that is meant a tradition with its own interpretive strategies and forms of argument. Art historians in different countries vary in what they study, and there is a wide latitude in the kinds of interpretive methods that are employed. (Most scholarship, I think, takes iconography as its principal model.) But there is no such thing as an independent narrative or scholarly approach to the writing of the history of art that can be understood *as* a history of art. There are ways of writing about art's history that developed in India from the seventh century, and in China from the Han Dynasty; but those texts are not recognizable as art history, and a simple proof of their distance from current practice is that no art historian who chose to emulate those texts could get a permanent position in a university. None of the Chinese specialists I know who teach in Western universities were hired because of their ability to deploy indigenous historiographic methods; but part of their qualifications would normally be the ability to negotiate the principal Western methods, such as formal analysis and iconography. (Still, this is a contentious subject—it is debated, for example, by the Chinese specialist Craig Clunas—so I will just leave it here as a proposition.)

Some of the most ambitious books in art history in recent years attack this question of the Westernness of art history from different perspectives, and there is no clear consensus yet. There is Hans Belting's *Bild-Anthropologie: Entwürfe für eine Bildwissenschaft*, which expands art history in the direction of a Continental sense of anthropology;[8] John Clark's *Modern Asian Art*, which looks at east Asian art using institutional critique to evade Western categories;[9] and most ambitious of all, David Summers's *Real Spaces*, a monumental attempt to create an opportunity for a global art historical practice founded on Western ideas. All these books raise the most fundamental questions concerning the alternates to art history as we know it, and by doing so, and still remaining clearly Western, they demonstrate an underlying unity in art history.

Any one of these five reasons could be used to urge that art history is, or could become, a truly global enterprise in somewhat the way that physics is. For better or worse (since I am not judging here, just describing), art history could be thought of as a field whose subject matter changes with its location but whose assumptions, purposes, critical concepts, and narrative forms remain fairly consistent around the world.

To the degree that this is so, each national or regional practice of art history has connections to all the others. Art history is in fact something like a language or a game, and therefore it matters when it is not played with the full set of rules, or (in the language metaphor) spoken with a full vocabulary.

Notes

This is a very rough draft, intended for speaking; I have retained the colloquialisms of the talk (given at the University of Maryland in November of 2005) in part to keep a record of the event, and in part because this is the text to which Jim Cahill responds (in Chapter 2). A different version appears in my *Is Art History Global?* (New York: Routledge, 2007). This particular lecture was first given at the opening of the Irish Art Research Centre at Trinity College, Dublin, May 2004. A retrospective look at the issues raised by *Is Art History Global?* appears as "Can We Invent a World Art Studies?" in a book titled *World Art Studies: Exploring Concepts and Approaches*, edited by Wilfried van Damme and Kitty Zijlmans (Amsterdam: Valiz, 2008), 92–102.

1 (New Haven: Yale University Press, 1998).

2 (New York: Routledge, 2002).

3 See above, Introduction, n. 7.

4 (New Haven: Yale University Press, 1999).

5 See *Partisan Canons*, edited by Anna Brzyski (Durham N.C.: Duke University Press, 2007).

6 (New York: Pantheon Books, 1960).

7 (Chicago: University of Chicago Press, 2002).

8 (Munich: Wilhelm, 2001).

9 (Honolulu: University of Hawai'i Press, 1998).

2
Visual, Verbal, and Global (?): Some Observations on Chinese Painting Studies

James Cahill

Part I: The Verbal–Visual Issue

This first portion of my paper is an argument for the importance of a visual approach, in conjunction with the verbal or documentary approach—certainly not instead of it—in Chinese painting studies. My choice of this topic was occasioned by a situation I know about principally through correspondence and conversations with Chinese colleagues, but also from my own observations: the verbal–visual controversy in art history circles in China's academia today. And in that context, I must begin by acknowledging the technical and physical difficulties that our colleagues in China have had in setting up programs for studying their own tradition of art. I became acutely aware of those problems when I went around art academies and universities there in the 1970s and 1980s; and I understand from Chinese colleagues that despite some improvement, the problems are still serious: slide collections are not widely available to academics; expensive reproduction books are in limited availability; major painting collections are still not as widely accessible as we are accustomed to enjoying in the United States, and so forth. About all this I can only feel the deepest sympathy, and I join others in hoping that new technologies, such as relatively inexpensive visual databases of digitized images, will alter the balance toward more incorporation of the visual into the teaching and scholarship of Chinese painting in China.

Everything I write, then, in commenting on this controversy—on the basis of my limited understanding of it and coming down heavily on the side of the visual, or at least of better balance—acknowledges this problem in China and is addressed only at deliberate, theoretically argued choices to downplay the visual. My understanding of this controversy, and especially of the powerful anti-visual faction in Chinese academia, is based also on a paper that Professor Ding Ning of Beijing University has contributed to James Elkins's long-term project "The Art Seminar," and which I read through the kindness of Elkins. Professor Ding's paper, titled "Verbal Above Visual: A Chinese Perspective," begins by outlining the historical background to what he calls the "emphasis on the verbal" in Chinese scholarship, as opposed to the visual, which he says has been "effectively marginalized." He goes on to describe the present situation in graduate programs in art history in China, without himself ever coming out in favor of their heavily verbal emphasis; in fact, he asserts in his final paragraph, "The interpretation of images should be the primary and uppermost task of art history." But he does not hold out much hope that this will come about soon or easily.

I was made aware of this widespread disinterest in the visual from the time I began lecturing and publishing in China: journal editors came up after one of my lectures (illustrated with slides) and wanted to publish my text, but were unconcerned about the pictures, even when I pointed out that the lecture was virtually meaningless without them; translations of my writings were published in China with a crucial painting missing from the illustrations, and nobody seemed to notice its absence, even though it is discussed at length in the text. I must add, however, so as not to exaggerate the real situation, that I have also read excellent recent writings on Chinese painting by Chinese specialists who make skillful and effective use of visual materials, and I have worked with publishers there who are sensitive to the need for adequate illustrations. What I am arguing against is only a tendency, or proclivity, one also recognized by others, and acknowledged by those engaged in it.

Studies of Chinese painting in the United States and Europe since around 1950 have undergone a remarkable development as a number of scholarly traditions have converged. From China, artist-connoisseurs such as Wang Chi-chien (C. C. Wang) and Chang Dai-chien, collectors such as Wan-go Weng, and scholars such as Wen C. Fong, Nelson I. Wu, Wai-kam Ho, and Chu-tsing Li, later Ju-hsi Chou, Mayching Kao, and Shen C. Y. Fu, have brought with them their backgrounds in Chinese connoisseurship and scholarship. Osvald Sirén, a Finn who lived and worked in Sweden, applied to Chinese painting what he had learned from Bernard Berenson and others. German art historians, notably Max Loehr but also Ludwig Bachhofer, whose work was carried on by his students, especially Harrie Vanderstappen, applied to Chinese art history the methods of the great German foundations of art history. From Japan, scholars such as Shūjirō Shimada and Kiyohiko Munakata brought to the field some of the special strengths of the Japanese tradition of appreciating and writing about Chinese paintings. The British school of writing about art and aesthetics was drawn on productively by Michael Sullivan, John Hay, Roderick Whitfield, later Craig Clunas and others. American scholars, notably Laurence Sickman, Alexander Soper, Sherman Lee, and Richard Edwards came from the art history and sinology programs in our universities to make major contributions to Chinese art studies. (I leave out American specialists younger than myself, which means virtually all those extant—a clever tactical move, I think.) And all of us American scholars learned from these people, as well as from specialists who continued to work in China, Japan, and Europe; and all of us, whatever our backgrounds, learned from each other, trying to incorporate some of what we found most useful into our own work. The interaction among us and the approaches we represented, although often contentious, has always, I think, been beneficial; and the outcome, although still far short of real synthesis (an ideal that in any event can never be realized, nor should it be), is a rich, multicultural, and pluralistic product, less a method than a cluster of different methods, transcending any of the lineages that went into it. It cannot by any means be dismissed simply as "Western art history," since it is far more than that.

Now, while all these different strands that have fed into the present state of Chinese painting studies have followed different patterns of research in documentary materials, they have also brought with them different ways of looking at the paintings, reading the paintings, dealing with them visually. The important thing for my present argument is that they all have seriously pursued the visual, alongside their diverse research into written materials, and that this has been central to most of the achievements that have led up to our present, I believe fundamentally healthy, state.

The first grand get-together of Chinese painting specialists, a two-day "Palace Museum Exhibition Post-Mortem Symposium" organized by myself and held at Asia House in New York in October 1962, was almost entirely visual: a number of us, including most of those I listed earlier, argued for two days about paintings, especially early landscapes, that had been in the great "Chinese Art Treasures" exhibition from the National Palace Museum in Taiwan, debating issues of dating, authorship, and authenticity. We did this almost entirely on the basis of visual observation, with slides of the paintings to which we could refer on the screen before us and our audience. This was, I feel, a good start for the field, and it was followed by a long period during which arguments of that kind continued, for better or worse, to be central to our interactions. When asked why this was so, we were inclined to reply that any other mode of dealing with the paintings, if pursued before we had established a relatively solid foundation of general consensus on dates and attributions for the key works, would be like building on sand. That is the answer I would give, for instance, to Svetlana Alpers in the later 1960s, after I had moved to Berkeley, when she wondered why we were still pursuing this hopelessly backward kind of art history. Historians of Western art, for whom this was no longer remotely a problem, heirs as they were to several generations of hardworking Europeans (and a few Americans, such as Berenson) who had built for them the kind of comfortable foundation we were now trying to build for ourselves, found it hard to understand our preoccupation with establishing a more-or-less secure "corpus" within our materials of study. We are still far short of having accomplished that desirable goal; but we are a lot closer to it than we would have been if we had ridden off madly in all directions, so to speak, from the beginning.

Chinese specialists who lean toward the verbal approach also, of course, have their own system of dealing with authenticity problems, one that belongs within a distinctly Chinese tradition: it relies heavily on seals and inscriptions, colophons and catalog references. Without wanting to downplay the importance of that system, I would see it as a supplement, never a substitute, for judgments based on visual studies of the paintings. It has been used effectively by some Western scholars as well, notably Richard Barnhart, who combines it with high-level visual studies.

The next point I want to make, and make strongly, is that even those who have thought of themselves, and have been thought of by others, as primarily book-readers have managed to combine their strengths in that pursuit with valuable kinds of engagement with the paintings. Let me exemplify that statement with three names (and I hope that the only survivor among them will not object to being in the list): Wai-kam Ho, Shūjirō Shimada, and John Hay. John, to take his case first, is perhaps the most widely read among us in general aesthetic theory, and the one who has most brilliantly brought his broad and deep understanding of it into his writings. But when he has had occasion to write about paintings, he has done that also in unexpected and enlightening ways, as when he reads Huang Gongwang's "Fuchun Mountains" scroll in terms of Chinese geomancy.

Wai-kam Ho was trained in the two best Chinese history programs of his time in China, at Lingnan and Yenjing Universities, before he came to this country around 1950 and took another degree in Chinese history and Asian art at Harvard. It would be superfluous and presumptuous to speak of the extraordinary strengths of his writings, which must be known to this audience. When I chaired a Chinese painting delegation during a month-long visit to China in 1977, Wai-kam was the only one among us who took no photographs of the hundreds of paintings we saw; instead, he studied them intensely while we were popping our flashguns, and wrote constantly in his notebook, noticing details that the rest of us missed. Wai-kam, while basically a historian, adapted with difficulty (he was notoriously unhurryable) but in the end successfully to his role as museum curator, exercising his visual faculties in helping Sherman Lee to choose and write about paintings for the Cleveland Museum of Art, and in organizing exhibitions, with the great "Century of Tung Ch'i-ch'ang [Dong Qichang]" (1992) as the climax.

I will admit that Wai-kam was one of those I had in mind when I expressed in a 1976 article some impatience with heavily-text-based kinds of scholarship, which I referred to as "artless studies of art."[1] But that was a brief methodological complaint, balanced by things that Wai-kam found to complain about (with good reason) in my own writings, and did not hurt our relationship, which was over the years one of mutual respect.

Shūjirō Shimada was at his strongest when dealing with the kinds of paintings especially preserved and appreciated in Japan, the Song–Yuan period works, most of which had been brought there centuries earlier and with which he was closely familiar from long study; those were the main materials for much of his teaching at Princeton. But he also knew intimately Japanese collections of Ming–Qing paintings such as the former Kuwana Tetsujō collection, most of it later owned by Hashimoto Sueyoshi, and the great collection of Sumitomo Kan'ichi with its masterworks by Bada Shanren and Shitao. He took me to see these and other collections during my Fulbright year in Japan in 1954–55, when he was teaching at Kyoto University a course that involved a close reading of Guo Ruoxu's *Tuhua Jianwen Zhi,* using Soper's new translation as a supplementary text. Here were visual and verbal approaches separately exemplified at their highest; and his long article on the *yipin* or "untrammeled" style, which I later translated, offered an equally exemplary model of how they could be combined and made to interact. Like other Japanese scholars of his generation, Shimada wrote only about paintings he had studied in the originals—his book on Song–Yuan painting, like Yonezawa Yoshiho's on Ming painting, used only works in Japanese collections. This was both a strength and a weakness, the weakness not to be overcome until, from the later 1950s on, Suzuki Kei, Kohara Hironobu, and others of the younger generation began to travel abroad and see collections there. But above all, Shimada's practice represented a dependence on firsthand visual experience of the works, and expressed a deep trust in that experience.

I was surprised at first to see Shimada making careful sketch copies of paintings he was shown; later I realized that this was a common Japanese practice. I encountered it again in Nishimura Nangaku, a *kanteika* or "authenticator"—professional connoisseur—whom I was taken to meet while I was working on the early Nanga-school master Sakaki Hyakusen, since he had written about that artist. When I showed him photos of Hyakusen works in the United States, he made sketch copies of them from the photos before he delivered his judgments on their authenticity. The same practice was common, of course, to the Kano-school painters who had performed the same function in earlier times, and who have left us albums and scrolls of *shukuzu*, reduced-size sketch-copies, that they had made from paintings they were shown; these are still valuable as records of works now mostly lost.

Behind this practice, which is peculiarly Japanese—I cannot recall seeing a Chinese connoisseur, or a German art historian, doing the same, although there may well be those who did it—behind this lies the Japanese concentration on the visual image over the execution of the work, a concentration that sets their mode of appreciation apart from the Chinese. In its extreme form it prefers the simple, isolated image that is central to both Zen and tea-ceremony taste, producing as it does a sharp, immediate visual experience that works like a metaphor for Zen enlightenment. (It was some adherent of that taste and doctrine who cut the fisherman in his boat from a Ma Yuan painting to suit it for hanging in the toko-no-ma of a tea-ceremony room, another who cut off the left end of Yujian's painting of the "Waterfall on Mt. Lu" to simplify and focus the image, another who cut up what was presumably a Muqi handscroll to produce the famous "Six Persimmons," "Hibiscus," and "Chestnuts" pictures.) The Japanese have not until very recently, by contrast, paid much attention to those areas of Chinese painting that were, for Chinese literati connoisseurs, the highest peaks of the art: Huang Gongwang, Ni Zan, and other Yuan masters; Shen Zhou and Wen Zhengming in the Ming; Dong Qichang and the Four Wangs and their following in the later periods. Such works were not totally absent in Japan, but they were rare, and generally underappreciated, except by certain Nanga artists who had become dimly aware, largely through reading, of this disparity between Japanese and Chinese connoisseurship. On the whole, the Japanese never quite understood or adopted the Chinese brushwork aesthetic until quite recently; their appreciation of Chinese paintings came mostly through their responses to them as pictorial images, apprehensible by the eye and not to be intellectually theorized as they were in China.

The difference between this mode of appreciation and that of Chinese connoisseurs such as C. C. Wang and Chang Dai-chien, with both of whom I also spent a lot of time looking at paintings, was striking. It is true that Chang Dai-chien made small sketches of passages from well-known paintings from memory while we talked about those paintings during my first meeting with him in Kyoto in 1954; and it is true also that Chinese professional artists commonly made small sketch-copies, or *fenben*, from paintings they saw for later use. The difference lies in a certain divorcement of these Chinese artists and connoisseurs from those who practiced academic scholarship, a divorcement that may have prefigured, I now realize, the visual–verbal controversy in present-day China. The Chinese have, that is, their own practitioners of visual approaches, but they tend not to be those who teach art history in universities.

The importance of the visual within Chinese painting studies in the United States is indicated also by the time, effort, and resources that have been devoted to building slide collections and photographic archives, and disseminating these materials to art history programs and museums. Unhappily, as I noted at the beginning, nothing comparable has been possible in China, and that failure is in some part responsible for the relative weakness of the visual approach in art history there. The ease and inexpensiveness, for us, of making 35 mm color slides from Chinese paintings—their paper and silk surfaces, for one thing, did not reflect light from a flashgun as varnished oil paintings do, so the problem of glare was avoided—and the need for multiple shots of a single work (whole and details, leaves of an album or sections of a handscroll)—have made these a prime resource for our research and teaching, more so for some of us than the black-and-white photos on which earlier art historians depended.

As my students will recall, I began every seminar with a long slide-show, which may have gone on over several two-hour sessions: showing slides of paintings of the kinds we were to deal with and talking about them, trying to instill a common visual acquaintance with our materials in the seminar participants, along with a tentative organization of these materials and equally tentative observations about them. Often these opening formulations had changed a good deal by the end of the seminar. But they started us off on the right basis, I think: ideas and information were linked from the beginning with the paintings. I am not offering my practice as any kind of model, but as a working method it still seems to me a good one. In my Anhui-school seminar, the one that led to the 1981 "Shadows of Mt. Huang" exhibition, four pairs of students explored issues raised by the paintings and the historical circumstances around them: the relationships of the paintings to Anhui pictorial printing; to the topography of the region, especially Huangshan; to developments in painting theory in that period; and to economic factors and patronage, the Huizhou merchants and their culture.[2]

Slidemaking is, of course, rapidly becoming obsolete, replaced by digital imagery. This means that Chinese scholars and teachers can, if they choose, leapfrog the slidemaking era entirely and adopt the new technologies, as their funding and facilities permit.

Another argument for the visual approach is this: if visual mastery of special areas of art is not taught, who will become the museum curators, the dealers, the auction specialists? Arnold Chang, who was in charge of Chinese painting for Sotheby's auction house in New York during the great period of the 1970s and 1980s, was enrolled in my heavily visual three-semester Chinese painting course and seminars at Berkeley, then studied traditional Chinese connoisseurship with C. C. Wang, wanting, as he saw it, to "get the best of both traditions." Will future aspirants to that kind of career be able to enjoy similar training? What are the possibilities open to anyone who wants to pursue careers of these kinds in China, where auctions of paintings and calligraphy are booming?

Museum curators, of course, can come from backgrounds other than art history programs. One type of specialist found among our ranks has been the sinologue-in-the-museum: Wai-kam Ho was a good example, and Aschwin Lippe at The Metropolitan, whose doctoral dissertation was a translation of the Li Kan treatise on painting bamboo, but who went on to organize the first exhibition of a regional school of painting, his Nanking-school exhibition held at China House in New York in 1955.

I comment below on Max Loehr's strengths. Here I note merely that the contributions of the German art historians to the visual approach scarcely need be pointed out, since they virtually invented it. Osvald Sirén, at one time the best-known European specialist in Chinese art, should have been a central figure in visual studies of Chinese painting, since he was a pupil of Bernard Berenson and set out to do for Chinese painting what Berenson had done for Italian. But Sirén never had a really good eye for painting, as Alexander Soper pointed out in a review of Sirén's seven-volume *Chinese Painting: Leading Masters and Principles*, which had been published in 1956–58. I had worked with Sirén on that in Stockholm for three months in early 1956, and knew too well his weaknesses, not only in judging authenticity (he had purchased two terrible "Xu Wei" fakes, along with others as bad, for the collection of the National Museum in Stockholm) but also in distinguishing individual and regional styles within Chinese painting, and in writing perceptively about them. Nor were those weaknesses compensated by sinological strengths: he scarcely read Chinese, and depended on others for translations and information from texts. He was essentially a compiler, a gatherer;

I remember talking with Jan Fontein in Amsterdam on my way back from working for Sirén, and saying that for our generation he was like the person who goes through the blackberry patch picking all the berries that are within easy reach, leaving it for us later people to scratch our hands getting the harder ones.

Vastly superior models among Western scholars were two of my colleagues at the University of California in Berkeley, Svetlana Alpers and Michael Baxandall: I attended many of their lectures, read their writings, talked with them at every opportunity, argued with them (especially with Svetlana), but also received invaluable guidance from them. Svetlana's *Art of Seeing,* Michael's *Painting and Experience in Fifteenth Century Italy,* along with their other writings: one could hardly do better in choosing models for joining visual studies of painting to historical research and theoretical concerns. Michael and I became friends, sharing a favorite pop-thriller writer (Ross Thomas), and attending each other's lectures; I quote him probably more often than anyone else I quote outside the Chinese art world, mostly because what he writes is always intelligible, and because he addresses productively the major problems, offering original and workable ways of negotiating some of them, along with admonitory rules for how not to do it. I mention this personal example simply to point out the obvious: our visual treatments of Chinese paintings must depend heavily, for some part of their methodology, on the much-longer-established and more-highly-developed practice of our Western-art colleagues. If we oblige our students to take courses and seminars with those colleagues, as we should, that is the reason. And if they end up improperly applying patterns they learn from Western art history to their Chinese materials, the gain, I feel, still heavily outweighs the danger.

Another virtue of the visual approach is that it permits us to explore areas of Chinese painting that are ignored, or nearly so, in Chinese texts. All serious students of Chinese painting and its literature know that Chinese writings on painting are unmatched, at least until very recent times, in their volume and sophistication, But we know also that these writings are partial in both senses: they are partial to the literati or scholar-amateur artists and their works, and they write about only a part of Chinese painting, paying little or no attention to large areas of it that we may want to study today. A visual approach allows us to work where documentation is lacking, using the paintings themselves, the relationships between them, and their analyzable imagery as our data. Some of these areas will belong to the kinds that traditional Chinese connoisseurs consider low-class, but that should not deter us. I myself still believe that distinctions can and should be made between significant works of art, and pictures that belong rather to studies of visual culture, but it is probably best not to assign any work or group of works to one or the other category too quickly or too firmly. A great many paintings exist, especially in foreign collections, that have been turned into "fakes" by dealers who added spurious signatures and early attributions to what were originally honest Ming–Qing works; often we can restore these to their proper art-historical positions, even determine their authorship, on the basis of their style and imagery. C. C. Wang was expert at this; Richard Barnhart has done it in some of his work, as have others, including myself. Others who have dealt with undocumented or poorly documented materials include Marsha Haufler in her studies of paintings by women or late-period Buddhist works, and Lothar Ledderose on the "Kings of Hell" series mostly preserved in Japan. Still others have done unexpected things within the canon on the basis of visual evidence, in ways unauthorized by the literature: Wen Fong's "structural analysis" studies and his collaboration with Sherman Lee on the *Streams and Mountains Without End* monograph, Ellen Laing's studies of the paintings of Qiu Ying, Jerome Silbergeld on Gong Xian and the Li–Guo school in the Yuan, Richard Vinograd's writings on Yuan landscape and on portraiture, Jonathan Hay in his recent book on Shitao and his articles on Jin Nong and Luo Ping—all these, along with many others, have gone far beyond where written sources could carry them in illuminating and expanding important areas of Chinese painting history.

My own work in recent years has been mostly of this kind, a radical departure from my early period in which, for instance, I scanned reams of Song and later writings searching for quotes and clues that could be used in putting together a tentative account of literati painting theory (which made up the long opening section of my doctoral dissertation). Now I scan auction catalogs and other sources of "low-class" and vernacular paintings of the kinds that make up the materials for my book *Pictures for Use and Pleasure: Vernacular Painting in High Qing China,* and for my project of trying to define a body of Ming–Qing paintings done mainly for an audience of women, as well as for other projects similarly risky and largely unsupported by written evidence. Studies of intercultural exchanges in the arts—China and the West, Japan and China—of the kind that some of us have engaged in, and that have opened up in a healthy way in recent years, are likely to be similarly dependent on readings of the visual materials, and to go more or less undocumented, because of the touchiness of these issues and the reluctance of many writers, especially those verbally oriented, to recognize that the interchanges took place at all. The lack of textual evidence cannot be taken as a deterrent to our pursuing these studies—if the visual evidence is compelling, open-minded and open-eyed viewers will accept it, and the skepticism of others will in the end be inconsequential.

I learned long ago to shrug off—and I would strongly advise others to do the same—the frequently heard criticisms of visually oriented studies on the grounds that they lack any solid foundation. I remember well Noel Barnard, with whom I was working in the early 1960s on the Freer Gallery's catalog of its Chinese ritual bronzes, deriding the stylistic approach of Max Loehr, which I was trying to apply in my catalog entries on style and chronology, as merely a matter of personal feeling, with no objective basis or value. Robert Bagley, a Loehr student, was met with similar reactions when he tried talking about bronze styles with Chinese specialists while working on The Metropolitan's "Great Bronze Age of China" exhibition of 1980. My own writings on painting have frequently encountered similar responses. The typical charge is, "He doesn't have any real evidence," by which the speaker or writer means, of course, written or documentary evidence. One feels frustrated, typically, because a visual argument that is entirely convincing, even blindingly obvious, to anyone open to reading visual data will make no impression on those who are not; one can only point, saying "Look! Look!" and collapse into despair when they don't look, or won't. And as often as not, the one who complains about "lack of evidence" knows perfectly well that because the aspect or area of painting under consideration lies outside the limited range of what the traditional Chinese critics and theorists felt to be worthy of their attention, there isn't going to be any written evidence for it. To insist, then, on documentation as the only legitimate basis for studying that area of Chinese painting is in effect to rule out serious consideration of it—which is exactly the underlying purpose and message of such criticism: Stay within the boundaries that we and our predecessors have drawn for you! That implicit admonition should be taken as a strong motivation for moving even more determinedly into the would-be forbidden territories, opening them up for further investigation, breaking the taboos wherever we find them.

Other than that, there is nothing I know of that we can do in the face of determined mistrust of the visual except to go on teaching our students what we ourselves know to be true about it, and continuing to practice visual studies of Chinese painting (along with textual and theoretical) as responsibly and convincingly as we can, both to provide useful models for others who may wish to do it, and simply to keep the practice going.

I will end this section by stating several things that I hope will happen before too long, as they will need to if I am to have the pleasure of watching them happen. First, I hope that the visual–verbal controversy can be divorced, in the thinking and arguing of both Chinese and foreign scholars, from the issue of foreign versus indigenous modes of art history; they need not be linked, and should not be. Our discussions could then proceed with less danger of touching uncomfortably on cultural sensitivities. Second, I hope that more of our colleagues in China will recognize that Chinese painting studies as they have come to be practiced in the United States and Europe, and increasingly in other parts of the world as well, are not by any means simply "Western," but embody methods and insights brought by Chinese as well as Japanese and Western scholars who have been engaged in them. For those in China now to adopt from these studies what seems useful to them, of their own volition, should thus carry no onus of betraying the indigenous tradition. Third, I hope that as digital imagery and other new technologies encourage Chinese scholars to move toward a better balance of visual and verbal in their work and their teaching, they will develop distinctively Chinese ways of looking, of engaging visually with the paintings, drawing on the great Chinese tradition of visual study and connoisseurship of individual works. (I certainly do not mean to imply that this kind of balance and synthesis is not being accomplished at all today, but only that it is not yet widespread enough to constitute a general collective practice.) By combining this Chinese mode of visuality, in which the reading of seals and inscriptions becomes a part of the visual experience as one appreciates their design and calligraphic quality as one reads their texts, with attention as well to brushwork and other aspects of style and to the painting as a picture, adding to these the Chinese specialists' unmatched mastery of the documentary sources, they will bring into being a practice that can be considered a truly Chinese history of Chinese painting. The interaction between that and the present multicultural one practiced outside China will, I think, be healthy and highly productive.

Part II: Elkins's Proposals for "Globalizing" Chinese Painting Studies

Sometime in 1991 I began a correspondence with someone I had not met named James Elkins, who had sent me an essay he had written titled "Chinese Painting as Object Lesson." I read it with great interest, having had thoughts in a similar direction myself, and sent him a very positive response, along with some suggestions for minor improvements. His essay began:

> Chinese landscape painting can be an "object lesson," that is, an analogy for understanding the course of Western painting from antiquity to postmodernism and beyond. It is possible, I will suggest, to make a reading of the Chinese tradition, and specifically of its developing sense of its own history, that runs parallel to essential developments in Western concepts of the history of painting.

I myself still believe this contention to be true, and well stated. Its author, however, has in a complicated way pulled away from it without really renouncing it. After his essay in its original form had been rejected by several journals (for what I believe to be bad reasons), he substantially rewrote it under the title "Chinese Landscape Painting as Western Art History." This also—except for the selections in Chapter 3 below—remains unpublished in English, but has been published in Chinese translation.[3] In this he takes a very different direction, arguing instead that any history of Chinese painting written today must by necessity follow the patterns of our familiar Western art history, so that (if I understand correctly the implications of his argument) what he saw before as "object lesson" and "analogy" are no more than products of the (Western) way in which the art-historical account is written. This argument has led, in turn, to his present concern with the possibility of a "global art history" or "world art history" within which writings about the art of non-Western cultures might escape this subjection to European modes of thinking and writing about art, and not have imposed on them the narratives of Western art, such as those centered on space representation and illusionism (the latter associated especially with the writings of Ernst Gombrich.) I do not mean now to engage myself in this problem as such, but only to respond to two of his proposals for ways this "global art history" might be achieved, as Elkins sets them forth in his review of David Summers's 2003 book *Real Spaces*.[4]

I must insert here a proper disclosure: I am not myself widely read in aesthetics or philosophy more generally, or nearly so widely in the general literature of art history as is Elkins, who is an art-historical and art-theoretical polymath and omnivore. I have an uncomfortable feeling that in my conversation with him, I will sound like someone responding with trivialities to matters of serious import. I can only say that my arguments as they will be made below, however naïve they may sound and however weak in theoretical grounding, are not trivial for me, but represent deeply held convictions formed over quite a few years of teaching and writing. Anyone who feels that an untheorized art history is not worth practicing will be frustrated by what follows. Also, my pairing of teaching and writing represents accurately my view on that matter: the two practices have scarcely been separate in my work. So references below to art history are to both pedagogy and published scholarship: these are, for me, merely different ways of reaching an audience, a readership, a body of students.

In the final pages of his review of Summers's *Real Spaces,* Elkins offers five possibilities for responding to the problem of moving toward a global art history, from the most "intellectually conservative" to the most radical. He sees *Real Spaces* as midway along the scale. I myself would, I am afraid, have to be located still further back, either still committed to his first, "Art history can remain essentially unchanged as it moves into world art" (he finds this position the "most potentially destructive of the coherence and interest of art history") or groping into his second, "Art history can redefine and adjust its working concepts to better fit non-Western art." I would suggest that good art historians working in non-Western fields do this second without necessarily formulating it as an objective, and without separating themselves clearly from the "potentially destructive" first option.

Elkins's third option—"Art history can go in search of indigenous critical concepts" and, as he elaborates with examples, adopt the native terms for these into its vocabulary—is attractive in theory but, I think, impractical if carried much beyond present practice, to the point where it would constitute a new mode of art-historical writing. Is each foreign writer on a non-Western artistic tradition to choose and employ a set of native terms for what he or she sees as the key concepts, and expect the reader to learn them all—along with the different set of terms used by each other foreign writer? I am certainly not opposed to introducing the native words for a limited number of ideas and qualities that are unfamiliar to foreign readers, and explaining them—I could make a list of the ones I myself introduced in early writings on literati painting theory, and others have done the same. But we mostly explain the indigenous concepts using our own vocabulary, pointing out how empty or void are not exact equivalents for the Chinese *kong* (Elkins's example) but continuing to employ what we take to be the closest equivalents. We explain the non-Western concepts as best we can—in my case, concepts derived mostly from reading Chinese texts, or from colleagues' readings of them—and try to take account of them in our own writings. But we can never assume simply that these provide a "right" way of interpreting the foreign works of art, as opposed to our own "wrong" way. (Later on I will give reasons for saying that.)

Elkins's fourth option, "Art history can attempt to avoid Western interpretive strategies," also sounds attractive but still breaks down, I think, when we consider how it would be applied. He writes that Professor Cao Yiqiang of the China Academy of Art in Hangzhou is "interested in adopting elements of a ninth-century Chinese art historical text by Zhang Yanyuan, called *Record of the Famous Painters of All the Dynasties*," in constructing an art history based in the Chinese tradition. "Adopting elements" is a fine but limited objective; going much further would, I think, be like contemporary specialists in Italian painting basing their inquiries only on those issues that concerned Vasari. It might not, on the other hand, be so radical a move as Elkins believes. He returns to Zhang Yanyuan's book a few pages later to remark that what makes it "so different from contemporary art history is its author's [Confucian] insistence that painting promotes filial piety and the health of the community." But those sentiments are largely limited to the introductory section of Zhang's book, which, as is common in introductions to Chinese books, proclaims pieties that are left behind once the author turns to his main matter. (My colleague Cyril Birch, a Chinese literature specialist, once advised one of my students about these prefaces that she should "take them very seriously but don't believe them.") Once Zhang begins the substantive discussions that make up the main body of his book (along with treatments of individual artists), he is as absorbed as we cultural outsiders might be in such matters with the styles of great and lesser masters, the distinguishing of schools and artistic lineages, standards of quality, and formulating a kind of "narrative" for the early periods. Elkins contrasts Zhang's purported "Confucian purpose" with "current scholarship on Chinese painting, with its emphasis on politics, identity, and patronage." But in fact we can learn quite a lot from Zhang's book about politics and patronage, if not identity, as factors in the context of painting up to his time, and not much about Confucianism. Cao Yiqiang himself writes that Zhang Yanyuan's book is "strikingly similar" to Vasari's, and notes that Zhang "surveyed this development [of early painting] from the point of view of a gradual improvement in the representation of natural life—he claimed that 'a better likeness was obtained in later portraits,' for instance..."[5] (Zhang Yanyuan could, as I cannot, adopt that approach without being accused of imposing the approach of Gombrich onto Chinese painting.)

The Chinese literature on painting is extensive, highly sophisticated, and in considerable part devoted to concerns that match well with our own. It would seem all the more self-evident, then, that there would be little loss and much to be gained if, in our studies of Chinese painting, we were to follow Elkins's fourth option, "attempt to avoid Western interpretive strategies," and embrace the assumptions and attitudes that underlie Chinese writings about it. And yet I have come to believe, after some decades of working in the field and being actively engaged in the directions it has taken, both here and in China, that there are several compelling reasons why that is just what we should not do.

The first and basic reason is that the extant Chinese writings about painting, which must necessarily be our guides and sources for whatever understanding we can reach of traditional indigenous approaches, can never be accepted simply as telling us what "the Chinese" thought and believed about the paintings. For one thing, even when the artist and the writer are the same person (as in the case of Dong Qichang), the exigencies of writing, the pressures on the writer to take positions in accord with factors in his time, place, social class, and so forth, were strong, even constituting determinants, which might be quite different from the factors operating on the artist as he painted. (Baxandall remarks, "Even [the artist's or maker's] own description of his own state of mind . . . [can] have very limited authority for an account of intention of the object; they are matched with the relation between the object and its circumstances, and retouched or obliquely deployed or even discounted if they are inconsistent with it.")[6] That is, painting and writing about painting in China often go in quite different directions. I have even come to believe, although I would be hard put to argue it on a theoretical ground without falling into the pitfalls that beset anyone making this kind of argument, that many of the most interesting and significant developments in Chinese painting, the complex artistic stratagems used by painters that can make their works so fresh and absorbing, go quite unrecognized and undiscussed in Chinese writings of their time and later. This is true despite the amazing richness of the Chinese literature of art and the frequently sharp observations made by its writers.

A major reason for the gap between painting and writing about it is that the prestigious writers were, virtually by definition, members of the literati class, and so were committed, especially from the Yuan period onward, to its particular viewpoint and special system of values. Their writings are imbued with the doctrines of literati or scholar-amateur painting, doctrines that were formulated in some part to support the practice of the literati artists, to deflect attention from their weaknesses and proclaim their strengths as defining the loftiest criteria of value.[7] I have observed elsewhere that at a time when so little else of the old, self-serving rhetoric of elites has been allowed to stand, this one has enjoyed a surprising tenacity. And I have been working, along with others, to recognize and try to reconstruct, necessarily in a very limited way, the large areas of Chinese painting that were deliberately excluded from the literati writers' account of it, and so have stood a poor chance of being preserved. Trying to understand, and give some voice to, the preferences and attitudes of the silent non-literati majority of consumers of Chinese paintings, the ones who did not write the books but acquired and enjoyed most of the pictures, is in my belief a legitimate pursuit. It can, of course, be realized only very tentatively and imperfectly, but the same is true of many other legitimate pursuits.

Those who advocate a narrow dedication to "the Chinese tradition" in studying Chinese painting—and who, as we learn from the paper by Professor Ding Ning cited earlier, make up the strongest faction within the present-day practice of art history in China's academia—seem to assume that the ways in which "the Chinese" understood and appreciated the paintings can be ascertained by reading the surviving literature about it. But that is only partly true, because, as noted earlier, that literature is, with a few exceptions, heavily partial in both senses: it applies only to a part of its assumed subject, Chinese painting, and it is thoroughly partial, i.e., biased, toward that part, and dismissive of the rest. Everyone knows the example of Chan or Zen painting, which, because it was not valued by Chinese critics and collectors, would be virtually lost to us if it were not for the preservation of a large body of it, including some masterworks, in Japan. Other big and important areas of Chinese painting have not fared even that well, and have to be put together from surviving, mostly misidentified scraps.

If, then, we were to move to a mode of studying Chinese painting dependent on Chinese writings on the subject, most of the advances we have made over the past half-century in working for a better balance and looking into neglected areas of Chinese painting would be sacrificed, and some of the most promising directions that Chinese painting studies have taken would be blocked. I tried to identify some of these neglected areas in a 1997 lecture delivered at Yale, the Hume lecture, titled "Toward a Remapping of Chinese Painting," and much of my own work in recent years has been on the undocumented areas. I will return to this issue in a moment; I want first to point out another basic flaw in the idea that surviving Chinese texts on painting can be accepted as conveying to us fully the thinking of artists and critics of the time the paintings were done.

The writings of Dong Qichang and other major Ming–Qing and earlier critics, theorists, and colophon writers are based on their wide acquaintance with major paintings—many hours or days of studying them, traveling widely to see collections, developing a level of connoisseurship which even when it may be flawed was deep and extensive. Their writings were done in relation to this, and were based on this—a kind of visual archive in memory, which allowed them to make judgments of works they saw by comparing them with the large databanks stored in their heads, and to write about different schools and artists and styles by drawing on this. They wrote often about particular paintings, and even when they didn't, their writings were charged with their close visual knowledge of a great many individual paintings. And they assumed a comparably broad visual experience of major artists and paintings in their readers—who, if they were reading the colophons at all, must be members of that small elite who had access to old and original works—and they made references to them on that assumption.

The problem is that in that pre-photography age there was no way for them to convey their deep visual engagement with paintings in their writings. Woodblock reproductions were of virtually no use, since they could not transmit the aspects of the paintings that mattered most to them. Copying by hand was an option, as in the well-known Xiaozhong Xianda or "Great Revealed in the Small" album, reduced-size copies of early masterworks owned by Wang Shimin with facing inscriptions by Dong Qichang; but the limitations of copies were also severe and well recognized. So the writings of these people come down to us more or less bare: imbued with, but physically lacking, the visual element—only as texts. And later people, through the Qing dynasty (when the great early paintings were mostly absorbed into the imperial collection, and accessible only to a very few in the court) and down to recent times, have had little or no opportunity to see and study major early works. In the 1930s, 1940s, and later a few collectors and connoisseurs and museum people, such as the late C. C. Wang and Xu Bangda, have been able to see more; but academics mostly haven't, and opportunities for students are even fewer. So they get a false and vastly reduced sense of what Dong Qichang and the others really knew and felt and believed. And they sometimes write as though staying within the realm of words—theories and arguments and colophons, divorced from real visual engagement with the paintings—were adequate and even desirable, since (they argue) it continues a native Chinese tradition. But it continues only in a greatly diminished form, robbed of what it was really based on in the visual experience of the writers they study.

For us outside China, then, to embrace the "indigenous Chinese" tradition of art history, as we would necessarily have to derive it from these texts, would oblige us to come down heavily on what I firmly believe would be, for us, the wrong side in the verbal–visual controversy discussed earlier.

Moreover, as I pointed out in the first section, what is dismissed by some academics in China as a "Western" or "foreign" way of studying Chinese painting is really the product of some sixty years of richly multicultural interaction between specialists who came from a number of traditions, Chinese and Japanese as well as German, English, and others. That the interaction took place largely in the United States has more to do with the economic and technological advantages we have enjoyed, along with the immigration of so many major art historians and collectors to the United States during and after the Second World War and the growth of major collections here, than with any factors particular to our own culture. To partake of the achievements of this very fruitful interaction can only augment and enrich, I believe, without in any way betraying, the more exclusively Chinese tradition of scholarship. Setting up the two as somehow irreconcilable alternative choices seems to me in itself a falsification of where we stand. (To write that is, of course, to contradict directly James Elkins's contention that Chinese art history can only be Western art history, an argument that after a lot of thinking I still cannot entirely comprehend and certainly cannot follow.)

An Under-Recognized Function of Art History

Now, on to my reasons for believing that any mode of art-historical teaching and writing that does not involve close readings and analyses of the works of art themselves is short-changing its readers and students. In arguing this, I have sometimes used analogies: one could, in principle, study and teach poetry without reading any poems, much less attempting close readings of poems, but that would be a very impoverished and ineffective way of teaching poetry. No one can adequately understand, for instance, uses of metaphor or allusion in poetry without being provided good examples of their usage in particular poems, just as (I once argued) any full and balanced understanding of Dong Qichang's advocacy of *fang* or creative imitation must be based on a visual study of how it works in particular paintings.[8] The same is true of music: we can read articles or hear lectures on composers and compositions and historical developments, and those are by no means without value; but teaching music without playing musical examples for the students to hear would deprive one's teaching of what should be its heart. (I have also pointed out, however, that we historians of the visual arts have a great advantage over teachers of poetry or music: where they must discuss the poem and then read it, or talk about the composition and then play it [in whichever order], we can enjoy a perfect three-cornered simultaneity: the painting, perhaps with details, on the screen, ourselves talking, and the students or lecture audience listening to us and gazing at the painting, all at once. This is an advantage we should exploit as fully as we can.) In any case, what matters is that the learner be afforded immediate experiences of the works themselves, whether the experiences be visual, aural, or literary; reading or hearing about the works can never suffice.

The objection will be raised: why need any teacher's voice be there at all? Isn't it better for the student/viewer to have a fresh, unmediated experience of the work? And that objection would lead to another proposal for avoiding a "visual art history," a proposal that I will introduce only to try immediately to shoot it down, since it is another that sounds plausible in theory but has fatal weaknesses when one thinks of how it might be put into practice. The proposal is this: why not adopt the Chinese verbal mode of teaching, and let the students and readers, equipped with the knowledge they have gained, go on to seek out the paintings and look at them on their own? Everyone who has eyes can look at paintings; why does anyone need to be "taught" to do it?

The answer to that lies in the paradox that Michael Baxandall somewhere writes about as the "man in the bus" situation: the man is excitedly pointing out to his fellow passengers what they can see outside with their own eyes. What, then, is his function, if any? When we teachers stand before a painting (or a slide image of one) and talk about it, are we doing no more than that? But Baxandall, and any good art historian, knows that ideally we are doing much more: we are conveying a reading of the painting, perhaps some kind of analysis of it, that opens new areas of perception in the viewer/listener's mind.

This brings me to a function of art-historical lecturing and writing that is scarcely taken into account in the Elkins discussions, as I read them, or more generally in theoretical accounts of art history, but that has been centrally important to my writing and teaching and the reception to it. I recall a student in one of Max Loehr's classes on Chinese painting asking me, partway through the semester, "What's so good about this? He just stands up there and describes the painting, things we can see as well as he can." In fact, what Max Loehr did over the semester was implant in us a visual understanding of the course of Song and earlier painting, especially landscape, its issues and stylistic developments and structures of relationships as he saw them, that has been the basis for my own accounts of it ever since, different as those have been from his. The way he taught the ritual bronze vessels of Shang–Zhou China, never neglecting archaeological or epigraphical evidence but laying out also a convincing morphology of décor styles and shapes, established in our minds a framework within which the individual object, seen as a "move" within a Kublerian series,[9] might be intelligible and deeply satisfying, in a way that it could never be without that context. It was not that he fitted the styles into some preexisting Wölfflinian or other pattern or "narrative," but that the study of morphology of forms in related series in European art had alerted him to possibilities that non–art-historians did not recognize: for example, that an abstract pattern can metamorphose over time into an image—a pair of circles, for instance, into the eyes of an animal mask. And after outlining the earliest development of Chinese ritual bronze décor styles on this pattern, Loehr was proven to be basically right, in a way independent of cultural traditions, when later excavations of pre-Anyang sites largely corroborated his proposed sequence of styles. Three other scholars, the preeminent bronze specialists in China, Japan, and Europe (as was recalled in a tribute to Loehr's achievement by Alexander Soper),[10] had all got it backward by assuming that the series must have begun with the representational image, which could then "dissolve" into an abstract pattern. This was not, then, a matter of the Western art historian imposing the patterns he knew onto the foreign materials, but of his having been sensitized, through his training, to possibilities to which those without that background were blind.

Loehr himself made this point strikingly at the beginning of the first seminar he gave in Ann Arbor, which was on the Shang–Zhou bronzes. He put a pile of unlabeled photographs of these on the table and invited us to arrange them into some kind of sensible order. As the only one in the seminar who had already been exposed to the bronzes, I stayed out. All the others were graduate students with backgrounds in other fields. By the end of about an hour, they had sorted the photos into an order that was a not-bad approximation of what we knew from other evidence to be the historical sequence of styles and shapes. Loehr had, of course, chosen examples that were susceptible to this kind of ordering, but his point was nonetheless made.

The writings of Bachhofer, Loehr, Soper, and others on the early periods of Chinese landscape painting drew in this way on visual and conceptual skills that had been developed in part through their study of other traditions of pictorial art, a consideration that in no way invalidates their work. Later studies making use of new archaeological finds and other materials have refined, in part corrected, but not replaced the narratives they laid out. None of them, on the other hand, was able to deal effectively with post-Song painting, to which I have recently applied the term "post-historical";[11] and it is there that the Chinese narratives, with their emphases on local schools or movements, "imitating" old masters, the aims and doctrines of literati painting, the brushwork or "hand" of the individual master, and other factors independent of any Gombrichian "pursuit of likeness," seem to be the suitable referents for an art-historical account. They are in fact the referents on which I have mainly tried to base my own accounts of the later periods of Chinese painting. But these, in turn, are mostly unsuited for dealing with painting of the early periods, where traditional Chinese connoisseurs are at their weakest.

Elkins sets up a bad model for cross-cultural work in art history, one in which foreign patterns of constructing "narratives" are imposed onto the indigenous tradition, and assumes that because all attempts must follow that model, the whole enterprise is contaminated. I would rather believe that there can be good and less good, appropriate and less appropriate, ways of applying an outsider's understanding to a foreign body of art, and that we must make our choices as perceptively and honestly as we can, trying to avoid a priori assumptions about how this or that choice will distort our subject.

Lecturing and writing of the kind I advocate can open new circuits, so to speak, in the minds of its listeners/readers, like installing software that allows them to read and understand a new set of texts that were inaccessible or meaningless before (I am not a computer person and the analogy may be faulty), equipping them to respond in a sensitized and cultivated way to other, related works of art. I would argue—and the idea is a common one, virtually a truism—that much of the value of a work, as a quality of the experience of it by a viewer, derives from its relationship to others made before and after. This is especially true of works by artists who belong to a self-conscious artistic tradition (as Elkins recognized the Chinese and European traditions of painting to be) and who are taking part, whether or not consciously, in vast games—not divorced from their lives in the real world, like the players of

Hesse's Glasperlenspiel (the "Glass Bead Game"), but deeply engaged not only with the past of their culture but also with their own time and place and society, within which their work is created and experienced. And the place of the work within that context, from which a major part of its value derives, will not be perceived fully unless the mind of the reader/viewer is prepared by lots of previous experience of related works, and lots of thinking—his own or a teacher's, ideally both—about the relationships between these: What are the really original creations (Kubler's "prime objects")? How do others derive from them? What are truly successful and satisfying solutions to the formal and aesthetic "problems" that obtain within this series? Of course, other contexts than the visual can also be fed into this mind-conditioning process as well, and should be: contextual matters, for instance, of the kind Baxandall writes about in his "inferential art history."

A good teacher, who has arrived at a clear and convincing set of formulations of all these and conveys them effectively to her or his students, can take the students a long way in this process. The student does not, of course, accept the teacher's account as the final word, as I did not accept Loehr's; but he or she has a model and a tentative structure to accept, modify, or reject—any of these being better than beginning "cold."

And that is what is wrong with the idea that the student can simply come to the work of art visually unprepared and experience fully its expressive impact and aesthetic value. I have met people who claim they can recognize quality in any work of art of any time and tradition; this, again, is not entirely untrue, especially if they have had enough previous experience with other kinds of art, but is only a limited truth. Examples I have used of sensitive and intelligent people "coming cold" at an unfamiliar body of art and being unable to make qualitative and other distinctions within it include the Chinese connoisseur Wang Chi-chien going around the European painting galleries of the National Gallery of Art with me in the early 1960s and remarking that the paintings all looked more or less alike and "have no brushwork," and John Canaday responding in a *New York Times* review to my "Fantastics and Eccentrics in Chinese Painting" exhibition of 1967 by writing that the paintings, beautiful as they were, did not look so different in his eyes from all the Ming–Qing paintings he had seen before—what was so "eccentric" about them? I have cited also a reviewer of a concert of Indian music who noted that when the musicians played an erotic raga the Indians in the audience were unable to sit still, while the non-Indians sat "like bumps on logs." Music is an especially telling case: someone who has not listened seriously to classical European music, for instance, cannot tell Mozart from Beethoven, much less Mozart from Haydn. Discernment is not, of course, the whole content of the appreciation and enjoyment of art, but it is a major component of it, virtually a requisite.

Art history, then, is in some part a matter of implanting the right set of visual referents in the viewer/listener's mind so that the work will be perceived in relation to those, and pointing out the relationships as you have come to understand them. For reasons I have never understood, theorists are inclined to leave out this function when discussing art history; perhaps they feel it belongs properly to pedagogy, or to criticism, and so is beneath their notice. But the truly successful art historian (or literary historian, or music historian), the one whose lectures and writings are exciting to listeners and readers, the one who gets letters saying "You have changed my life," is the one who understands the importance of this process, has built up in his or her mind the formulations and structures of relationships for the bodies of art he or she teaches, and can convey these to others by instilling some form of them, with enough time and slides, in their minds. Individual teachers, of course, do this better or less well; all of them, I think, should at least attempt it, even when their principal strengths are elsewhere. Many will simply adopt existing "narratives," whether the traditional

Chinese one or some adaptation of one they learned from their teacher, or one put together from reading attempts by others to formulate new "histories." Many, perhaps most, will modify existing accounts to put more emphasis on their own strengths and interests. What matters is that the students will have a visual grounding into which they can fit their experiences with paintings, and which they can in turn adapt and use if they themselves become teachers. Teachers of the history of Chinese painting have fewer well-established and widely accepted "narratives" to choose among than their colleagues in Western art studies, a circumstance that makes their choices all the more interesting and important.

To reinforce my argument, let me quote a passage by a literary historian named Geoffrey Galt Harpham that I read recently and found myself resonating with.[12] After writing about the consequences of "the anti-humanistic spirit that, in varying degrees, animated all [the theorists who have dominated literary studies in recent decades]," with their "determination to undermine concepts of human creativity, human freedom, and the human capacity for self-awareness," he ends by reasserting some old beliefs about the value of literature and the teaching of it: "The distinctive form of aesthetic pleasure we take from the literary experience gives us the sense that we are being deepened, empowered, and enriched even as we are being entertained or charmed. Such a complex experience is difficult to theorize, professionalize, or politicize, but it is a vital and essential dimension of literary study and should be maximized wherever possible." What good teachers of literature teach, he believes, "is not just a set of facts about an archive of texts, important as the record of literary history is; they also inculcate an informed and disciplined responsiveness not directly connected to advantage, utility, or immediate needs. Transmitting the literary heritage in all its astonishing variety, scholars are engaged in the constant rekindling of the capacity to experience aesthetic pleasure and the sense of imaginative freedom, even wonder, that accompanies that experience. . . . Such a project may not satisfy many short-term interests, but it is not without honor, and those who are engaged in it have no need to question the value of their work."[13]

Within such a project, the structures or patterns ("narratives" if you will) into which one organizes the materials are not, I think, nearly so determined as Elkins argues by one's cultural tradition and background. He would have it that all Western (European and American) art historians are inextricably bound to the Gombrichian narrative built around gains in illusionism. I myself, as I argued earlier with references to Bachhofer, Loehr, and Soper, believe that that is not an inappropriate approach, if applied very loosely, for Chinese painting through Song, since it corresponds in a general way with what, in my understanding, the Chinese artists are "up to" in this early period (see Zhang Yanyuan cited above, who agrees.) But it makes no sense after that; my "histories" of Yuan and later painting have taken their form, I think, from the materials they treat and the issues as they are discussed in Chinese writings and as I see them, not from any preexisting Western model. That I have constructed a "narrative" for these later periods is true, but it has not, so far as I can see, derived from the Gombrichian or Wölfflinian or any other pattern that I have been forced to impose on them simply by being a Western art historian.

If someone objects, and someone will, that the procedure I advocate is necessarily going to be shot through with the special assumptions and biases of my time and situation, I will agree, but add that I do my best to let it or make it derive from the body of art itself, or from my limited understanding of it, and of pertinent factors in its cultural setting. They will say: but you can never make it all the latter, so as to eliminate the former; I will reply, yes, but it is worth doing anyway. Baxandall (to cite him once more) somewhere points out that to avoid attempting something because you cannot do it perfectly is like telling a runner not to run the hundred-yard dash because he cannot run it in no time at all.

There is no reason I can think of why art history in this sense, as I have tried to practice it and believe it should be practiced, cannot be global, if one means by that, applicable to any body of interrelated works of art, of whatever culture and period. Of course the practitioner, in preparation for teaching and writing, will attempt to understand the relevant indigenous concepts that will inform his or her formulations, and will strive to avoid imposing "narratives" absorbed through the study of some other culture onto the art of this one—as distinct from the practice, praised earlier in the writing and teaching of Max Loehr and others, of drawing on one's familiarity with such patterns in other cultures in recognizing them in the material being studied. I will be the first to acknowledge the difficulty of making the distinction (yes, I know about unconscious biases) and of practicing what I advocate, and to admit my own failings sometimes in attempting it. But I am not persuaded by arguments that it is basically impossible, and so not worth even attempting.

It should be unnecessary to add that the visual ways of dealing with works of art cannot in any way replace documentary research; the two kinds can comfortably coexist within the working methods of any scholar who chooses to let them, the one augmenting and sometimes correcting the other. It often happens—I might say ideally happens—during a research project that the two kinds of data become all but inseparable within one's mind; one is constantly checking information and clues from reading against the paintings and their relationships, or the reverse, trying to resolve productively any tensions that may seem to arise between them. One may lean this way or that—textual scholars are inclined to trust always the texts, those visually oriented, the paintings—but any disparity between them in fact constitutes new data, to be used as one will, and can lead to further levels of enlightenment. That our Chinese colleagues are vastly better equipped than we by language, background, and training to deal with the textual materials is beyond question, and we depend on them heavily for all the information and insights that texts can provide, along with what we can derive on our own. But those of us committed also to a visual approach would be happy if our conclusions based on visual evidence could be given comparable credence and weight.

We would be happy also, as remarked earlier, if the whole visual–verbal issue could be removed from the arena of the controversy over foreign versus indigenous traditions. What might follow that divorcement, by allowing a more open discussion, could lead, I believe, to great advances in the study of Chinese painting. It could open the way, as I suggested at the end of the first section, to a new, fuller but still truly Chinese practice of studying Chinese painting, based in the Chinese tradition of textual research but also recreating in contemporary scholarship the kind of visual mastery with which the Chinese connoisseurs and critics of former times, the ones who wrote the texts, were so richly endowed. Jim Elkins's contention about Chinese painting studies necessarily being Western art history would thus be confounded; and he himself, I suspect, would be pleased to watch this happen.

Notes

1 "Style as Idea in Ming–Ch'ing Painting," in *The Mozartian Historian: Essays on the Works of Joseph R. Levenson*, ed. Maurice Meisner and Rhoads Murphy (Berkeley: University of California Press, 1976), 137–56.

2 James Cahill, ed., *Shadows of Mt. Huang: Chinese Painting and Printing of the Anhui School* (Berkeley: University Art Museum, 1981).

3 *Xifang meishushixue zhong de Zhongguo shangshuihua* (Hangzhou: China Academy of Art Press, 1999).

4 *The Art Bulletin* 86, no. 2 (2004): 373–80.

5 Cao Yiqiang, "Approaches to Chinese Art History," in *Art and History: Haskell's Historical Achievements and the Development of Art History* (Hangzhou: China Academy of Art Press, 2001), 198.

6 Michael Baxandall, *Patterns of Intention: On the Historical Explanation of Pictures* (New Haven: Yale University Press, 1985), 42.

7 This is not simply my own observation; Cao Yiqiang writes in the same vein: "Whereas the professional masters of the past have left us almost nothing in writing about their art, the literati painters have produced a massive body of treatises on their own painting. . . . Our knowledge of ancient Chinese art history is only transmitted through their writings and their interpretations. It is inevitable that our views are prejudiced by their attitude towards their professional counterparts." Cao, "Approaches," 186.

8 "Style as Idea" (above, n. 1).

9 I refer here to the concept of a "linked series" as set forth in George Kubler's book *The Shape of Time: Remarks on the History of Things* (New Haven and London: Yale University Press, 1962).

10 "Early, Middle, and Late Shang: A Note," *Artibus Asiae* 28 (1966): 5–38. The three scholars are Li Chi, Umehara Sueji, and Bernard Karlgren.

11 "Some Thoughts on the History and Post-History of Chinese Painting," *Archives of Asian Art* 55 (2005): 17–33.

12 Geoffrey Galt Harpham, "Politics, Professionalism, and the Pleasure of Reading," *Daedalus* 134, no. 3 [special issue on professions and professionals] (Summer 2005): 68–75.

13 It is also good to see—*New York Times* for Sunday Oct. 19, Book Review section p. 8—the chair of Yale's English department assuring us that "the Age of Theory is over in America," and criticism like Helen Vendler's, written "in lucid prose" and able to "verbalize our experience of great writing," is acceptable again. I am uneasy about the "verbalize," or at least would not like to see it applied to art criticism, but the news is heartening.

3
Chinese Landscape Painting as Western Art History

James Elkins

[*This is a selection of excerpts adapted from my book,* Chinese Landscape Painting as Western Art History, *which has so far appeared only in Chinese:* Xifang meishu shixue zhong de Zhongguo shanshuihua.[1] *That book is organized into about 100 numbered sections; I have retained those numbers here. I have interpolated some comments, and added a note at the end on recent developments. A revised version of that book is forthcoming from the Hong Kong University Press.*]

From the Preface, added in 2005.

Chinese Landscape Painting as Western Art History is an attempt to see how Chinese landscape painting appears through the lens of art history, a discipline that I will claim is partly, but finally and decisively, Western. My subject is Chinese landscape painting, and I would like to understand it as well as I am able, but I am equally interested in how the history of any non-Western art can be represented. Saying that the history of Chinese landscape painting appears only through, or as, a Western discipline will certainly seem mistaken or polemical, and probably also perverse. So it may be helpful to say right at the start that this book grew out of an inextinguishable interest in Chinese art: an interest that refused to let itself shrink from a possible "minor field" into an avocation or pastime—an interest that slowly grew until it became, in an illogical fashion, an emblem for art historical understanding in general. I am not a specialist in Chinese art, but I find myself intrigued and often confused by the ways art historians present Chinese painting, and also by the very conditions of such understanding and representation.

That, at least, is my excuse for writing about Chinese landscape painting, as if it could also be an inquiry into art historical representation of any sort. The two problems have become entangled in my mind: the "general" philosophic question of representing other visual practices, and the "specific" example of Chinese landscape painting. At one moment Chinese landscape painting is just an art among many, and in the next it is the exemplary moment in which Western art historical understanding encounters another tradition very much the West's equal in duration and complexity. At such times it becomes especially difficult to understand what it means that the major art historians, from Panofsky to Gombrich, from Schapiro to Belting—the historians who had the interest and means to look beyond Western practices—remained centered on Western art. Can Chinese landscape painting ever appear as the *central* instance of painting? If it can, then it remains to be said why it does not. And if it cannot, then we need to start coming to terms with an inherently Western structure of historical understanding that prevents Chinese painting from being more than the most important, complex, fascinating *example* of non-Western painting.

And one note especially for China specialists: I propose here, not that the study of Chinese painting is exclusively a Western project, but rather that it is mainly so. Westernness and Chineseness are relative, overlapping, and subject to change without notice. As I write this, in November of 2005, it has recently been announced that China intends to build one hundred world-class universities. (The announcement responded to a study that found that there can be one world-class university for every eight million inhabitants of a country. In Ireland, where I was living at the time, that report precipitated a small crisis: in a country of only four million people, could there be even one world-class university?) No one can predict what mixtures of Chinese and Western methods will develop in the coming decades: but I do not believe that organic growth will solve the problem I address in my book. The very idea of writing an art history of some country or region is Western in the ways I will define, and that means all historians of Chinese art are, and will remain, culpable of trading in Western practices. A guiding assumption of this book is that it is better to try to understand those practices than to assume they will be rendered harmless by the many distractions of new art, new colleagues, new books, and new philosophies. . . .

2

I begin with a recent occasion that bears on [my] book; then I will go back to the beginning and recount [my] book's staggered development. The recent occasion was a two-day conference, with just four speakers, convened by Jason Kuo at the University of Maryland at College Park, in November 2005 [*That is the conference that inspired this book,* Stones from Other Mountains]. That event came fourteen years, fourteen rejection letters, over twenty reader's reports, and five complete revisions after Jim Cahill first saw the manuscript, in 1991. As a rule of thumb in academic publishing: up to ten rejection slips, and you may have a work of genius that no one recognizes; over ten, and you have a problem with your manuscript that you're just not addressing. By the time of the Maryland conference, even Jason Kuo's graduate students were suggesting the book might be better off unpublished.

The conference was intended to discuss the state of scholarship on Chinese painting. There were papers on the subject of Chinese art studies since World War II and on the globalization of art history, and Jim Cahill and I held a fifty-minute public conversation. We talked at some length about Craig Clunas's writing, and the many things that separate it from

Jim Cahill's. [*That conversation inspired the letters that appear in Chapter 4 of this book.*] I realized then that my book would need yet another introduction if it were to stand a chance of persuading a spectrum of readers: it would have to say something about the encroachment of visual studies into Chinese art history, and the gradual dissolution of painting and bronzes in a brew of lacquer, porcelain, funerary sculpture, clothing, bas-reliefs, advertisements, films, performance art, and tourist photographs. I would also need to cut from my book material that could not be persuasive to scholars interested in visual studies. That would be the manuscript's fourth introduction, and its fourth round of cutting. The problem I was trying to pose was not getting less important, but it was becoming less audible and weaker, shrunken into a lean shape and hidden beneath its elaborate armatures.

3

. . . I am going to argue that despite our best efforts at enlightened multiculturalism, all attempts to write the art history of non-Western cultures result in Western narratives that serve Western purposes and are supported by Western ideas. In other words, in relation to postcolonial theory, I will claim that closer attention to the dynamics and theory of cross-cultural writing will not purge, uncover, or even meliorate cripplingly Western motives and concepts. That isn't to say Western scholars can't say true things about other cultures: it's to say that our motives, our methods, and the institutions of our scholarship are all Western.

To that thesis I need to add a caveat that I think may sound not only unhelpful but unlikely in the extreme: I think that as far as the last two centuries of art history are concerned, the phrase "non-Western cultures" should be taken to include virtually every country outside France, with the occasional exception of Germany, Italy, England, and America. In other words, there is no such thing as an art history of nineteenth-

and twentieth-century Finnish art, or Argentinean art, or Sudanese art that is not wholly driven by French, or German, or American ideas and interests. And if someone in some isolated village in the Sudan had managed to write a history of modern Sudanese art uninfluenced by Western historical texts, it would be illegible as art history.

My position implies several critiques of the effects of postcolonial theory. It seems to me, for example, that postcolonial theory disguises hopeless interpretive situations as occasions for learning and analysis; that it fosters the illusion that we have a grasp of the art of non-Western countries; that it makes it seem as if a history of world art might someday again be possible as it was thought in the nineteenth century; and that it implies art history is diverse and malleable enough to refashion itself in all sorts of new contexts. . . .[2]

47

There are histories with gaps, when centuries pass with no evidence of human activity. The European "dark ages" is the exemplary case, though its darkness is now widely contested and redistributed among a number of different cultures. The mid-third millennium BC in the Middle East, the founding centuries of Rome, and "Dynasty 0" in Egypt are also examples of periods whose sequences may always be inadequately known. Elsewhere and further back in history the gaps grow wider, and the known objects fewer and further between. In Paleolithic Europe there are so few artifacts dispersed through so many years that it is better to speak of a history of voids, occasionally punctuated by objects. Instead of a history of sequences, broken by a few dark ages, Paleolithic archaeology is almost compelled to try to tell a history of darkness, interrupted at long intervals by isolated images.

These problems are endemic to prehistory and early history, both in archaeology and art history. What happens at the end of the Ming Dynasty and throughout the Qing is different in kind. Dark ages are times from which objects have disappeared, but the history of Chinese painting from the mid-seventeenth century to the beginning of the twentieth is replete with images. There is a profusion of painters, schools, and styles, and if art historical accounts were written in proportion to the amount of surviving material, the Qing would hold center stage in Chinese history.

Instead narratives of Chinese art tend to fall silent after Dong Qichang. There is a traditional sequence that continues with the generations after Dong, including the "individualists" and several groups of "eccentrics," and then ends around the middle of the eighteenth century. A few alternates give life to that sequence: some accounts also note the influence of Western printmaking and painting, or conclude by nodding in the direction of representative twentieth-century painters to show that the tradition is still alive. But many books effectively end about two hundred years before the present.

48

A short essay by Arthur Danto called "The Shape of Artistic Pasts: East and West" draws a comparison between modernism in China and in the West. Danto observes how the past is made of "modes of available influence," and he proposes that "modernism, alike in China and the West, meant the dismantling of these narratives and reconstitution of our relationship to the past." Danto defines modernism in terms of historical perspectives: it begins, he says, "with the loss of belief in the defining narratives of one's culture."[3]

I can't use Danto's formulation here, close as it is to some themes I intend to explore, because it is at once too general and too focused. Since I have been looking rather strictly at historical perspectives of artistic strategies, I do not want to broaden the critique to embrace "defining narratives" of all kinds. Many threads weave together in the succession of artistic practices and in their slow unraveling, and the intricacy of the dissolution of painting is what impels me to keep to a somewhat narrow path.

On the other hand, I also want to be a little unclear about the historical limits of modernism or of later Chinese painting, so as not to end up in a one-to-one correspondence between a "Chinese modernism" and the Western one. (Throughout the book I have been avoiding the phrase "Chinese modernism." Like the Renaissance, *modernism* is a term that makes sense in the West, and is analogic and problematic elsewhere. It wouldn't do to assume China had or might have "a modernism": it would beg the question of the meaning of such parallels.) History did break at the inception of modernism, but not as suddenly as it is sometimes claimed. Perspective, for example, was never merely "overturned" or "discarded" as modernist writers would sometimes have it.[4] Despite the importance that has been attached to years such as 1905 and 1910 (in the West), it is seldom helpful to say exactly when a thing called "modernism" became a preeminent concern.

There is also a paradox lurking here, since later Chinese painting often seems marked by an excessive attention to tradition, rather than a break. Modernism is central to the West's understanding of its own art; later Chinese art is often optional. There are many differences, but somehow, if we step back far enough, Danto seems right: in both cases something went wrong with tradition.

49

To an art historian first encountering the silence that hangs about later Chinese art, the effect is spectacular. The *Propyläen Kunstgeschichte* provides an example; it is the German equivalent of the Pelican *History of Art*, though many of its texts are longer than their English counterparts. The volume on China, Korea, and Japan devotes a page and a half to nineteenth-century Chinese painting, and exactly one sentence to the twentieth century: "In the twentieth century all the élan is lost, and in every domain of art one finds only torpor and decline."[5] The two words *Erstarrung* ("torpor") and *Verfall* ("decline") are very strong: *Erstarrung* also means paralysis or numbing, and *Verfall* is dilapidation, or ruin.

It is impossible, I think, to overestimate the strangeness of this elision. Its precise parallel in the West would be a four-hundred-page volume on European art with two pages on painting since David, culminating in a single, intensely derogatory sentence on the art of the last hundred years.

50

Other books on Chinese art offer even less. Sherman Lee's short, widely read *Chinese Landscape Painting* (originally published in 1954) runs through the Eccentric Masters of Yangzhou—about whom more in a moment—and concludes: "With these, after all, not-so-strange masters, one nears the end of creative landscape production. . . . by 1800 landscape and all painting has run dry in theme, technique, and mood. And so the last of our talented painters, Ch'ien Tu [Qian Du], living on to 1844, sets himself a limited scale of dry brushwork within a severely limited size and so is able to keep touch and breath alive—just barely. . . . The Chinese view of nature was still a valid one and its pictorial expression depended upon other new and individual replies, but exhaustion made no answer."[6]

I wonder if any more elegiac passage has been written about Chinese painting: it is tiring just reading it, as if there is nothing left to see and no reason to continue trying. Terse and enthusiastic as it often is, *Chinese Landscape Painting* ends by falling asleep: the author's listless eye closes at the end of the last line, which is also the end of the book.

Lee's *History of Far Eastern Art* (fifth edition, 1994), the major one-volume textbook available for undergraduate teaching, also ends around 1840 with no further explanation. He provides a comparative timeline of art in China, Japan, Korea, Thailand, India, Indonesia, and "the West," which goes only as far as the mid-nineteenth century. It is tempting to read some significance into the fact that the last entry under the column for "the West" is Postimpressionism, as if Western painting also ended a hundred years ago.[7]

Nor has the situation changed in recent years. The art historian Ho Ch'uan-hsing ends a short summary of Qing painting with a page on the "Painters of Yangzhou" (the "Eight Strange [Eccentric] Masters") and one on the "late Qing Paleographic School"—painters such as Wu Changshuo (1844–1927) who revived archaic calligraphic techniques.[8] Ho's account does not mention painting between the mid-eighteenth century and the late nineteenth, even though its purpose is to survey the entire Qing dynasty. (He does say, in a typical gesture, that the period witnessed "an irreversible political decline."[9])

Wen Fong's sequence of naturalistic representation pays little attention to developments after Dong Qichang.[10] His *Beyond Representation* is a history of Chinese painting from the eighth to the fourteenth century, and so it is under no obligation to speak about the later Ming or Qing (as Lee's text is). But two paragraphs before the end of the 549-page volume, Wen injects a virulent judgment into an otherwise carefully modulated account: "And finally, during the Qing dynasty, stultifying and lifeless imitation became a way of art."[11]

Could a volume on European painting end with the sentence "And finally, after 1820 painting became stultified and lifeless"? Wen's judgment is not driven by the narrative that precedes it—no mention of the Qing is even necessary, given the text's concerns up to that last page—and it does not round out the narrative, or bring it to a provisional conclusion. Instead it implants in the reader's mind a vision of a rich tradition that suddenly and inexplicably collapses.

51

If the Qing eclipse were the result of a universal negative judgment, that would be strange enough. (It would correspond, in general terms, to the negative valuations of cultures that were once common in art history.) But most writers do not profess opinions about the period: instead their prose just begins to fade, as if it were especially taxing to write about the later Ming. The writing flags, and the descriptions slowly lose energy, as if the historians couldn't keep their eyes on the pictures. It's less a negative judgment than a kind of torpor. It seems difficult, in effect, to say anything about the tired, repetitive, formulaic paintings of the late Qing—they look so self-evidently like the typical products of decline.

If negative opinions are uncommon, reflective negative judgments are even less so. James Cahill wrote a moving peroration to his *Chinese Painting* in which he describes how "very sophisticated" aesthetic values replaced simple ones, "awkwardness" was "sublimated into a kind of skill," and "straightforward feeling" was expressed in "oblique allusions." Each of these traits is connected to a withdrawal from nature and a growing fascination with what Western art theorists called invention.[12] Most are acceptable and even sought after in modern and postmodern art criticism: but here they are linked with a negative valuation. In a lecture given in 1990, Cahill puts it plainly: "Painting as a whole, after the K'ang-hsi era [Kangxi era of the early Qing dynasty], undergoes a marked decline. To say this once more will annoy those of my colleagues who follow the different-but-just-as-good approach, but it is a conviction."[13]

52

Once again the older scholarship beckons, with its apparently outmoded opinions. Like other scholars of his generation, Laurence Binyon thought Chinese art declined after the Song: he didn't even want to look at literati painting, much less later Ming and Qing art.[14]

On the one hand, that kind of sweeping statement is the product of a prejudice that scholarship has outgrown. But on the other hand, it may well be the not-so-distant ancestor of our own blindnesses. The latter possibility opens the way to two conclusions: either art historians are gradually curing themselves, and managing to see more and more of the tradition; or else the tradition as a whole has been and continues to be marked by an irreparable decline. Perhaps those who speak ill of Qing painting do so "only by ignorance," but they may also be following the only available shape of history.[15]

Nor is this a phenomenon that is specific to the literati tradition, since the same kinds of apparent decline affect the professional Zhe School painters. At the end of a long study of Ming court painting, in a chapter called "The Disappearance of Academic Craft," Richard Barnhart spends a few pages on a late regional school he calls the "Min [Fujian] School." He describes the works as "scribbly, spontaneous, sketchy, and slapdash," and speculates that "such practices were probably necessitated by economic reality." As the market for court painting collapsed, painters could only "maintain a minimal standard of living" by "making and selling, say, ten paintings a week."[16] It is true that the art market was undergoing fundamental changes, and Barnhart also points out how difficult it is to reconstruct many painters' oeuvres; but it is also curious that his terms and critical descriptions so closely match what is said about literati painting. Is the "slapdash" manner of literati painting also an economic phenomenon? As it becomes "slapdash," historians have a progressively more difficult time keeping their attention on the works and even Barnhart (who usually tries to see everything, and to hold judgment in suspension as long as possible) flags; the chapter concludes several pages later.

I would go so far as to say that the decline of Chinese painting is subtly present in every narrative. When Fan Kuan's *Travelers Among Streams and Mountains* is praised, in the context of a general survey of Chinese art, as a "great picture" with an "overwhelming grandeur of conception," there is the faint but definite impression that later works fail by the same standards.[17] Only one historian I know sees a positive light in the middle Qing, though it is not unqualified: Jung Ying Tsao notes that the period is "not usually considered outstanding," but might be an "important transitional style" leading to new discoveries.[18]

Recently some writers have taken to simply laying out the material, rather than trying to judge it. Claudia Brown and Ju-hsi Chou write at length about late Qing painting without ever defending the interest of the paintings they catalogue; their *Transcending Turmoil* is a large exhibition catalogue, given over entirely to historical summaries, provenance, and translations of colophons.[19] It is as if simply showing the paintings would be enough to overturn the weight of historical and critical judgments that go against them. But in the absence of any advocacy, the result is inevitably more evidence of work that is "not usually considered outstanding."

Even twentieth-century work that could otherwise be compelling is buried by the downward pull of the traditional narratives. I want to make it clear that there is plenty of interesting twentieth-century Chinese painting; the question at hand is the manner in which the existing art historical narratives smother that painting by placing it at the end of a long decline, in a period characterized by overwhelming Western influence. Fu Baoshi (1904–1965) is a strong painter, but he is doubly hidden from narratives of world art: once by the Western narratives I'm tracing here, and again by contemporary Chinese criticism that denies—I think absurdly—that he was influenced by Western painting.[20]

53

What I have written in these last sections may seem too black and white. After all there is scholarship that takes nineteenth- and twentieth-century Chinese landscape painting seriously. Yu-chih Lai's study of Ren Bonian (1840–1896), while it's not focused on landscape paintings, is a sympathetic iconographic study of the painter's responses to the division of Shanghai.[21] But even though she cites Cahill's opinion of Chen Hongshou's *A Tall Pine and Taoist Immortal* (1635, Taipei)—namely that it evokes "the absurd world" of Ming society—she does not make use of the larger context of Cahill's argument or what it implies about Qing Dynasty painting; her citation seems mainly intended to get her own argument going.[22]

How are we to understand this passive, often invisible laying-down of narrative? I think I wouldn't be as surprised if most reactions were like Cahill's, because then the last two and a half centuries of Chinese painting would simply be poor work—though I would still want to know how such a thing could happen. But it's doubly intriguing when the painting seems to be merely uninteresting, as if artwork could somehow just be affectively neutral, neither good nor bad. Either way the phenomenon has no parallel in the West: we do not have a tradition that simply sinks from sight.

Hypothesis. The history of Chinese painting has an odd structure. In particular the Ming decline and Qing eclipse have no parallels in the West, and they may be fundamentally inassimilable. [*In the full text of my book, this is the fifth hypothesis. My whole book is structured around a series of six hypotheses.*]

I'm going to oppose that hypothesis to another one, its mirror opposite, because the very invisibility of the period makes it the focus of attention. I cannot imagine a reflective reader of Sherman Lee's books, or of Wen Fong's, who is not immediately fascinated with the possibility that a major tradition could somehow take such a wrong turn that it calls down the combined wrath and indifference of its major historians. Later I will be collecting the relevant traits into the last "moment" of the parallel of historical perspectives:

Counter-hypothesis. Late Ming and Qing artists appear to art history as a form of postmodernism.

54

Some of the most common explanations would have it that later Chinese painting suffered a natural decline. (Sherman Lee's description implies as much.) Thus William Willetts thinks that "pictorial schemas" in the Qing "degenerate into the most threadbare of clichés," precipitating the end of the tradition,[23] and Michael Sullivan suggests that the tradition unraveled because Qing painters after the first generation had nothing to rebel against.[24] Another historian says only that the artists "seemed to have lost contact with any sources of creative energy."[25]

This is the "biological fallacy," the notion that historical movements "grow" and then "decline" the way people or plants do. It borrows its terms from the arc of human life, and—as Panofsky has demonstrated—it often follows classical Greek and Roman schemata that divide a person's life into three, four, or five parts. Ideally the Tang or Song would be the vigorous youth, the Yuan the mature man, and the Ming the decrepit old man. No one says as much, of course, but the fallacy is pervasive in history and it fits the facts here as well.

Some Western scholars mix the biological fallacy with a moral judgment in favor of youthfulness. This is more explicit in earlier sources; thus Binyon speaks of "pedantry and conservatism" and "the ingrained weakness of the Chinese genius," and reserves his highest praise for the "lofty idealism" of the Song.[26] Ernest Fenollosa, too, writes about the degeneration from the "worthy" Song to the "decaying" later dynasties.[27] Usually the fallacy creeps into art histories in the guise of metaphors about death. Arthur Waley's history ends with Gong Xian (d. 1689), whom he calls a "tragic master," whose pictures have a "blank, tomb-like appearance," and he concludes "hactenus dictum sit de dignitate artis morientis."[28]

Thinking about this, it helps to ask what the "fallacy" actually explains. Do we understand a period better because it appears as a kind of natural decline? Is Qing art really like old age in any comprehensible fashion? I would rather say that the biological fallacy and its variations are descriptions, solace for a sad ending rather than analysis of the plot.

55

Among explanations there is James Cahill's argument that the Qing is marked by Western influence. (The first Italian engravings appeared in 1600, and the Qing began in 1644.) For some scholars, the influence of Western paintings and prints dilutes the Chinese tradition, and is cause for regret; for others, it is a delicate subject since it appears to subtract from the value of some Chinese artists. The longest shadow cast by this subject is the possible influence of Western prints on Dong Qichang, a possibility whose remoteness does not make it any less dangerous for a certain understanding of the tradition. Western influence is an interesting subject, since it can be so subtle or unlikely that it may not exist (as with Dong Qichang), or so blatant that it produces monstrous hybrids (as with Giuseppe Castiglione, the Jesuit court painter). It has proven difficult to tell the story, because Qing artists refracted Western chiaroscuro, perspective, modeling, and anatomy in ways that are unexpected and perhaps even invisible to Western eyes. Yun Shouping, for example, painted scenes that use Western perspective and chiaroscuro, but his work is so enmeshed in the Chinese tradition that it may not even make sense to pry Western from Chinese forms.

Western influence is a large subject, still mostly unexplored, but it may have its limitations in explaining the Qing eclipse. I am not sure I would want to assign the *lack of interest* in Qing painting to admixtures of Westernness. It seems to me that if Chinese–Italian admixtures were a principal trait of Qing painting, the period would be *more* interesting to art historians, and more challenging to interpret, than the art that had been made before 1600. Did Western art really only dilute Chinese art, making it flavorless and flat? (And wouldn't flavorless, flat painting be alluring, as it was for Ni Zan?) Or was something else at work?

56

The many negative terms and acknowledgments of descriptive defeat are balanced, oddly, by a single word: *guai.* I take this as another sign of historical anomaly, since it is unusual to collapse a period, or even a generation, onto a single word. Baroque and rococo are well-known examples of derogatory terms that have become empty place-markers for their periods; *rocaille* means "rockwork" and *Baroque* comes from the name of the painter Federigo Barocci—but no one thinks of rococo art as carved gemstones, or of Baroque art as work done in Barocci's style. Tenebrism comes to mind as a possible parallel for the centrality of *guai* (tenebrism names the shadows that took the place of visible forms the generation before), but the situation is historically unusual and has no clear precedents in earlier Chinese art.

Guai is usually translated as "eccentric," a word that passes nearly unchanged throughout European scholarship—*Exzentriker* in German, *eccentrici* in Italian, *les excentriques* in French.[29] Encapsulated that way, the word can seem more restricted than it actually is. In Chinese *guai* means "eccentric," but also "strange, rude, outrageous, wonderful, remarkable, unrestrained, extraordinary and uncanny."[30] For a Westerner writing in the second half of the twentieth century, those words seem natural, a perfect match for any number of postmodern preoccupations. *Rude,* of course, means "unpolished" or "unsophisticated," and as such it is one of the key terms of early modernism. The uncanny has special resonance for recent scholarship on surrealism and its postmodern echoes, and it has been the subject of a number of studies—most recently Hal Foster's *Compulsive Beauty.*[31]

Yet despite its immediate appeal and apparent potential as a descriptive term, the word *guai* also encrypts a negative judgment. As Hans van der Meyden points out, its locus classicus is in the Confucian *Analects*: "The Master did not talk about extraordinary things [*guai*], feats of strength, chaos and spirits." Whatever positive attributes *guai* has, it is founded on a negative judgment, and in that respect every synonym and hortatory usage is an attempt at restitution.

It is curious that *eccentric* usually appears in quotation marks, or in phrases like "so-called eccentrics." On the one hand, that can be understood as an acknowledgment that the painters in question were not merely eccentrics; but it also implies that they were really not eccentrics—after all, how could painters for nearly three hundred years all be eccentric? But if the "eccentrics" weren't eccentrics, then why do we still follow the nineteenth-century custom of calling them eccentrics? As I read it, the ongoing editorial decision to put *eccentrics* in quotation marks is a sign of indecision. It can be especially odd to see *eccentric* in quotation marks when the artists are being described as eccentrics. The twentieth-century painter C. C. Wang occasionally painted in the manner of the Yangzhou eccentrics, even though he thought it was "like singing too fast." Jerome Silbergeld's account of C. C. Wang follows the typographic convention and puts *eccentrics* in quotation marks, creating a strange effect: a traditional twentieth-century painter tries a brief exercise in eccentricity by copying "eccentrics."[32] Like the period they typify, the eccentrics both are and are not worthy of serious attention.

57

Another explanation for the state of later Chinese painting is the long shadow cast by Dong Qichang. Richard Barnhart and others have suggested that we are still under the spell of Dong's historiography, and therefore unable to "value professional painting over *wen-jen* painting, to see the merit in later painters who rejected Dong's values." From Barnhart's point of view "we have been . . . thoroughly brain-washed by a handful of critics," and "it is time to consider their pervasive and destructive influence." It seems, for example, that Dong's coinage of the phrase "Zhe School" (to describe professional and court painters) must be related to the undervaluation of Zhe School painting. The force of Dong's formulation is also brought home in that it has only recently seemed possible to assert that no "school" even existed in an academic sense.[33] Dong's influence can then be called upon to explain the ongoing relative neglect of later Ming and Qing painting, since—as Eugene Wang puts it—Dong's theories posit "an art-historical lineage with [Dong] himself as the ultimate end of history."[34]

Perhaps, then, we are faced with a lingering judgment, which has crept into Chinese historiography and even infected the painters themselves. If so, Barnhart would be right that whatever imbalance remains in Cahill's descriptions is due to Dong's influence; but the subject is tricky, since Cahill spends considerable time looking at professional painting of the kind Dong disparaged. Recent scholarship (especially Barnhart's) shows that such works are far from invisible, and the lingering negative judgments in some texts may not be as significant as the pages of attention that are being lavished on Zhe School painting, Buddhist painting, and other neglected forms.

I say "may not," because Barnhart is also right to go on insisting that even the most compelling description can be effectively undermined by the gentlest negative judgment. Nor will the current work on "less important" genres and artists have lasting historiographic force unless it comes to terms with the originary and ongoing imbalance between privileged and excluded styles. If we imagine Dong's doctrines as the skeletal structure of a building, then the current work on professional artists may be less a matter of rebuilding than of painting and embellishing what is already in place.

But the principal reason I hesitate to accept the idea that Dong Qichang and the theorists who followed are responsible for the Qing eclipse is the amount of time that has passed since Dong died: over three centuries. Until very recently, Dong's theories seemed unanswerable, and his painting unimpeachable.[35] Certainly the West can offer examples of theorists whose ideas still enthrall us after hundreds and even thousands of years. Western philosophy has been said to be nothing more than footnotes to Plato, and thinkers as deeply engaged as Jacques Derrida imagine themselves still partly "inside" Western metaphysics.

But there is a distinction to be made between acknowledging the unarguable nature of some conceptual systems, and making strong local judgments against certain parts of a system. Even if the very idea of Chinese landscape painting is effectively underwritten by Dong and his followers, and even if any discourse about Chinese landscape painting effectively speaks Dong's language, it is still possible to say—however ineffectually—that he is wrong. Dong's theories can't be that unanswerable if the first generations of Western scholars, from Ernest Fenollosa to Laurence Binyon, managed to ignore him almost completely, or if Ludwig Bachhofer could call him an "execrable dilettante."[36]

58

The ubiquitous word *eccentric* is an initial sign that we experience Ming and Qing painting as a form of modernism. A more substantial reason is the eclipse itself. Art that cannot be represented in terms of previous art, that so breaks the tradition that it appears at first invisible, that inverts values so effectively that it appears "unskilled," that sends historians scrambling for terms when their vocabulary fails, that seems at least for a generation or two not to exist: all these are markers of Western modernism from the Impressionists onward.

In one sense it is clear that the individualists and eccentrics are only carrying on what Richard Rorty calls the "conversation" of Chinese painting. (As Jan Fontein puts it, eccentricity is "a form of traditionalism," and the admiration and wonder aroused by eccentricity is nothing more than the "unconventional aspect of a very old convention."[37]) But at the same time the eccentrics seem to be doing it badly, or in a misguided way. The first critics of Impressionism and Postimpressionism reacted similarly: they knew that painting was at issue, but not how it was at issue, and the works were for a time effectively invisible to criticism. In the late Ming and in early modernism the very structure of historical schools and styles seemed in danger of collapse, so that painters had to be become "individualists," or (in the West) "independents."

And then came a situation analogous to late twentieth-century pluralism, which has produced a startlingly large number of movements (as witness the table of contents in any textbook of twentieth-century art) and a corresponding increase in individuals who do not entirely fit those movements. The Qing has at least as many "isms" as the twentieth century, although they are named differently—usually by place or number. There are the Masters of Anhui, the Eight Masters of Nanjing (the Eight Masters of Jinling), the Eight Eccentric Masters of Yangzhou, the Four Small Wangs, the Four Rens, the School of Shanghai, and so forth. (To some extent Chinese writers have always organized their history in this fashion, but most groupings—for instance the Four Talents of Suzhou of the Yuan—are later coinages.[38])

The eclipse itself, therefore, is another piece of evidence that we may be responding to later Chinese painting as a form of modernist rebellion. The eclipse is more than just a symptom of decline (though conservative critics of Western art continue to present modernism in those terms): it is a practice that has achieved such a profound critique of what has gone before that it seems at first to be a gap or a hole in history rather than an ordinary revolution or renascence.

59
As the Qing progressed, schools became shorter lived, individualists and eccentrics more prominent, and styles more diverse. It was an unstable ecology in which competition forced diversification. Each artist needed to accentuate the markers of his style to survive. Eccentrics and more-or-less independent masters sometimes experienced the field of painting as a network of narrow paths: that is, instead of developing broadly referential, catholic styles, they embarked in specific directions, carefully restricting and underscoring their innovations. This led to a constriction and simplification of the crystallized style definitions that the Yuan artists had first given to artists of the Tang and Song.

In the Qing, the traits by which styles were known were sometimes further limited to those susceptible of hyperbole. Thus Ni Zan's skeletal articulations continued to be important, while his sense of what we call plasticity and three-dimensionality were de-emphasized or altered. This restriction of personal style did not always mean that artists worked in only one style, but rather that they chose eclectically among a number of possibilities, each strongly emphasized and narrowed. The same happened in professional painting; in Barnhart's words, sixteenth-century Min School works are "uniformly slapdash and sketchy, given to dramatic gestures of brush and ink, like an exaggerated stage performance of something that had once been quite restrained."[39]

In Cahill's formulation, style had become idea: that is, the artists sought and adopted styles the way ideas have been transmitted in the West, as essential and sometimes exclusive carriers of meaning.[40] In broad terms, this inflated economy of styles marks the current art world in the West, where it is embraced under the name "pluralism" and seen as a healthy alternative to the apparently restrictive norms of earlier art.

60

Examples are available in the four principal "priest-hermit-individualists," Bada Shanren, Gong Xian, Shitao, and Kuncan; in the nearly contemporaneous Masters of Anhui (Hongren, Xiao Yuncong, Zha Shibiao, Mei Qing, along with Dai Benxiao); and in the slightly later Eight Eccentric Masters of Yangzhou (including Hua Yan, Jin Nong, Huang Shen, Li Shan, Luo Ping, and Gao Xiang).[41]

Mei Qing (1623–1697), for instance, "invented some six or eight motifs and varied them ad infinitum."[42] One of his "motifs" is a "rolling, rococo movement" "not unlike" Fragonard. Jin Nong's (1687–1764) compositions were called "most peculiar" and "quite startling,"[43] but at the same time they paid for their eccentricity by a restriction on versatility; to one scholar, the Eight Eccentric Masters are somewhat predictable since "the scope of their painting themes was narrow."[44] Huang Shen (1687–1768) had an "exaggerated," "nervous, flying touch," which "evidently puzzled his countrymen who called him 'too extravagant.'"[45] The traces of his beginning in Huang Gongwang, Ni Zan, and Wu Zhen have been almost burned away in his fiery, skittish brushwork.[46] Other artists took even more extreme measures. Gao Qipei is famous for painting with his fingernails: early in the day, they were sharp and suitable for fine painting, and later they were good for "broad stains and splashes" in the *pomo* technique.[47]

I think this is a familiar picture. Contemporary Western art observes a similar economy in which artists adopt strategies that are at once extreme and narrow. If I name a representative list—say, Barbara Kruger, Jenny Holzer, Jeff Koons, Christian Boltanski, Leon Golub, Nancy Spero, Annette Messager, Francesco Clemente, Damien Hirst, Wolfgang Laib, and Sigmar Polke—then what comes to mind, at least initially, is each artist's signature strategy. Jenny Holzer's LCD displays, Barbara Kruger's *National Enquirer* font, Wolfgang Laib's fields of pollen, Damien Hirst's cows in formaldehyde, Sigmar Polke's fugitive chemicals: those are the visual strategies that produce the effect of pluralism. Each is narrow in the sense that it is specific to the artist, and extreme in the sense that it is strongly different from any other strategy.

This is not to say that the Western artists are necessarily producing impoverished work—what are called one liners or one-note works. It may take time to spell out the actual relation between a given style and the fuller range of a work's meaning, and there is no necessary correlation between styles that are instantly recognizable and works that are overly simple. Postmodernism is not a shrinkage of meaning as much as an attenuation of meaning: meaning is differently shaped than it had been.

Strategy, a word I have been using throughout the book, is typically postmodern in its mixture of down-to-earth artist's technique and canny, politically informed decision. An artist "works in" a style or manner, but "adopts" a strategy or a stance. The very word evokes the labile state of affairs in postmodern art.

61

Not all elements of the crystallized style definitions were susceptible to the kind of hyperbole that the Chinese artists desired. The class of traits "susceptible of hyperbole" includes those that can be taken from already crystallized versions of the styles of historical figures, as well as those that can be multiplied until they become the single strategy for an entire painting, or an entire lifetime's work.

Three of the most prominent candidates were the anatomizing of Ni Zan, the archaizing of Zhao Mengfu, and the structural inventions of Dong Qichang. Hongren (1610–1664), for instance, practiced a "bare bones" style based on the style of Xiao Yuncong,[48] but derived theoretically from Zhao Mengfu's strategy in relation to *his own* past: "Hongren does to Xiao Yuncong's style what Zhao Mengfu did to Li Cheng's. . . . He depletes the color and flesh and leaves only the bare bones."[49]

The "gentle renunciation" and "mournful loneliness" that has been seen in his works is a benefit of the style: exaggerate the style of Ni Zan, and you increase the pathos of the result.[50] The "spindly trees" in Hongren's paintings almost crackle with brittleness, and the whole is airless and blanched. Looking from a Hongren to a Ni Zan is a relief, a return to actual water and palpable rock.[51]

The style that is "an essence of an essence, refined to the breaking point and always on the verge of disappearance" became a stock-in-trade for later painters. Zha Shibiao (1615–1698), another of the Masters of Anhui, practiced a "global mannerism," a hyperbolic extension of Wu Zhen's wet brush technique. In some paintings he let the wet brush become flaccid and weak, in distant emulation of Huang Gongwang's "insistently repeated brushstrokes."[52] In others he expanded the style nearly into a "full [Western] water-color technique."[53] Dai Benxiao, another of the Masters of Anhui, sometimes painted in very dry strokes, in an exaggeration of his contemporary Gong Xian's recommendation.[54] *Man in Cave* pictures a dry, crumbling world, and it is painted in a deliberately feeble and trembling manner. (It shows a mountainside, with two cutaway views into caves. In the lower center, a man sits meditating under milky stalactites.)

The Masters of Anhui are a typical group: they splayed themselves into as many styles as they could manage: very dry, very wet, very skeletal, very florid, very slow, very fast. Ni Zan, Zhao Mengfu, and Dong Qichang are touchstones for this kind of art because they lend themselves—for reasons that have yet to be analyzed—to hyperbole.

62

Western images may be another example of strategies that were "susceptible of hyperbole." Given the recorded reactions to Western images, it is reasonable to assume that prints appeared as objects already strongly marked by immoderate visual strategies. Chiaroscuro, in particular, might well have looked like an "eccentric" strategy akin to others that were already in play.

To Western eyes, early landscapes by Gong Xian (active ca. 1655, died 1689) are "strange, silent" and "ominous," and they may owe those qualities to a personal encounter with Western chiaroscuro.[55] That possibility, if true, would mean that that Dong Qichang learned from Western engravings, since Gong's forms can sometimes be read as details of Dong Qichang's "chiaroscuro" modeling. (Gong's leaden "close-ups" are also a form of exaggeration, since their portentous lugubriousness is made possible by the perception that Dong's forms could be anatomized or "magnified" into a compositional principle.)

Other exaggerated mannerisms spring from iconographic conventions. Bada Shanren (1626–1705) is an instance of the expansion of pictorial wit and irony—not to mention the interest in versions of the "artistic temperament"—that also characterizes Western art since the late middle ages.[56] As far back as Wu Zhen, elements of older traditions (especially the formulaic architecture inherited from the Northern Song) had been treated lightly or humorously by archaists.[57] Bada Shanren's painting explores the possibility that many other forms might be susceptible to ironic "mistreatment." The fact that scholars can disagree on assessments of his wobbly birds and fish (some seeing them as humorous, others as "angry-looking"[58]) is readily comprehensible given his hyperbolic wit.

63

The possible role of Western art, and the rise of humorous versions of themes that were once serious, are also signs that history itself was beginning to lose some of its overwhelming weight. The "eccentric" artists did not feel the pressure to align themselves with one or another style that preoccupied artists from Zhao Mengfu to Dong Qichang. History seemed more open, less fraught, more immediately and widely accessible. These are again hallmarks of postmodernism. From a postmodern perspective, history is no longer composed of schools and styles that come up out of the distant past like mountain ranges. A postmodern artist is more free to go where he pleases, and take shards or fragments from any artist's work, from any period. Ancient artists are as "close" as recent ones, and any mistake or forgotten convention can be exhumed and pressed into service for the next round of styles.

When historical styles lose their force, and negotiating or rewriting the past ceases to be a pressing issue for the formation of new modes of working, then history itself begins to seem a little distant and irrelevant. Shitao (1642–1718), the more radical of the Two Stones [Shitao and Shixi or Kuncan], marked his independence from history by a preference for the album leaf format, experimentation with color, and a loose, "Western," "no-method" brushstroke.[59] It may be that those strongly circumscribed sources of inspiration, and the telescoped sense of the past they entail, contributed to his sense that he was free of history, with no predecessors and no followers.[60] This, too, is characteristic of recent Western art, in which the world of the Renaissance and its pictorial concepts is largely divorced from current concerns, and in which artists make statements declaring their absolute independence from aspects of the past. Barbara Kruger's dissociation of herself from the Western male tradition of "genius" is an example.[61] Postmodern artists (and art historians) often lack interest in the art of previous centuries, and many lack curiosity about the historical anomaly of their lack of interest.

64

Now it may be time to put the argument together, since I want to say that the Qing eclipse and its hyperbolic economy are both modeled with interesting precision by a particular Western theory about a possible end-state of history. The model draws an equation between a prevalent construction of postmodernism and a problem in chess called the "endgame," and it begins with slightly earlier scholarship on the affinity between chess-playing and economies of artistic production.

In art history the chess model surfaces first in Hubert Damisch's *Fenêtre jaune cadmium*, a book of essays published in 1984. Damisch draws a parallel between playing chess and playing the game of art at any given moment, or in any given milieu. He distinguishes between the match or individual game, which he calls the *partie*, and the game itself, in its immutable rules and possibilities, which he calls the "game of Painting" (*jeu "Peinture"*).[62] The slight ambiguity between a match and a single game is tolerated because Damisch means to distinguish between *plays* that are made at particular historical moments, in particular conditions, and *play* that takes place continuously, since it is the name for the conditions and rules under which chess makes sense.

One of the problems this makes clear is the difference between playing *a* game of painting, and playing *the* game of painting. The Abstract Expressionists may have believed they were "returning to the very foundations of the game, to its immediate, constitutive given terms," even though what they made can be understood as the result of a particular game, a match in which certain locally meaningful problems were being worked out within a field of limited possibilities.[63] Occasionally it is also helpful to distinguish a match from a sequence of games within it. Thus Damisch speaks of the "match" of abstraction, which has been underway since shortly after the turn of the century, and the Abstract Expressionists' "games" begun fifty years after the match was first joined. So *parties* are either individual games or matches, though in other contexts Damisch calls them "plays" (in English), implying that a painter's works might be moves within a game rather than a game itself.[64] The slight slippage is important in putting Damisch's argument to work: as it stands in *Fenêtre jaune cadmium,* the chess metaphor is a way of thinking about two levels of play: one, the game apparently set in place by the medium itself; the other, a series of games apparently set in motion by individuals, schools, styles, and other historically contingent agents. The difference is fictional, but it gives a name to a distinction that is usually played out unnoticed, as if it were just part of the given conditions, the *données,* of art.

Imagining art history as a chess game is initially a way of avoiding Hegelian historical sequences and replacing them with a combinatoric model that has no single inexorable direction. Another advantage of the model is that it pictures a work (or an artist, or school, or period) as an event bounded by certain rules. Like a chess piece, an artist's work can move only in its neighborhood, and only in accord with capacities that are taken to be effectively inbuilt and unchangeable. (A knight, for example, cannot start moving like a bishop.) For that reason Damisch likes to speak about a "field" (*champ*) or "place" (*lieu*) where the game is played, moving at one moment right or left, forward or backward, but never merely or continuously forward as Hegel would have it.[65]

65

Yve-Alain Bois puts a slightly different stress on these ideas when he re-presents them (in the form of a review of Damisch's *Fenêtre jaune cadmium*) in his *Painting as Model.* There Damisch's work is given a powerful, sympathetic reading, and set out as four "models" for asking fundamental questions about the object and the act of painting. Bois calls the fourth model "strategic," and suggests it was born from Damisch's interpretation of Barnett Newman's apparently careless remark that "everything he had been able to do had meaning only in relation to Pollock's work and *against* it."[66] The difference between Bois's etiology and Damisch's Wittgenstinian interest is slight—the two are compatible, in this context—but also decisive, since it reorients the chess metaphor as a question of personal decisions and reactions. "A work has significance," Bois glosses, following Lévi-Strauss's account of masks, "first by what it is not and what it opposes."[67] It is the oppositions, then, that work to create new configurations, new strategic opportunities, and ultimately new "matches." As I read it, Damisch's account is more neutral, more concerned (as a chess master might be) with the configurations and patterns on the board. Bois's story is a little more engaged, in chess terms more concerned with offense and defense, with possibilities taken up and declined.

66

"Endgame" is a chess player's term, and I want to spend a few moments on its normative meaning to set the chess player's understanding alongside the model that has been elaborated in contemporary art theory.

A chess game becomes an endgame when there are so few pieces left that it becomes unclear whether or not either player can bring the game to a conclusion. There are situations in chess where neither player can force a mate, and situations in which neither player can force a draw. In such cases one player might want to continue playing, in the hope—perhaps misguided—that an end might present itself, and the other player would then be compelled to continue without such an illusion, or else resign out of sheer disinterest or fatigue. Endgame theories in chess are devoted to the conditions under which it is possible to force a mate or a draw, and in chess rules a game is officially a draw if neither player can force a solution in less than fifty moves.

Actual chess, therefore, puts limits on the endlessness that haunts visual theorists when they talk about what has come to be called "endgame art."[68] As it has been described by artists such as Sherrie Levine, the endgame condition is one of apparently endless reshuffling of possibilities that have been tried many times before. As Levine says, "the world is filled to suffocating" with images, so there is no longer any meaning in pretending that originality is possible.[69] The oppressive, slightly anemic sense of the endgame was captured decades before endgame theory by Samuel Beckett, whose novel *Murphy* begins with the wonderful, depressing line: "The sun shone, having no alternative, on the nothing new." Murphy, the protagonist, carries "somehow on" as Beckett himself did, thinking increasingly about nothing except the mechanisms of motion and their extension into the infinite future. The interminable waiting for Godot, and the wavering, eternal surveillance in *Ill Seen Ill Said* are also pictures of the endgame: its mood is antihistorical, quietist, pessimist, and always dully aware, as if the protagonist is suffering through a perpetual low-level siege.

67

The endgame model is tempting: it trapped Beckett, despite his fierce analysis of his moods, into a kind of strangulated attention on the absence of onward motion in works like *Nohow On*. It meshes with everyday studio talk, especially when artists speak about their latest "strategies" and "moves," and the "stances" they take in relation to various ephemeral issues and styles. The complicity between the historical understanding current in postmodernism and the notion of the endgame may be deeper than what we can so far understand. And yet if the endgame is to be made explicit and taken as a model, it may have several specific limits.

In particular I wonder if the endgame, and the *jeu "Peinture"* more generally, can do more than stave off the Hegelian sequence, and the attendant notion that the "game of painting" somehow is, was, or should be moving forward. Elsewhere I have argued that an antihistoricist model may not be an effective method of overturning Hegelian certainties, which tend to resurface in ever more devious forms; but at least the endgame provides a new conceptual field in which a non-

Hegelian art might seem to thrive.[70] One of the cracks in the anti-Hegelian armor of the endgame is the drive to win, and the question of the ultimate aim of any one move. In Damisch's model, the interest is more formal or structural, the way a *go* player is supposed to take pleasure in the shifting configurations of the board as the game develops. In Bois's account, the slightly greater emphasis on making moves, especially to oppose other moves, also presses the question of purpose. A chess player's purpose, after all, is to trap pieces: that is, to create a condition in which the opposing player is petrified. The game of *go* is even more ruthless, since its players aim to crowd their opponents so closely that they die. Actual endgames are played on a nearly empty field, but metaphorical ones are played on very crowded fields. It is no accident that Beckett was dogged by a condition of partial paralysis, in which he could only rock helplessly back and forth.

So I would rather describe the endgame as a condition in which two senses of history batter against one another: from one perspective forward movement seems impossible, and every new move looks like it has been made many times before; but for that very reason the slightest move forward is the object of intense interest, and nearly every thought is directed at the faint possibility that something might decisively end. It goes without saying that such a condition also encourages the most virulent forms of competition. In the game of *go*, the very same players who are supposed to be complacently experiencing the unfolding patterns of the board are also "secretly" competing against one another. *Go* is filled to suffocating with metaphors of suffocation, as players build walls of stone around their opponents' pieces in hopes of cutting off their avenues of escape and ultimately even the air they breathe.

Another limitation to the endgame (and to the chess metaphor in general) is brought out by its affinities with Wittgenstein's model of language games. Ultimately Damisch's source for the idea of a game is Wittgenstein, and he has allied himself with Wittgenstein especially in the recent catalogue *Traité du Trait, Tractatus tractus,* where the early Wittgenstein becomes the ironic model for a meditation on "games" of painting very much akin to the later Wittgenstein's notion of "language games." As I read it, Damisch intends the *Traité du trait* to be ironically Wittgenstinian, especially because he avoids the famous proposition 7.0 from Wittgenstein's *Tractatus* (the one that declares the place of silence "in" philosophy). At the same time Damisch is interested in playing with the "games" of marking (*traits*), including the Chinese "game." For Wittgenstein, the point of imagining or isolating a game is to elucidate the sense and function of such ideas as truth, grammar, and certainty—in other words, a game is an occasion for clarification. Here I read a deep cleft between Damisch and Wittgenstein, since I find that for Damisch games are of interest largely because they avoid the clarity of the Hegelian machinery. What counts is their complexity, not their precise configuration. This orientation helps Damisch remain as long as possible outside the ordinary machinery of art history, with its sequences, traditions and influences, but it also forces him to keep *actual* gaming at arm's length.

68

The endgame metaphor makes good sense of a number of traits of Qing painting. It explains the artists' ongoing attempts to crystallize the past, or to mine it for recuperable fragments of styles, because those actions imply that history itself is somehow broken. With the sequence of periods no longer in operation, any past accomplishment can be appropriated and used to energize a work, even if its effect wears off almost immediately. The intermittent awareness of an ongoing ending of a tradition also explains the increasing narrowness of artists' strategies, and their brilliance against the background of dull repetitions: if the "game" is reduced to a repetitious shuffling of pieces, a move needs to be sharp and focused to stand out.

These signs are also the symptoms of kitsch, and they are among the classic traits of the avant-garde as it has been understood since the early fourteenth century. As Karsten Harries once argued, a public immured in kitsch makes accelerating demands for pleasure, and eventually fails to even recognize strategies once thought to be outrageous. Its jaded eye sees less and less, until it is attracted only by the most spectacular and shortest-lived phenomena.[71] The avant-garde could be described in similar terms; E. H. Gombrich has done so in speaking about the "leaven of criticism" in Renaissance art, and how it impelled artists to take increasingly long strides with each new work.[72]

Both kitsch and the avant-garde can also be defined as movements with clear beginnings and no obvious endings short of political and ideological metamorphosis (or, in Damisch's terms, short of the inception of a new game). The endgame probably cannot be understood apart from kitsch or the origins of the avant-garde, since it borrows ideas from both. But it has a peculiarity that suits postmodernism especially well, and that is its relative lack of change over time. It is a kind of steady-state condition that is not prone to inflation: the anxiety in an endgame art is that the play might remain as it is forever, but the anxiety in kitsch is that things might not be able to move fast enough.

69

Especially as it is articulated by artists such as Sherrie Levine, the endgame raises a very interesting possibility, one that casts a dim light on postmodernism's sense of itself: by its nature, an endgame is taken to be potentially endless, and therefore, to the extent that postmodernism is experienced as an "endgame art," postmodernism itself may not have an end. A given "game" of postmodern painting might well come to an end, and even the game of painting itself might end (as Arthur Danto, Joseph Kosuth, and others have said), but postmodernism itself may never reach a conclusion.

Generally my sense of the literature is that postmodernism is imagined as a historical period, and that we are living through a fin de siècle of multiple possibilities that will somehow be subsumed under a solidly codified postmodernism or else decisively replaced by whatever is to come. In place of this diffident meliorism, the apparent endlessness of the Qing eclipse (it was interrupted only by the Revolution, and in conservative painting it is still underway) implies a different future for the Western game of painting. Perhaps—not least because we may believe it ourselves—our next few centuries will see more of the same hyperbole. Perhaps, in other words, the endgame is in fact interminable, and postmodernism is not only a period but a state that comes after periods. In this respect Chinese painting is an object lesson, a reminder that our post-Renaissance culture is still young, and that a rich ongoing disintegration may await us "after" postmodernism—at least until we can manage to tell ourselves other kinds of stories.

Abstract as this possibility is, wisps of it are in the air whenever the game metaphor is at work. It hints that postmodernism may be a different kind of concept than modernism, and not just the name of a period that follows modernism. The middle ages, the renaissance, the baroque, neoclassicism, romanticism, and even modernism would be names of periods, as they have always been taken to be; and they would be susceptible as ever to Hegelian notions of sequence and progress. Postmodernism, though, might be different: it could be the name of the "period" that arrives when the sequence of historical periods has played itself out. It was certainly that way in Beckett's mind: his condition was interminable by definition (or more exactly, it was indefinably interminable).

The best writing on the endgame is intimately related to the dawning—and necessarily incomplete—understanding that the endless listlessness is also a form of dying. Yve-Alain Bois sees the endgame as a Freudian work of mourning, in which painting slowly recognizes its investment in "millenarianist" hopes and turns to the slow business of "working through the end of painting." Louis Marin has also written about painting and mourning, and Jacques Derrida has taken mourning as the principal theme in Marin's work.[73] In *Les fins de la peinture* René Démoris asks about painting's aims, its intentions and ends, and though he recognizes that the nature of painting itself enjoins these questions, and that there can be no satisfactory answer, it might be argued that his questions have the urgency and persistence that comes from the long Western expectation that periods do end.[74] This is where metaphors of exhaustion and decline, so common in accounts of Qing painting, meet Western counterparts in a theory about a slowly gathering sense of impending—but indefinitely postponed—death.

70

To sum up: the later history of Chinese art is marked by brief, eye-catching and idiosyncratic schools, and artists distinguished by single hypertrophied traits or monomaniacally repeated tricks. China's past three centuries have seen a continual simplification of narratives of the past, together with a disintegration of historical connectedness. Their artists have had to try ever harder to obtain notice, resulting in an economy of improvised ideals, idiosyncrasy, exaggeration and eccentricity, and a concomitant shift away from conventional canons, normative ideals, serious purpose, and prolonged labor on single works.

The Chinese pluralism did not heal or define itself, and in this century the legacy of its diffuse confusion has been incorporated into social realism and other Western currents rather than clarified by them. An endless lingering "postmodernism" was the lot of Chinese painting before outside currents disrupted their sense of the problems and purposes of art. Despite vigilant and acute self-reflection regarding historical position and meaning (a trait shared by postmodern theory in the West) the Chinese painters did not imagine that they were in the midst of anything quantitatively different than the succession of styles and schools that comprised art history as they knew it.

Postmodernism in both cultures can be redescribed as an interminable final stage produced and defined by the very history that appears to say it must be otherwise—that is, the history that has always defined itself by dynasties or periods, manners or styles, artists or schools. Even the monotony of later Qing art makes sense in this model: as the years wear on, even the most strident voices sink into the background noise, and the most outrageous mixtures of styles blend into a uniform grey. Painting is still going, but, as Sherman Lee says, exhaustion has made no answer. . . .

71

Something about Chinese landscape painting stirs my interest in questions of art and art history, rather than the other way around. The problems come out of what is said about the paintings, and they return to the paintings as if for nourishment. Because of the nature of this inquiry I have not had the opportunity to say much about what attracts me to individual paintings—their technique, their visual force, their painters' lives—and it may often have seemed that I would rather talk about what history might be, or how it appears, rather than what it is or was. I understand those preferences as signs of the encounter itself: when it is seen as art history, Chinese landscape painting insistently raises questions that take a viewer away from viewing and toward reflection on viewing. Before I end, therefore, I want to draw a few conclusions about Chinese landscape painting itself.

I have never felt what I assume is perfectly ordinary for a specialist of Chinese painting: the conviction that I am understanding the painting in the way it was intended—not projecting inordinately, or generalizing inappropriately, but merely apprehending, with fair accuracy, what the artist meant me to see. To some degree that deficiency on my part is one of the effects of not reading Chinese, and so always being reminded of the veil of translation between my words and anything the artist might have said. (I have copied Chinese paintings, and then the sense of intimate understanding is present in full force.) But the larger reason is my interest in how Chinese paintings have historical and expressive meaning as Chinese paintings, and to Western art history.

Why should Chinese paintings spark this interest more than, say, Indian paintings or Mesoamerican images? Perhaps because the tradition of Chinese landscape painting seems so much like the tradition of Western art history: its myriad artists, schools, and interpretive texts are the familiar elements of Western art history. Studying a Chinese painting is very like studying a Western painting: there are contemporaneous documents, critical and appreciative texts, contemporaneous historians and other informants, social and political circumstances—and all that before it's even necessary to open a book of art history. I think that to an art historian, Chinese painting is always already art historical, and for that reason it continuously returns me to questions of interpretation. When it is otherwise (as it sometimes is when I am imaginatively wandering in a Chinese landscape, or when I am immersed in copying one) I also recognize that I am not experiencing the work as an object in history.

72

The match between the study of Chinese landscape painting and the expectations of Western art history is uncanny, in Freud's original sense of the word. Chinese painting is the doppelganger of Western painting, the perfect double that is somehow less than perfect, the twin who differs in some fundamental and secret way. Freud's idea of *Unheimlichkeit* is appropriate here, because Chinese painting is at one and the same instant *just the same* as art history (it conforms to art historical expectations at every point) and utterly different. This is more than a psychological effect: I think it is generated by the discipline itself, and is therefore one of the conditions for understanding Chinese art in general. I don't mean that Chinese painting has to be understood through Freud, but that it cannot be seen except as a near-miss for Western expectations. That is what I mean by the title of my book: Chinese landscape painting presents itself to us as Western art history, even though we know full well that it isn't, and that tension animates and generates art historical meaning. To ignore the uncanny resemblance, or to put it in footnotes, is to avoid the full game of art history.

My first hypothesis was that "Chinese landscape painting tends to appear as an example . . . and not a co-equal in the production or reception of art history itself," but that isn't quite right. Chinese landscape painting is not an example, but an exemplary encounter: it is the occasion in which art history finds itself most nearly mirrored, most nearly matched by a discourse that is clearly not its own.

And as in any cultural encounter (or any encounter with a ghostly twin) both sides begin to seem strange. Writing this essay has made me wonder again about my understanding of Western art history. It seems less easy, now, to look at a picture without thinking of the structures of history it implies. What does it mean to say a Western artist misunderstands tradition (as I think Wu Bin misunderstood his)? Which artistic strategies in the West have been "crystallized" (as in Wang Wei, or Li Cheng)? The Chinese tradition is not the only one that groups and opposes artists in unlikely ways. How is our sense of the Renaissance affected by the extremely unlikely triad of Leonardo, Raphael, and Michelangelo? In what ways does the Western sequence of periods conform to the supposedly non-Western sequence of shifting "renewal" and "synthesis"?

As Freud knew, the encounter with the *Doppelgänger* is an encounter with the patient's own history. As it unfolds, the patient comes to understand himself. In the end, of course, there is no ghost: only an echo chamber of hallucinations and unrealized desires. The Chinese example is far more frightening, because the "ghost" is real—perhaps, as I have suggested, it is more substantial than the patient. Encountering Chinese landscape painting is a way of wondering out loud what it means to want to write art history. What does it mean to assume that painting has a history? And above all: What does it mean to *want* painting to have a history?

73

So the encounter itself becomes the subject, and its problems overwhelm the investigation of the paintings. But does it also lead to new knowledge about the paintings? Is there also a truth-value here, a conclusion that might be drawn about Zhao Mengfu or Dong Qichang? I will offer three answers, one responding mainly to the principal argument; another more pessimistic; and the third, I think, the best.

[*In the full text of* Chinese Landscape Painting as Western Art History, *I propose that one of the best ways of comparing Chinese and Western painting, or art history, is by contrasting "historical perspectives." For example, the past, as it seemed to people in the Yuan (or more accurately, as it was reimagined by later writers) was composed of a recent past, the Southern Song, which seemed unusable, preceded by a more distant past, the Northern Song, which appeared to be a good model to be emulated. The structure of the past was therefore a distant past, followed by a gap, leading to the present. The same structure can be observed in the Italian Renaissance, when people looked and saw a recent past—the middle ages—that seemed unusable, preceded by a more distant period—classical antiquity—that provided models for emulation. My original idea in writing* Chinese Landscape Painting as Western Art History *was to consider whether this "comparison of historical perspectives," as I called it, might be an optimal way to compare Chinese and Western painting. It seemed much better, for example, than calling Southern Song "romantic" or comparing Guo Xi to Caspar David Friedrich. After I had written a second draft of the book, I began to wonder whether the comparison of historical perspectives was as neutral as it seemed. That doubt is raised and examined in the chapters of my book that are omitted from this excerpt.*]

Unlike some parallels, the comparison of historical perspectives is not immediately intended to find out some truth about the paintings. It is principally a discursive tool, a strategy for finding out how Western art history guides the exposition of the development of Chinese painting. Even so, nothing in the comparison entails that Chinese art is epistemologically inaccessible. It seems unlikely, for instance, that the Chinese senses of their past could be entirely different from the ways they are presented in Western art history. There is even evidence that art historians are sometimes more Chinese than the Chinese themselves, for instance when we stress "eccentricity" even though the term becomes widespread only after the fact, or when we insist on pairings such as Li–Guo even though things were initially much more open-ended.[75] In regard to the parallel of historical perspectives my own opinion is that Cahill's account is mostly right, and that the Chinese sense of their past does correspond, by and large, with the history as he presents it. Art historians do learn about the Chinese sense of history when they read his texts and those of art historians who are in accord with his historiographic descriptions.

Certainly this leaves other questions unasked. One of the things that it means to say a historical account is true is that it makes sense within a certain kind of writing, and a certain sense of history. (More on that in a moment.) It also implies that the account is adequate or sufficient to its task, meaning that it represents its subject fairly well, with no egregiously misplaced emphasis. But by its nature, emphasis continuously shifts. In the book from which this is excerpted, I take exception to some comparisons not because they seem untrue, but because their emphases are decidedly Western. When Wen Fong frames the history of Chinese painting as a sequence leading from surface to depth, and then to "eccentric" elaboration, I wonder how much of his account was made possible by mid- to late-twentieth century concerns about formalism, the flat picture plane, the dissolution of perspective, and the turn from naturalistic depiction. Although it is clear that Chinese painters were concerned with such issues, I am also interested to know what happens when Chinese painting is presented as an art that can be described primarily or optimally as a negotiation of surfaces and fictive space. Space is a ruling metaphor in modernist scholarship in a way that it never has been in past centuries, and so in reading accounts such as Wen Fong's I try to watch for signs of a rearrangement of the hierarchy of critical terms, and a typically art historical interest in the dynamic of plane and recession.

The analogous question arises in Cahill's books whenever historical perspectives are important to the narrative. On many occasions Chinese scholar-painters were preoccupied with their positions in relation to the past. It may be a Western emphasis, however, to gather perspectives into sequences and string them into overarching narratives about the succession of painting from the Tang onward. Needless to say my own account does that in a deliberate, mechanical fashion, and no such construct appears in any one text of Cahill's. It's the way an argument might return to such a principle, or build from it in a consistent fashion, that makes me see a Western preoccupation.

74

My initial purpose in spinning out the comparison of historical perspectives was to see what the most neutral, unobjectionable comparison might look like when it is more fully developed. As I put it in the fourth hypothesis, the idea was to look at a comparative principle that seems (at least in principle) to be above suspicion, and to show how it is part of the machinery of Western art history. Looking at things from that perspective, the entire parallel of historical perspectives may be just as thoroughly Western, just as much a projection, as Rowland's prose-poems about Li Cheng's "demon groves." I don't think we can quite see it that way, even though many details seem unlikely when they are spelled out; from the vantage of twentieth-century scholarship, the parallel of historical periods points to a deep structure within art history itself. Yet in time, I suspect it may appear more superficial.

Art historians tend not to spend much time thinking about themselves, or unearthing the unanalyzed assumptions they bring to their work. Reading older art history, it can be glaringly obvious how art historians were products of their time and how their conclusions say more about themselves than about their subjects. Fenellosa's writings appear that way, and to a lesser degree so do Binyon's and Rowland's. We no longer read them to find out about Chinese paintings. Instead they are of historiographic interest, since they are part of the history of the reception of Chinese art. And from an even more distant perspective, the entire project of art history starkly contrasts with Chinese accounts of their own art written before Western contact. From that vantage everything we do is Western, down to the Wade-Giles or pinyin transliterations and the halftone reproductions with their Western-style captions.

It is not easy to take this obvious lesson to heart. It means that art history is not only impelled by the cultural milieu of its authors, but largely determined by it: so much so that in a few decades' time it will seem that twentieth-century art history was more a diary of Western impressions than a contribution to the understanding of Chinese art. Though it seems impossible now, the time may well come when future historians read accounts by Wen Fong, Cahill, and others (as well as texts I have written on Western art) as signs and symptoms of the latter half of the twentieth century in America. These are stark and unpleasant thoughts, and they lead with a dull unarguable logic to the conclusion that comparisons are primarily opportunities for unnoticed self-representation.

75

That is the difficult truth that so seldom appears in the course of ordinary art historical research. It strikes me that the reason the two alternatives of naïve truth and wholesale projection become such a stark opposition has to do with the nature of the subject. When Panofsky considered Dürer, or Dvořák looked at El Greco, they saw something of themselves, and they knew as much. That "salve," as I called it, helped hide the two extreme possibilities (that Dürer or El Greco simply were the people they seemed, or that they had no resemblance to Panofsky's or Dvořák's imaginings). In contemplating Chinese painting there is no "balanced equilibrium," as ecologists say, and a historian's thoughts may oscillate wildly between the inordinate anxiety over projecting modern or Western ideas, and the indefensible complacency entailed in making parallels as if they were only heuristic aids. At least that is why I have presented such bald alternatives, and entwined the history of Chinese landscape painting with the more "general" issue of comparison, or representation.

Another, and perhaps even more difficult truth is that once they have been sighted, the twin poles of naïve acceptance and disaffected relativism do not fade away. Ultimately—outside the discipline of art history—the project of writing art history is Western, and so we necessarily distort the Chinese sense of their history. From that point of view, it's very unlikely that any of these parallels have force. They probably say less about recurring patterns of history across cultures than about patterns we instinctively understand and try to find in other cultures. Every once in a while it is important to say as much, and to step back from the profession in order to ask what it wants to do. The resulting disorientation is more thorough than anything postcolonial historians want when they search for ideological distortions, since they also want to get on with the business of writing art history. From this farthest viewpoint, *all* of art history is a Western project, one with no place in pre-contact China. Chinese landscape painting, even when we are most vigilant, even when we pare our more obvious Western usages or corral them into footnotes, and most especially when we are satisfied with some measure of veracity, *is* Western art history.

76

Overt comparisons, such as the one I have proposed, are like narrow searchlights playing on the dark ground of our habitual thinking. We are drawn toward comparisons, and if it weren't illogical I would say we are especially drawn to comparisons we don't recognize. Comparisons, parallels, analogues, and metaphors are the foundation of understanding, even though historical understanding turns against them whenever it can.

Yet parallels are tricky things. A discipline too wary of comparisons is apt to repeat them unawares, and shy away from cross-cultural inquiries. If the only interest of cultural comparisons is to deconstruct them, or to reveal their inherent violence or distortion, then it can come to seem as if a continual vigilance against comparisons is an adequate response to the (then curious) fact that they continue to reappear.

The *structure* of comparisons, I would rather say, is built into the discipline in ways too deep to be excavated: and so the virtue of looking for the best available comparison, on the largest possible scale, and following it to see where it leads (instead of censoring its operative terms, and shutting it down prematurely), is that such an inquiry can help show us part of the inevitable shape of art historical understanding. The really interesting questions for postcolonial theory concern the structures we cannot avoid, and the optimal ways of thinking about them.

Why do art historians tend to be so wary of comparisons, especially when they begin to sound too serious or systematic? Why attack them so vociferously, or avoid them so studiously? Partly because they are evidence that something non-Western is being seen through Western eyes, and also partly because they are so vulnerable to critique. I'd like to suggest another reason as well: comparisons draw fire because they are symptoms of a condition that we sense is endemic to the discipline. Like a tic, they register a deeper problem. Even though at any given moment the comparison itself is what seems faulty, the deeper issue is the shape of our imaginations, which has generated the problem to begin with. This is where we come up against inscrutable words like "art," "history," and "the West." And that brings me to the final hypothesis, which is more a caution against the overenthusiastic hunt for ideological bias:

Sixth hypothesis. There are reasons to keep trying to understand how art history is Western. But any such attempt will remain within Western art history, and if an account succeeds in throwing off Western assumptions it will no longer be recognizable *as* art history.

In other words: the repertoire of comparisons effectively *is art history.* It can be criticized, amended, prefaced, suppressed, analyzed, dissected, "atomized," and silenced, but it cannot be expunged without altering art history as we know it. The cardinal overconfidence of some recent cultural theory is that self-criticism will yield a new narrative, effectively shorn of Western perspectives. I doubt it.

Postscript, January 2008

The literature on Chinese landscape painting continues to grow exponentially. Most recently, there was the critical exchange in *The Art Bulletin,* regarding Jonathan Hay's essay on what he calls "mediation."[76] I am trying to keep up with the literature, as well as an outsider can, and I have been helped immeasurably by Jason Kuo, Rick Vinograd, Jenny Purtle, Jerome Silbergeld, Maggie Bickford, Wen Fong, Marty Powers, and a number of others. But of course it is impossible to keep up. All I can say in my defense is that the field of Chinese studies is changing rapidly, but the changes are all superficial when they are seen from the perspective I have been pursuing here.

The institutions, departments, conferences, professorships, examinations, seminars, monographs, interpretive methods, archival interests, narrative forms, self-descriptions, disciplinary affiliations, committees, professional associations, and teaching methods of Chinese art history remain Western. The very idea of studying Chinese painting in such a way as to produce a printed record of its history, which will stand together with printed records of the history of other countries' art, is itself Western. All other changes, such as the rise of postcolonial theory, social art history, patronage studies, phenomenology, and "mediation," are cosmetic. The enterprise itself, and the grounds of its sense, are Western, and that needs to be a theme in all our writing.

Notes

1 Translated from the English by Pan Yaochang and Gu Ling (Hangzhou: China Academy of Art Press, 1999).

2 This line of argument is pursued in my *Stories of Art* (New York: Routledge, 2002), which also refers in passing to questions of Chinese art.

3 Arthur Danto, "The Shape of Artistic Pasts: East and West," in *Philosophical Imagination and Cultural Memory: Approaching Historical Traditions*, ed. Patricia Cook (Durham, N.C.: Duke University Press, 1993), 125–38; quotations are on p. 132.

4 This is argued with further references to such texts in my *Poetics of Perspective* (Ithaca, N.Y.: Cornell University Press, 1994), 259–60.

5 Jan Fontein, "Die Kunst der Chinesen," in *China, Korea, Japan*, ed. Jan Fontein and Rose Hempel, vol. 17 of *Propyläen Kunstgeschichte* (Berlin: Propyläen Verlag, 1968), 11–74, quotation on p. 74.

6 Sherman Lee, *Chinese Landscape Painting*, 2nd ed. (Cleveland: Cleveland Museum of Art, 1962), 132.

7 Sherman Lee, *A History of Far Eastern Art*, 5th ed. (New York: Prentice Hall, 1994), 10–11.

8 Wu Chuangshuo is also known as Wu Changshi.

9 Ho Ch'uan-hsing, "The Ch'ing Dynasty" [part four of a survey of Chinese painting in the Palace Museum, Taipei], *Arts of Asia* 16 (1986): 112–21, quotation on 121.

10 The early essay "Toward a Structural Analysis of Chinese Landscape Painting" (*Art Journal* 28, no. 4 [summer 1969]: 388–97) ends with a reference to Qing painting, but its last illustration is Dong Qichang.

11 Wen C. Fong, *Beyond Representation: Chinese Painting and Calligraphy 8th–14th Century* (New York: The Metropolitan Museum of Art, 1992), 497.

12 James Cahill, *Chinese Painting* (Geneva: Editions d'Art Albert Skira, 1960), 192, 194, and idem, "Afterword: *Hsieh-i* as a Cause of Decline in Later Chinese Painting," *Three Alternative Histories of Chinese Painting*, The Franklin D. Murphy Lectures 9 (Lawrence, Kans.: Spencer Museum of Art, 1988), 100ff.

13 James Cahill, "On the Periodization of Later Chinese Painting: The Early to Middle Ch'ing (K'ang-hsi to Ch'ien-lung) Transition," paper given in Kyoto, 1990. Courtesy the author.

14 See Laurence Binyon, "Painting," in *Chinese Art: An Introductory Review of Painting, Ceramics, Textiles, Bronzes, Sculpture, Jade, Etc.* [contributions by Binyon, Roger Fry, Osvald Sirén and others] (London: B. T. Batsford, 1925), 5–12, especially 12; and Laurence Binyon, "Painting and

Calligraphy," in *Chinese Art* (London: Kegan Paul, 1935), 1–30, especially 28.

15 Werner Speiser, "Painting," in *Chinese Art: Painting, Calligraphy, Stone Rubbing, Wood Engraving,* ed. Werner Speiser et al., trans. Diana Imber (London: Oldbourne Press, 1964), 52.

16 Richard Barnhart, *Painters of the Great Ming: The Imperial Court and the Zhe School,* with essays by Mary Ann Rogers and Richard Stanley-Baker (Dallas: Dallas Museum of Art, 1993), 325.

17 Michael Sullivan, *The Arts of China* (Berkeley: University of California Press, 1973), 131.

18 Jung Ying Tsao, *Chinese Paintings of the Middle Qing Dynasty* (San Francisco: San Francisco Graphic Society, 1987), 20.

19 Claudia Brown and Ju-hsi Chou, *Transcending Turmoil: Painting at the Close of China's Empire, 1796–1911* (Phoenix: Phoenix Art Museum, 1992).

20 Twentieth-century Chinese painting is the subject of part of a work in progress. I noted the denial of Fu Baoshi's Westernness in Hanghzou in 1998; but one of his surviving students, Yan Bo, told me Fu Baoshi never denied he was influenced by the West, and he took it as a natural component of his work.

21 Yu-chih Lai, "Remapping Borders: Ren Bonian's Frontier Paintings and Urban Life in 1880s Shanghai," *The Art Bulletin* 86, no. 3 (2004): 550–72.

22 Ibid., 554, quoting James Cahill, *The Compelling Image: Nature and Style in Seventeenth-Century Chinese Painting* (Cambridge, Mass.: Harvard University Press, 1982), 143.

23 William Willetts, *Chinese Art* (New York: Braziller, 1958), 305–6.

24 Sullivan, *Arts of China* (above, n. 17), 224: "The art of Shih-t'ao [Shitao], and indeed of all the Individualists, represents a private protest against the new academicism of the literati. But as the Ch'ing [Qing] settled deeper into that stagnation which seems to have been the fate of every long-lived dynasty in Chinese history, the lamp of individualism burned more and more dimly. During the nineteenth century the growing foreign menace produced not more action but paralysis at the centre, and patronage shrank to almost nothing. A handful of literati kept the tradition alive, however, until in the twentieth century there took place a revolution over which the artists themselves had little control."

25 Torao Miyagawa, *Chinese Painting,* trans. A. Birnbaum (New York: Weatherhill, 1983), 149.

26 *Painting in the Far East: An Introduction to the History of Pictorial Art in Asia, Especially China and Japan* (London: E. Arnold, 1923), 189.

27 *Epochs of Chinese & Japanese Art* (New York: Dover, 1963 [1912]), 2:51–52, 141, 144, 147. To Fenellosa, the Southern Song was the epitome of

Chinese painting, and the *wen-jen* were "pedants," "Confucian atheists" who clung to their "simple and uniform" ideal of the past (ibid., 140ff.).

28 Arthur Waley, *An Introduction to the Study of Chinese Painting* (London: E. Benn, 1923), 251.

29 Sometimes also *Sonderlinge*, "recluses." Fontein, "Kunst der Chinesen" (above, n. 5), 71.

30 Hans van der Meyden, "Jin Nong—The Life of an Eccentric Scholar and Artist, A Study of His Socio-Cultural Background," *Oriental Art* 31, no. 2 (1985): 174–85, quotation on 174.

31 (Cambridge, Mass.: MIT Press, 1993). My review, *The Art Bulletin* 76, no. 3 (1994): 546–48, addresses the question of what it means to describe an entire movement (in this case, surrealism) using a single term (the uncanny). See also the ensuing exchange, "Construction and Deconstruction in Psychoanalysis," *The Art Bulletin* 77, no. 2 (1995): 342–43.

32 Jerome Silbergeld, *Mind Landscapes: The Paintings of C. C. Wang* (Seattle, WA: University of Washington Press, 1987), 98.

33 Barnhart, *Painters* (above, n. 16), 2.

34 Review of *Latter Days of the Law: Images of Chinese Buddhism 850–1850*, ed. Marsha Weidner, *The Art Bulletin* 78, no. 3 (1996): 556–59. The situation has suggestive parallels with Hegel's meliorist views of history, since the internal structure of both accounts does not give explicit place to later readers. Hegel neither denied nor described a succession beyond the Prussian government and the "final" state of the Spirit.

35 Speiser, "Painting" (above, n. 15), 7–189, especially 52, 54, and 56.

36 *A Short History of Chinese Art* (New York: Pantheon, 1944), 127.

37 "Kunst der Chinesen" (above, n. 5), 71, 72.

38 Fong, *Beyond Representation* (above, n. 11), 469.

39 *Painters* (above, n. 16), 325.

40 James Cahill, "Style as Idea in Ming–Ch'ing Painting," in *The Mozartian Historian: Essays on the Works of Joseph R. Levenson*, ed. Maurice Meisner and Rhoads Murphy (Berkeley: University of California Press, 1976), 137–56; the concept is also adumbrated in his *Compelling Image* (above, n. 22), 184ff.

41 For a fuller list of the painters in the group (originally more than ten) see van der Meyden, "Jin Nong" (above, n. 30), especially 184–85 n. 6; for illustrations see *The Selected Paintings and Calligraphy of the Eight Eccentrics of Yangchou*, ed. Chang Wan-li and Hu Jen-mon, 8 vols. (Kowloon: CAFA Company, 1970).

42 Lee, *Chinese Landscape Painting* (above, n. 6), 124.

43 Ibid., 129.

44 Yoshiho Yonezawa, *Painting of Sung and Yüan Dynasties* (Tokyo: Mayuyama, 1952).

45 Lee, *Chinese Landscape Painting*, 129.

46 The sources are suggested by Yonezawa, *Painting*.

47 Klaas Ruitenbeek, *Discarding the Brush: Gao Qipei (1660–1734) and the Art of Chinese Finger Painting* (Amsterdam: Rijksmuseum, 1992); the quotation is from a review in *Oriental Art* 39, no. 2 (1993): 54–55, quotation on 55.

48 Speiser, "Painting" (above, n. 15), thinks Xiao Yuncong may not have been Hongren's teacher; see also James Cahill, *Distant Mountains: Chinese Painting of the Late Ming Dynasty, 1570–1644*, vol. 3 of *A History of Later Chinese Painting* (New York: Weatherhill, 1982), chapter 2.

49 Lee, *Chinese Landscape Painting*, 123; I have converted the Wade-Giles romanization in the quote to pinyin.

50 Speiser, "Painting," 145.

51 "Spindly trees" is from James Cahill, *Fantastics and Eccentrics in Chinese Painting* (New York: Asia House Gallery, 1967), 48.

52 Richard Barnhart et al., eds., *Three Thousand Years of Chinese Painting* (New Haven and London: Yale University Press, 1997), 169.

53 Lee, *Chinese Landscape Painting*, 124, and pls. 98 and 99 facing p. 116.

54 The connection with Gong Xian is mentioned in Cahill, *Fantastics*, 50.

55 See Cahill, *Compelling Image* (above, n. 22), 146–83; idem, *Fantastics*, 73. Marc Wilson, *Kung Hsien: Theorist and Technician in Painting*, Nelson Gallery and Atkins Museum Bulletin, vol. 4, no. 9 (Kansas City, Mo.: Nelson Gallery, 1969).

56 See my "Uccello, Duchamp: The Ends of Wit," *Zeitschrift für Ästhetik und allgemeine Kunstwissenschaft* 36 (1991): 199–224 and 10 plates. For Bada Shanren, see Wen Fong, "Stages in the Life and Art of Chu Ta (A.D. 1626–1705)," *Archives of Asian Art* 40 (1987): 7–23. For madness, see James Cahill, "The 'Madness' in Bada Shanren's Paintings," *Asian Cultural Studies* (International Christian University Publications vol. III-A) 17 (March 1989): 119–43, and my "La Persistance du 'tempérament artistique' comme modèle: Rosso Fiorentino, Barbara Kruger, Sherrie Levine," *Ligeia* 17–18 (October 1995/June 1996): 19–28.

57 This is said of the architecture in Wu Zhen's copy of *Autumn Mountains* after Juran (Taipei). See James Cahill, *Hills Beyond a River: Chinese Painting of the Yuan Dynasty, 1279–1368*, vol. 1 of *A History of Later Chinese Painting* (New York: Weatherhill, 1976), pl. 24.

58 Sullivan, *Arts of China* (above, n. 17), 222.

59 Lee, *Chinese Landscape Painting*, 111–13. Shixi (Kuncan) was the other of the Two Stones.

60 Quoted for example in Miyagawa (above, n. 25), 147.

61 See the statement in the "Picturing 'Greatness'" exhibit (New York: Museum of Modern Art, 1988); I have discussed the untenable nature of such claims in "Persistance" (above, n. 56).

62 *Fenêtre jaune cadmium: Les dessous de la peinture* (Paris: Editions du Seuil, 1984), 167.

63 Ibid.

64 Ibid., 170.

65 A painter such as Ad Reinhardt, acutely aware of the limited field of possibilities, defines "un champ—on serait aujourd'hui porté à écrire: un lieu—commun, partagé: le lieu, le champ d'un jeu où ceux qu'on à cités, bien d'autres encore, auront été impliqués, chacun pour sa part et avec ses intérèts, suivant sa stratégie propre." Ibid., 157. I thank Laure Faber for bringing this passage to my attention.

66 Ibid., 154, quoted by Yve-Alain Bois in *Painting as Model* (Cambridge, Mass.: MIT Press, 1990), and in "Painting as Model," *October* 37 (1986): 125–37, quotation on 134.

67 Bois, "Painting as Model," 135.

68 Yve-Alain Bois, "Painting," in *Endgame: Reference and Simulation in Recent Painting and Sculpture* (Boston, 1986). The term has been taken in a different sense by Leo Steinberg, "Picasso's Endgame," *October* 74 (1995): 105–22.

69 "From Criticism to Complicity: *Flash Art* Panel," ed. P. Nagy, *Flash Art* 129 (summer 1986): 49.

70 For the anti-anti-Hegelian argument, see my *Our Beautiful, Dry, and Distant Texts: On the History of Art as Writing*, 2nd ed. (New York: Routledge, 2000).

71 Karsten Harries, *The Meaning of Modern Art* (Evanston, IL: Northwestern University Press, 1968).

72 His "The Leaven of Criticism in Renaissance Art" is discussed in my *Master Narratives and Their Discontents*, Theories of Modernism and Postmodernism in the Visual Arts 1 (New York: Routledge, 2005).

73 Louis Marin, *To Destroy Painting* (Chicago: University of Chicago Press, 1995); Jacques Derrida, "By Force of Mourning," in *The Work of Mourning*, trans. Michael Naas and Pascale-Anne Brualt (Chicago: University of Chicago Press, 2001).

74 In connection with Bois see *Endgame* (above, n. 68) and the review of *Painting as Model* by Akira Mizuta Lippit, *MLN* (*Modern Language Notes*) 106, no. 5 (December 1991): 1074–78, especially 1077; René Démoris, *Les fins de la peinture* (Paris: Editions Desjonquières, 1990), reviewed in Jacques Berne, "Comment parler de la peinture aujourd'hui?" *Critique* 47, no. 534 (November 1991): 874–81.

75 I am thinking especially of Jerome Silbergeld's essay contrasting Yuan style choices with those codified in the Ming, "A New Look at Traditionalism in Yüan Dynasty Landscape Painting," *National Palace Museum Quarterly* 14, no. 3 (1980): 1–30.

76 "Interventions: The Mediating Work of Art," *The Art Bulletin* 89, no. 3 (2007). Hay's essay, "The Mediating Work of Art," is at pp. 435–59; my response, "The Mottled Discourse of Chinese Studies," is at pp. 482–86.

4
The Cahill–Elkins Exchange

1A. James Elkins to James Cahill

[*James Elkins's note: this text was improvised in December 2005, taking Jim Cahill's material in Chapter 2 of this volume as a point of departure. Actually this text has a complicated prehistory. It has four points of reference:*

1. My review of David Summer's Real Spaces *in* The Art Bulletin *(86, no. 2 [2004]: 373–81). I recommend reading that review first, because it is presupposed in what follows.*

2. My book manuscript "Chinese Landscape Painting as Western Art History," excerpts from which appear as Chapter 3 of this volume.

3. A book I edited called Is Art History Global? *as vol. 3 in a series called The Art Seminar (New York and London: Routledge, 2007). It centers on a round-table conversation with David Summers, and it includes forty assessments of the conversation by scholars around the world, including Craig Clunas.*

4. The public debate Jim Cahill and I had in November of 2005 at the University of Maryland, College Park, Maryland. Time there was too short to incorporate much of what needed to be said. This text continues and elaborates that occasion.]

Chicago, December 10, 2005

Jim,

I want to set the tone for this exchange by adopting the letter format. It's better, I think, than an impersonal scholarly debate, and it might capture something of the conversation we had in College Park.

Because you've written at such length, and combined two papers into your response [Chapter 2], you'll appreciate it is difficult to know where to begin. As in any lengthy summary of one's own work I find some things wholly accurate and others in need of reframing before they can be addressed.

I'll begin with four areas where I think we agree.

1. Current art history has turned away from large-scale problems. Your project, of writing a dependable art historical account of the full range of Chinese painting, has a scale that is matched by only a few other scholars aside from the writers of freshman world-art survey textbooks.[1] It is useful, at the outset, to name some of the pertinent exceptions.

a. *Art Since 1900* is by far the most historiographically and philosophically articulate history of modern art.[2] However it is not unambiguously a single text, with a single purpose. Its four authors begin with four anonymously authored introductions, each setting out a different (and partly incompatible) set of methodological concerns; and it ends with a roundtable in which the authors acknowledge those differences. On the other hand, it is unmistakably consonant with the postmodernist project of the journal *October*, with its privileging of Surrealism and its stance against high modernism, and in those respects *Art Since 1900* is nominally unified.

b. David Summers's *Real Spaces* is a fundamental revision of the conceptual foundations of any world art history; it is in the tradition of Dagobert Frey and George Kubler, and has no contemporary parallels. [*See my book review, mentioned above.*]

c. Craig Clunas's *Art in China,* to take an example more topical to our discussion, is at once a history of Chinese art, and—as he says—an attempt to write about what was made in China, without stressing the coherence of the many kinds of production, or implying that the accidents of national definitions and self-definitions add to a conceptually coherent history. It serves the textbook market, but it is ideologically distinct from the majority of textbooks on national art, which tend to assume the unity of their subjects.

Jim, your books add up in a way that is virtually unheard of in scholarship of the last twenty-five years, and in addition you propose their cumulative project explicitly, instead of permitting the simple accumulation of pages to imply some larger purpose. I'm stressing the explicitness of your larger goal because that, even aside from your methodologies and choices of objects, is what sets your project apart. I have written several things that involve large claims—about "all" of modernism in one case, and "all" of images in another.[3] I am also editing a book series that asks all its contributors to address large-scale issues that they had not previously addressed.[4]

I think we can both agree that, all other issues aside, the explicit avowal of a larger purpose is itself extremely rare in current art history. This presents, I think, two interesting questions:

—How might art historians who do not embark on such projects, but whose interests make them conceptually dependent on such projects, justify their skepticism? (My qualifier is intended to point to the fact that large-scale questions are not pertinent to all of art historical research.)

—Is your sense of large-scale unfinished work in Chinese painting similar to that of the authors of *Art Since 1900,* or *Real Spaces,* or my own work? I think that despite the very large and very apparent differences, it is. This question, which seems somewhat coarse and unguarded, is, I think, a necessary question, because it forces the issue of the conceptual coherence of art history as a whole.

2. I think we also agree that Chinese art history, as written in China, continues to be based on texts. To that I will only add that the Chinese self-understanding of their own work does not always correspond to this description. There is also, complicating this issue, the existence of a poetic kind of writing that gets called "criticism" or "connoisseurship" but counts, for some Chinese readers, as visual. (I am thinking for example of Jiang Hong's book *Shang tu pin hua,* which is full of a painter's poetic enthusiasm for images.) I should also add that Ding Ning's paper, which you refer to, belongs to a separate project, a book called *Visual Literacy*.[5]

3. I think we also agree that my initial project in the book that was to be called "Chinese Landscape Painting as Object Lesson"—namely a comparison of historical perspectives—is still valid. I still believe in it, and the reworkings of the MS in light of postcolonial theory have only made me skeptical of my motives for wanting to insist on it. Skepticism of one's motives is not the same as skepticism of the object in question. (I'm thinking, somewhat apocalyptically, of Robert Oppenheimer.)

4. And I think we can agree that there is no such thing as a purely Western art historical practice. Thinking of what counts as Western or non-Western must be a matter of incremental awareness of one's presuppositions. As you say, "we must make our choices as perceptively and honestly as we can, trying to avoid a priori assumptions about how this or that choice will distort our subject." I can also almost agree that "[w]e begin from the West, but the materials show us where to go": but really, that is only part of the story. Materials—the unexpected stuff of historical research—shows us that we cannot keep going as we had planned. It is different to say that the materials show us where to go, because that implies the materials take over. I think some of our disagreements might

begin here, because I would rather say we can be deceived into thinking the materials have taken over, because we cease to recognize our own interests and assumptions in the new occasions. And again this does not mean that what we find is wrong: it is an example of a place where our own interests become invisible and therefore, as Marx would say, "natural."

Now I have completed my list of four points of agreement, and at the same time I have begun to note what I would think of as disagreements. Let me stop there, to keep this brief, and maybe start to give it the character of a conversation.

Best,
Jim

1B. James Cahill to James Elkins

Vancouver, December 2005

Dear Jim,

Your response to my "position paper" is, as always, temperate, reasoned, stated concisely where I tend to be verbose. And I agree that we are in agreement on the points you lay out, with a few places where we may still diverge, as below. I will try to be (uncharacteristically) brief.

Your observation about my books "adding up" and making an "explicit avowal of a larger purpose" corresponds, in a sense, to what I wrote about aiming at providing for readers and students a large, coherent "narrative" into which they can fit their experiences with Chinese painting. I assumed idealistically when I first began that everybody seriously in the field was doing the same, or should be, and I aimed at "mastering it all": gathering reproduction books, making large numbers of photos and slides, compiling indexes to control these, giving a four-semester lecture course in Chinese painting history, etc. When I finished my projected five-volume Later Chinese Painting series I was going to start back through Song (the Southern Song book would be titled *A Pure and Remote View*). I wanted to "map out" areas that could later be explored in more detail—Japanese Nanga painting as well as Chinese—and am still doing it (with what I am calling vernacular Chinese painting, and with images of women in later Chinese painting). As I wrote, you specialists in Western art have had this done for you, in large part, by more than a century of hard work of a kind nobody wants to do any more, so that you don't need projects with a "larger purpose," at least of that kind. (The book on 20th century art you cite would be an exception, of course; and your own large-scale [or huge] project, if I understand it right, is more in the methodological-theoretical-critical realms than in conventional art history, although you do that too on a high level.) Whether or not my colleagues in Chinese art realize this, we still do need the "larger projects." Such a work as Craig Clunas's *Art in China* is a different kind of project, with its own aims and values; the other, older kind still needs to be done (especially for the early periods of Chinese painting.)

About your part-agreement with, part-objection to, the idea that "the materials show us where to go"—that's a good statement of the problem. For Chinese painting, one can say that the jumping-off point is the end of Song: up to there, scholars of the earlier generation such as Bachhofer, Loehr, Soper, early-period Sherman Lee, could deal with it relatively effectively, to some extent by adopting familiar patterns of "progress" toward better representation. But they had no way of getting beyond that, and were more or less helpless for the later periods. (Loehr was moving toward a better understanding of Ming–Qing painting in his later writings.) We who have tried to work out a "narrative" for the later periods have indeed aimed, as you put it, at "letting the materials show us where to go." But when the materials include our readings of Chinese writings on these later periods, some of them by the artists and others of the time—then, even though we still face the danger of being "deceived into thinking the materials have taken over," and although we can indeed "cease to recognize our own interests and assumptions" in our new formulations—if those materials include the native (Chinese) accounts of this later art, along with whatever other textual research we carry out—how can we do better? This is what I tried to do in my writings on later Chinese painting, and with full awareness of perils and weaknesses, I can't see a better way I might have done it. That there are dangers in moving into an area where "our own interests become invisible, and therefore . . . 'natural'," I am perfectly willing to acknowledge. But to state a danger doesn't invalidate the whole project; it's just something that, as I wrote, one tries one's best to avoid. A project of writing about the later periods of Chinese painting in ways that would not incur that danger (following, perhaps, your proposals to which I responded in my "position paper") would so impoverish the whole enterprise as to be, for me, quite unacceptable. (Or maybe I misunderstand your proposals; if so, correct me.)

And what, after all, are the dangers? You rewrote your "Chinese Painting as Object Lesson" (which I still wish had been published in something like its original form) "in light of postcolonial theory" because you were, as you say, skeptical of your motives in writing the original. But supposing you hadn't rewritten it, had stayed instead with the "comparison of historical perspectives" that you "still believe is valid"? What is really at stake? Your "apocalyptic" invocation of Robert Oppenheimer suggests the answer: for him, the deaths of some hundreds of thousands of people, maybe lots more; for you, some frowns from colleagues still ruled by the strictures of postcolonial doctrine. (I named two of them in an earlier, private correspondence and won't do so here.) I was more or less aware, when I published my lecture arguing for a "post-history" of Chinese painting,[6] of what direction the responses would probably take: Yes, very interesting, but we aren't doing that kind of art history any more, with revolutions and significant turning points and grand coherent narratives. I respect these responses, as the counterviews of colleagues whose way of thinking differs from my own; but they wouldn't deter me from publishing it. To make what one believes to be a valid point in a publication is to open the way for others who agree with its validity to develop it, and those who don't to try to alter it or deny it—any of these healthier than blocking its publication, I'm certainly not blaming you, but I do blame the editors of journals that rejected your essay, and the outside referees who recommended against it. They have deprived our field of a provocative and valuable if controversial study.

Let me say finally, before concluding, that I was pleased to see your book *What Happened to Art Criticism?* cited approvingly in the essay in last Sunday's *NYTimes Book Review*.[7] What you say about the crisis in art criticism is surely true; does it follow inevitably on the crisis in art? I used to tease modernist colleagues by remarking that if only someone had said, at the right moment, "Good joke, M. Duchamp, ha ha ha, now let's go back to making art," the whole 20th century would have been very different. Instead, everybody said "Oh wow!" and it's been downhill ever since. I also recommended, after listening to a string of lectures by candidates for our modernist position, that anyone who uses the formulation "His/her work is important because it calls into question (or challenges) the whole established (blah blah blah)" should be eliminated from our list—that was never an adequate raison d'être for a work of art, and shouldn't ever have been taken seriously. A significant work of art can do this among other things, but its artistic value lies elsewhere, and still needs to be defined.

I will look forward to more from you.

All the best,
Jim

2A. James Elkins to James Cahill

Cork, Ireland, January 7, 2006

Dear Jim,

Thanks, as always, for that very accurate & friendly letter, and greetings from sodden, half-frozen Ireland, where I'm starting the teaching term. (The students here begin classes on January 3, which seems more barbaric than Christian.)

Let me start out this time with what you say at the end. The idea that work is important because it "calls into question" or "challenges" some established practice (actually, "interrogates" is my favorite of those verbs) is certainly central to the discussion of modernism and postmodernism. For someone like Thomas Crow, conceptual difficulty is a hallmark of the most ambitious and interesting work in the wake of conceptual art; he has actually argued that the most important philosophic work currently being undertaken around art takes places in and through conceptual and postminimal artwork, rather than in philosophy departments. In a different mode, but in the same category, there are theorists like Irit Rogoff who argue that encounters with artistic practices can effect the most radical conceivable transformations in one's own assumptions, and that, as a "theorist of the contemporary," she is concerned with the transformative possibilities inherent in art—especially those possibilities that might lead the critic or historian to entirely reconceive their own role in relation to the artist and artwork, producing previously inconceivable collaborations. From either Rogoff's or Crow's points of view—and they are otherwise very different—the most significant art is the most challenging art. It not only "calls into question": it overturns, restructures, and repositions the fundamental concepts that enable any discourse about art to go forward.

Why am I going on about this? Because the position you take so clearly, that "it's been downhill ever since" Duchamp, is a radical opposite to the radical conceptualizations of people like Crow or Rogoff. The middle ground, the normative position of the plurality of art historians, is, I think, exactly as you characterize it when you describe the job search: people are interested in work that is challenging, ambiguous, complex, and difficult.

So I'll propose, for the sake of our exchange, a spectrum or scale between your position, the common range of positions, and those of scholars like Rogoff or Crow. It could be pictured like a bell curve: Irit's position, certainly (if not Crow's), is a statistical rarity, and so is yours. I think this is a good place to start, because it can potentially include everyone. (And by the way, you aren't alone in your valuation of Duchamp! There are many people who are serious about both painting and art history who hold versions of that view, although most of them are either artists, or else they teach outside North America and Western Europe. I have material on them in my book *Master Narratives and Their Discontents,* in a chapter on people who value skill above other criteria. Another good source for the kind of "bell curve" or spectrum I'm positing here is Thierry de Duve's *Kant After Duchamp,* especially the first chapter, in which he imagines a viewer from Mars, and then a succession of viewers who look ever more closely and sympathetically at Duchamp. But we can go into those possibilities later, if we want to.)

So, to bring the subject back to Chinese art: I noticed throughout Jason's conference, and especially in Rick Vinograd's paper [*see Chapter 5 of this volume*], that Craig Clunas's name kept being mentioned as someone importantly different from you. Yet at the same time, he was referred to as someone whose work is simply different from yours, as apples are different from oranges—different in a way that prevents a valuative comparison. That is how he appeared in Rick Vinograd's paper [Chapter 5 in this volume], which sounded, as someone in the audience said, as if it were coming gradually toward a conclusion that it did not quite reach. I am not sure that is quite the right way to put it, but I would say that Rick was enumerating points of divergence without stressing which ones might be amenable to one-to-one comparison. Which differences, in the metaphor, were comparisons of apples and oranges, and which were comparisons of apples and apples? (Therefore, of course, good apples and rotten apples?)

The idea that Clunas's work is best described as "different" is one that you also have—in your last letter you said as much: "Craig Clunas's *Art in China* is a different kind of project, with its own aims and values."

So here's what I propose, in order to bring the conversation further: let's see what happens if we try to make valuative comparisons between *Art in China* and your own work. I propose this for three reasons:

1. Clunas's work really is, I think, the most conceptually coherent alternative art historical practice in Chinese art history. He isn't a random choice.

2. The field of Chinese art history is our subject, even before and apart from the question of global practices of art history, and so we need to address its internal differences head-on.

3. The best collegiality, I think, is honest debate. I know the politics of a specialized field often prevents people from speaking too directly about their disagreements, and I'm certainly not proposing anything polemical.

So I'll pose this question, to start: From your point of view, what is wrong with *Art in China*?

I'd be interested to know if you think that his enterprise, as it's embodied in that book, is part of a different field, or if it is better described as building on things you and others have done. If it's the latter, then there must be some conceptual dependence: it wouldn't just be that he and others are using dates, provenances, and attributions you've established. If it's more the former, then I would be curious to know if you think that there are other approaches just as different, just as disconnected from yours, as his is.

And as a postscript to this letter, I'll add that my own position in regard to the internal differences within the field of Chinese art history is one of intellectual curiosity. I'm mainly interested in understanding how many kinds of approaches there might be said to be. As you know, I am puzzled by the existence of Chinese kinds of "connoisseurship" and writing that aren't given weight in the West, or aren't even recognized as historical approaches. I mentioned Jiang Hong's book as an example, and I'd like to come back to it sometime. That is just to say that in this context, my main interest is to find a way of speaking that might enable us to make direct comparisons between your work and Clunas's. And if that is impossible—if it isn't diplomacy that is preventing direct comparisons, but genuine difference—then I'd like to know how the study of Chinese painting has become so diverse that contemporaneous practitioners have effectively no common ground.

I do have a stake in the surrounding question of the globalization of art history, and my position there is more than intellectual curiosity. But on this subject, of the ways Chinese painting is described, I am an observer. But that doesn't mean I don't want to argue!

And finally, as a postscript, I'll say briefly what my own sense of the field of Chinese art history is, at least that portion done in the West, in Western universities. I think that what gets called "postcolonial theory," as exemplified here by Clunas's book, is in fact the single greatest challenge to older scholarship: it is connected to what you do, but as its direct contradiction and opposite. It isn't just a change of conversation or emphasis, although it's necessarily that as well. It doesn't just alter the terms or the artworks that are of interest. When editors and colleagues say, as you put it, "Yes, very interesting, but we aren't doing that kind of art history any more, with revolutions and significant turning points and grand coherent narratives," they are not being wholly honest or coherent. What they should say is, "We are trying to build an account of Chinese art history that is entirely independent not only of your findings but of the ideology and values they imply." The fact that they don't—such things are not commonly said, or even I think conceptualized in that way—makes the field very interesting, and poses challenges for someone like me who would like to see if honest conversations can be held across the spectrum. But that's my own sense of it: I'd like to start with yours, and we can develop these as we go.

Best (and happy 2006!),
Jim

2B. James Cahill to James Elkins

Jan.–Feb. 2006

Dear Jim,

Again, your response is admirably terse and informed where mine was rambling. You raise the right points and illuminate them with references unknown to me, such as those to the Crow and Rogoff writings and their "radical transformations." And your discussion of that issue is enlightening, far more informed than my response can be.

Two things in it, however, that I want to correct or take issue with. One is the implicit (perhaps not intended) inclusion of me with the people your chapter was about, who "value skill above other criteria." I don't think that accurately states my position. The other is that my belief about "calling into question" (or "interrogating," a good term since it has less the sense of denying) puts me into the category of a "statistical rarity," outside the "plurality of art historians" who are "interested in work that is challenging, ambiguous, complex, and difficult."

The fault is largely mine, for not making clear what I meant at the end of my communication. I certainly wasn't arguing against the value of art's being challenging and complex etc.; that would be like being against motherhood and apple pie, i.e., a pretty much universally accepted position. I did write, though, that this was "never [*I should have added "in itself" to avoid misunderstanding*] an adequate raison d'être for a work of art," and that is what I believe. I've always told my students: doing the radical thing is the easy part—even the minor artist can do that. What is difficult is somehow reconciling the radical thing with producing a solid, satisfying, moving work of art, which typically will manage to preserve something of older values along with its innovative features.

As a musical analogy (of the kind I often turn to) I could use Edgar Varèse, who in the early 20th century was a radical rule-breaker with his semitones, extreme and unresolved dissonances, etc. But who listens to him today? Whereas Stravinsky did radical things along with writing great music, with solid roots in the past, and is the one we listen to and are moved by (and, if we are composers, learn from). In my own field, the Anhui school of landscape will serve. When we had our exhibition "Shadows of Mt. Huang" in Berkeley in 1981, there was no question of what painting knocked everybody over: it was Hongren's great "Sound of Autumn" in the Honolulu Academy—from casual visitor to *S. F. Chronicle*'s art critic, who went wild over it. Other artists had done the radical thing decades earlier: Wang Zhirui, Li Yongchang (neither in our show) or Hongren himself in early work; they eliminated all washes and texturing, making the landscape out of stark geometricized linear forms. And they were no doubt the ones who elicited the "Oh wow!" reactions, and certainly the ones who made the "radical transformations" and broke the rules and forced people to rethink—all that. But it was Hongren, later, in this one great work and to a lesser extent in his others, who used this new sparse, linear manner to build a landscape that also evoked the effects of space, mass, monumentality, that were high among the values of previous landscape. And who set the model for other artists of the school to follow, in their different ways.

I could produce other examples; those should suffice. You or I could have thought of exhibiting the urinal, if we'd been in tune with other French avant-garde jokes of that time; neither of us could have created Picasso's Cubism. And, given the choice between the urinal and a major Picasso Cubist oil, how many would go for the urinal? Once it has done its interrogating (and is invoked for that purpose endlessly afterward), not much is left. (And if you respond: it's not the object, it's the idea—and so on into conceptual art—then we part ways again.)

So, in holding a view defined that way, I really think I belong to a statistical plurality. And the *New York Times* review I mentioned last time, citing you about the crisis in art criticism, surely points that way, with its list of prominent critics who have gone over to the skeptics. Another of the lines I used to use to irritate some modern art people was: Art began to go wrong at that moment when artists managed to convince everybody else that art should be defined as whatever artists choose to do. I am profoundly convinced that we can and should come up with much more useful and valid definitions than that (however much we may disagree on how to formulate them), and that applying still-valid criteria from them would suffice to eliminate from serious consideration a lot of stuff presented as art. The Princeton musicologist Ed Cone, whom I got to know during his year in Berkeley, once made the proposal that we should simply remove the designation of "art" from objects or works presented as that, and see if they could stand on their own. That, too, would surely eliminate a lot of foolish stuff—performances that wouldn't make it as entertainment or drama and are simply boring, objects that nobody with sense would really want around his or her house. And I hope you won't counter that such judgments would have a stultifying effect on art by discouraging innovation, pointing out once more that critics of Beethoven's time didn't appreciate his music, etc., because that one has been too often misused to carry weight any more, I think.

Thomas Crow is a brilliant art historian and theorist (we tried to get him to Berkeley, without success) but I think his argument about conceptual and postminimal art and their underpinnings as extensions of philosophical discourse risks too much turning the production of art into an intellectual game played by a limited number of artists (of that persuasion) and critics, leaving everybody else out. I wouldn't discourage them from playing it, but I would continue to be among the ever-growing majority who balk at seeing that as the most significant kind of art production going on today.

I recall reading that Andy Warhol originally meant to do enlarged cartoon panels, but learned that Roy Lichtenstein was already doing those, so a New York woman dealer suggested the Brillo box, or was it the Campbell's Soup can, and the rest is—what? When not even the idea was the artist's own, and the object scarcely original except in size and medium, what are we left with? (Don't bother to respond at length—I've read Danto etc. and know roughly what the answers are supposed to be. My question is rhetorical.)

Your idea of contrasting my old *Chinese Painting* and Craig Clunas's *Art in China* is an interesting one, and with the usual reluctance to even seem to criticize an esteemed colleague's work (in public at least), I'll agree to that as a working plan. But first, another comment on global art history and its proponents. Shane McCausland (Princeton PhD, now has joined you in Ireland, Chester Beatty Library) begins his good article on the copy by two Japanese Nihonga artists of the British Museum Gu Kaizhi-attributed scroll in the latest *Art Bulletin* (Dec. '05) with a paragraph hailing the British Museum's recent redefining of itself as a "universal museum" of world cultures as a healthy new direction that "would seem to mark a historical break with the imperialistic attitude of the modern great powers toward other cultures." I certainly wouldn't disagree with that statement in itself—I worked during my years as a CAA executive board director to open the way for more non-Western art, besides managing as a member of the National Committee for the History of Art to get one International Congress, the one in D.C. (but that one only, they backslid afterward under French pressure), opened to Asian art specialists, and so forth. But I would be very sorry if McCausland's statement were read to mean that the alternative to your global art history, or his or anyone else's, should be branded as "imperialistic." That would be Bush administration tactics (if you're against the Iraq war you're unpatriotic). Nothing was more natural than for a culture to pay most attention to its own art tradition; China, Japan, India, have all done that, as has Europe/America. Lots of factors—more international travel, publication, exhibitions from abroad etc.—have changed that parochial (not necessarily imperialistic) attitude, a welcome development. And the new openness takes various forms, of which your idea of "global art history" is one. But not by any means the only morally defensible one.

OK, on to Craig's book and mine, differences between them. Let's eliminate the main apples-and-oranges factor: his deals with all kinds of art objects and artifacts, mine only with paintings. I've never attempted a general book or long study of that kind, and don't have the knowledge to do it well; Craig does—partly, I suppose, from his V&A background. (When *Superfluous Things* appeared I wrote him an unsolicited fan letter about how admirably this broke with the older V&A tradition of refined aesthetic and connoisseurial approaches.)

The plan of *Art in China* follows, I think, a very controversial one that the Chinese section in the V&A used for a new installation of its galleries—when? my memory is bad—the late 1950s? later? Anyway, making separate cases or areas for arts of the tomb, the temple, the court, the elite, etc. It aroused an uproar among old-guard museum people in London. I remember thinking that it was a promising new idea, and deserved its try. It also has its strengths as the plan of a book, throwing emphasis to aspects of the works or objects that otherwise would be neglected, bringing out new relationships. But what of things that don't fit? The great Fan Kuan landscape for instance—not tomb or court or elite—is that why it's not there? I would rather stay with a plan, chronological or other, that allows me to choose freely what I want to include and write about. But that implies an object-oriented and connoisseurial approach, exactly what Craig is escaping from. And his plan permits the inclusion of pieces that wouldn't fit into the kind of "narrative" I would write.

To get at the deepest difference between his book and mine, I would have to go back to the argument I made at great length in my paper for the Maryland symposium [in November 2005], and don't want to make at length again: about how the good art historian, as I see it, should (among other things) open the reader's/listener's mind to responses more informed, cultivated, sensitive, by calling attention to features and aspects of the work that wouldn't otherwise get through to someone unfamiliar with that kind of art. My *Chinese Painting* book has done that for a great many people, as I know from letters, and from people telling me after lectures about how it was the beginning of their appreciation of Chinese painting. I recall Fritz Mote (Princeton Chinese historian) telling me that he understood from my book, for the first time, what Ni Zan's paintings were really about, and I've had the same kind of report from others, how reading what I wrote about Ni Zan, along with Huang Gongwang and the more austere kinds of literati painting generally (all this based, of course, on my own long period of searching out and reading relevant Chinese writings), opened their eyes to a whole new aesthetic mode, one crucial to later developments in Chinese painting, in a way no one up to that time had even tried to do. (Bachhofer's dismissal of Ni Zan as an "execrable amateur"—followed even, for a time, by someone so good as Sherman Lee—is sometimes recalled in accounting for this.) And I did indeed devote substantial space (pp. 109–13) and careful writing to these two and their innovations, partly to prepare for much that followed. I reproduced the section of Huang's "Fuchun" scroll that seemed to best exemplify the points I made, and a typical, strong Ni Zan landscape (although not the one I would choose today.)

Now, Craig's purposes are elsewhere, and they are perfectly valid purposes that aim at enlightening the reader in other ways. He reproduces, small, a longer section of Huang's scroll, which doesn't permit a close reading of brushwork, and is otherwise (for me) the least interesting part of the scroll: the ending, which Huang (perhaps impelled by circumstances related in his inscription) finished off quickly and relatively sloppily. Craig's paragraphs on the scroll (pp. 150–62) tell his readers about matters that mine don't, such as its history, the possibility of reading it as a landscape of reclusion (some of this from John Hay's study of it, I think), and the probable social circumstances of its production and reception. All worthwhile, matters I've pursued myself in later writings. But he doesn't try, as I did, to make the writing and the visuals work together on the reader/viewer's eyes and mind for a deeper understanding of this kind of painting. And Ni Zan isn't there at all, except as one name in a list of names. Craig has good discussions of literati painting and its implications elsewhere in the book (Su Shi, Dong Qichang) but his non-historical approach means that he wouldn't attempt to define the Yuan turning-point—or, as we older scholars saw it, the "Yuan revolution"—in landscape painting. That such concepts are obsolete was made clear, as I noted before, in the responses to my *Archives* piece on the "post-history" of Chinese painting. Does it seem odd that we are encouraged to recognize and credit "radical transformations" in recent and contemporary art, however ephemeral they may be, but are discouraged from recognizing the ones that really mattered, had productive and even epochal outcomes, in the past? Not odd at all, I suppose, if one accepts the replacement of diachronic modes of understanding by synchronic ones, and all the rest.

And that brings us to your last, perceptive interpretation of what colleagues who say, in effect, "We aren't doing that any more" are really saying: "We are trying to build an account of Chinese art history that is entirely independent not only of your findings but of the ideology and values they imply." Yes, I think that's exactly right; and it means that the kind of writing I've been arguing for in all this becomes impossible, since, in spite of all our efforts to ground it in our understandings of Chinese concepts that we take to underlie the paintings, we can't escape intrusions from our own conscious or unconscious biases, and so forth. This is a perfect example of what I've always argued is the fatal flaw in the whole postcolonial (etc.) enterprise: the implicit belief that finding some ideological impurity in a certain practice invalidates the whole practice and dictates the discontinuation of it. So what I have argued for throughout these exchanges as a little-articulated but highly beneficial capacity of the best art-historical writing (and lecturing) is ruled out, unless it is done by Chinese writers—who, for reasons I tried to outline in my first Maryland paper [part 1 of Chapter 2 in this volume], aren't in a position to do it effectively unless they give up their insider's status by adopting elements from "foreign art history." Under these conditions, opting for ideological purity would be as clear a case as I can imagine of throwing out the baby with the bathwater. For my part, I'm not convinced that the bathwater is nearly as toxic as the postcolonial people try to persuade us it is; and even if it were, getting rid of it wouldn't begin to compensate for the loss of the baby.

This hasn't answered some of your questions and comments, and we can come back to them later. I think you are in a better position than I am to answer some of them—I'm too emotionally engaged, as all the above testifies. Still, I hope that this exchange will prove to have value for others than ourselves, even as it leaves unanswered some of your larger methodological questions.

Best,
Jim

P.S. If I say pessimistically that I can't imagine we will resolve our differences, it's because I think we would give different answers to a basic question: What is art? Mine would sound more like Walter Pater than like Tom Crow, I'm afraid. Or, to take a middle position, Susanne Langer, whom I was very taken with in my college years, and whom I still quote sometimes. And I will compound the backwardness by saying that I still believe that there is such a thing as an aesthetic experience, to be distinguished from other kinds of experience, and that it can be defined, up to a point. I once sat in on a course in aesthetics taught by Abraham Kaplan from UCLA. He used Dewey as a text, argued that defining the aesthetic experience is the right first step to answering the "What is art" question, and then saying: the art object is the object that evokes/permits/gives this kind of experience. Susanne Langer's argument is in that line, but takes it much further in seeing the content of art as form symbolic of feeling (or significant patterns of experience), and the need to create such symbols, in art and religion, as a human need as basic and universal as sex. Your "conceptually coherent" (ref. to Clunas) brings up, again, the problem of the effect of theory on creative work—writing art history is partly that, surely—and whether it should be a criterion for judging that writing. You may not have meant it as a criterion, but it sounds like one.

P.P.S. Jason Kuo asked me whether I mean to continue the exchange with you, and I answered: I'm perfectly ready to continue with the interchange with Jim Elkins, and await his response to my latest, which you received. I do think we have to get off the big what-is-art, has-contemporary-art-gone-wrong issues, on which we can't resolve basic disagreements, and get back to his global art history argument. My fault for spinning it off course. I will leave it to him to handle the re-direction, and respond more relevantly next time. OK? Just to let you know.

3A. James Elkins to James Cahill

An Uaimh, Co Meath, Ireland, April 9, 2006

Dear Jim,

Well, sorry for being silent so long. This is my last year in Ireland, I have decided, and I have had to tell everyone at the university. At the same time, I've been teaching (the compact Irish 12-week semester is over) and I've just finished three edited volumes that are now off to the publishers. We held another roundtable for publication, this one called "Renaissance Theory". . . .

All by way of excuse. Now back to business. I wonder if it will surprise you to hear that Chinese art history was on my mind during the "Renaissance Theory" roundtable. I opened with a sketch of the different kinds of disagreement in different fields in art history. I said that twenty years ago, Dutch 17th c. studies were riven by Svetlana's book. French 19th c. studies used to be the place everyone looked for methodological models, but now it seems the victory has been won by a kind of social art history—even though there are "outliers" (I used the statistics metaphor a lot) like gender theory and elements of Michael Fried's phenomenology. Modernism, I said, has its deep divisions, but a "victory," at least for pedagogy, has been won by the textbook *Art Since 1900*, with its *October* model of the century.

Chinese art history, I said, seems driven by two different kinds of splits. One is between scholars who were trained in Western institutions and teach in Western institutions, and scholars trained in China and Taiwan, who practice either a text-based interpretive practice (and this is, of course, a way of naming the practices against which you've campaigned) or a combination of aesthetics, art criticism, and art history (and that is, of course, my interest, which I know you don't see that way; I still like Jiang Hong's book as a test case). We can leave that first kind of split to one side for a while, not least because it is documented in the second edition of Jason's book. The other split—the other kind of difference within the field, I said, is within Western-trained scholars of Chinese art, and it's a split between, very roughly speaking, postcolonial and poststructural theory, on the one hand; and formalism, structuralism, and other visual accounts on the other. When I said that, I was thinking of our exchange, and I was hoping that someone later in the roundtable would pick up on it and note a parallel with Renaissance studies. In the event, no one did, but the analogy I was hoping for did develop without reference to the Chinese example.

That panel was put together by Bob Williams (Santa Barbara) and myself. We spent a long time thinking about Continental European or South American scholars we might invite, and in the end we had none. All our 7 panelists were from Ireland, Canada, and the US. The audience properly took us to task for that, but it didn't worry me because the format of the book allows for 40 respondents, from all around the world, to tell us what they think of us. The point is that Bob and I couldn't think of anyone in those countries (including, note, the home countries of the Renaissance) who was engaged in self-reflective discussions about the discipline and its historiography. Italian and other continental scholars have a wider range of references (as one of our panelists, Matt Kavaler, noted), but they tend to study "the objects themselves" and not their own motives or their own places in the history of the objects' reception. Bob and I knew that we couldn't have the kind of conversation we wanted with those people. We both hope that the conversation we actually taped will provide those 40-odd respondents plenty of things to argue against, but we knew we wouldn't make headway at a roundtable if we found ourselves talking to people interested mainly in facts, dates, styles, forms, and provenances—people for whom the specialty of Italian Renaissance art history has nothing to do with nationalistic motivations, and for whom it isn't helpful or relevant to consider what it means to study the fifteenth century in the twenty-first, or to write essays about the art that would have puzzled the original artists.

Needless to say there isn't an exact parallel with you and Craig. What I mean is that, as I said in my last letter, I think there are reasons for saying your book and his book are not just somehow more or less different, but fundamentally different enterprises. The differences among the two groups of Renaissance scholars are different kinds of differences—they involve terms, languages, methods, even generations—but the distances between the two groups is as great, and it is not irrelevant that some of those differences turn on the sense of art, the purposes of art history, and the ways that art history can, or should, be talked about.

I'm harping on this analogy, and on the idea of examining kinds of differences within fields, because I know that collegiality in any field, especially in a small specialty, prevents these things from being said. And I know Craig a bit, and I can well imagine him rolling up his eyes at all this. There are many things to be said for a plurality of approaches, and many good reasons not to be doctrinaire about differences. (You're very generous and accommodating in what you say about Craig's book.) But art history as a whole, and in Chinese studies in particular, cannot be as forceful in its claims, and as clear in its aims, as it might be unless these differences are aired. That, I suppose, is my main objection to the paper Rick gave in Maryland [*see Chapter 5 in this volume*], not anything he actually said. His comparison was a kind of détente, I think really impeccable, and acceptable to both sides, but it hid substantive ideological differences.

So let me risk, as the perpetual outsider, the one who has the least to lose by sounding ham-fisted, at least two items on a list of the distinctions between the two books, as I see them.

1. The nature of art. You articulated the first one as succinctly as anyone could: "I still believe that there is such a thing as an aesthetic experience, to be distinguished from other kinds of experience." Now I don't have to imagine what Craig might say to this, because for our purposes it's enough for me to conjure what a number of scholars I know might say. Something like this: "I have no reason to deny that kind of claim, or even to object to the discourse it enables. But I probably wouldn't insist on it in so many words, because to do so would be to present an entire history of political and social decisions, claims, dogmas, and notions, as if they were simply or merely true. An aesthetic experience, if I were to

want to say I had such a thing, would become, I suppose, an object of interest in its own right. Why was I tempted to feel that way? Why did I think that the object in question was 'beautiful'? What sequence of readings, what genealogy—as Foucault said, meaning what apparently natural lineage of historical moments—led me to think such a thing?"

Jim, I doubt you're in a minority of art historians in having aesthetic experiences, and I don't think that you think you have those experiences somehow outside of history or culture (as Kant did), but I imagine you're probably nearly alone among art historians in being willing to say "there is such a thing as an aesthetic experience" without feeling it also necessary to say something about your reflections on the historical conditions of your experience. It is a very deep, and I think unbridgeable, gulf.

Please pardon me for continually referring to the books I'm editing, but of course parallels spring to mind. I won't even bring in *Art History versus Aesthetics,* which is vol. 1 in the same series as *Renaissance Theory*: that book is out now, and in it you could see this problem played out at length. The people on that panel, and the respondents in the book, are all interested in contextualizing or relativizing aesthetic experience—in other words, they all distance themselves from an actual aesthetic experience to the degree that they always pose Kant as a figure in history, rather than a person who articulated something that is as true for him as for us. The exceptions (plenty of them in that book) are all philosophers, except Thierry de Duve.

Volume 4 in the same series will be *States of Art Criticism,* and a crisper parallel occurs to me there. In that roundtable, a parallel issue arose: the question of judgment. I was concerned, as you know from my pamphlet and the *New York Times* piece, about the fact that contemporary art critics don't usually judge artworks. One of the two roundtables for that book was set up in part to confront that issue. I had two journalists (Ariella Budick, who writes for *Newsday*, and James Panero, of the *New Criterion*) and a very opinionated and judgmental critic (Dave Hickey) at the same table as two very academically minded, poststructuralist theorists (Michael Newman, my co-editor, and Stephen Melville). Michael and Steve would, generally speaking, be interested in meditating on the conditions of judgment. They would, in a sense, agree with what Rosalind Krauss said back in 1971: art criticism, she thought, should from that moment on not be about judgments but about the conditions under which judgments seemed plausible. Dave, Ariella, and James were in the business of judging: good, bad, beautiful, ugly. We tried, Michael and I, to get a conversation going that might bridge the sides, and we just couldn't.

The question for us, I suppose, is what effect your assertion about aesthetics and the purposes of art history had on your book, and what effects Craig's cultural relativism (as I'll describe it, roughly speaking) had on his. That brings me to the second point.

2. The absence of the canon and its narrative contexts. I'll do this more briefly, for now. It can ramify into larger issues, but at the moment what I intend by the poisonous word canon is not just the set of works and artists that are, or were, common to beginning pedagogy and serious scholarship (several of whom you mention in your last letter), but also the context, the "discursive field" as Fried likes to say, that surrounds them and gives them sense. That field—this is why this second point can expand so rapidly—includes the principal and contending readings of the works and artists, and also the "master narratives," as I like to call them (*Master Narratives and Their Discontents*, 2005) that are used to link them together into art historical prose.

All that is missing in Craig's book. His bit of *Fuchun Mountains* is not an excerpt from the canonical object in the sense I have described it, but an excerpt from another discourse. There is no aesthetic, formal, stylistic, humanist significance at the core of his interest. His concern is political, social, institutional, economic, and market-oriented. *Fuchun Mountains*, and literati painting more generally, are in the book as activities among many others, not as central works that inform much of the rest of painting, or Chinese art in general. Postcolonial theory (about which I have different concerns and objections than you), institutional theory, sociology (which we mustn't forget: Pierre Bourdieu looms large here), and other concerns necessarily revalue the "canon" in such a way that it actually dissolves. It may seem to reappear in apparently familiar guises that really aren't familiar at all, but actually it's not reappearing: *Fuchun Mountains*, as it has been known in art history and in your books, does not actually appear in *Art in China*.

Or let me put it as a metaphor: if your books build a large-scale account of Chinese painting, Craig's *Art in China* and his other books have no such intention, and more—they intend, by omission, not to contribute to such an account. *Fuchun Mountains*, in Craig's book, is like a part of a Roman column and a bit of mosaic, out in the countryside, half-buried in the earth. Together they indicate a Roman house was once on the site, and with a few other shards and fragments—a mention of Ni Zan, perhaps—they can provide evidence that a Roman town was once on the site, complete with roads, canals, baths, towers and gates, fora.... But *Fuchun Mountains*, in the wider sense of its significance rather than the narrow sense of its naming, is not in *Art in China*, and the landscape of *Art in China* has no Roman buildings. It's a landscape from a different time, with different architecture.

That's my blustery, overly strong, outsider's way of putting something that, as we both know, is also nuanced and involves many overlaps and points of comparison. Craig's book, I think, is deeply, fundamentally, different from yours and not compatible—not susceptible to détente.

I'll just close by quoting a bit of your letter that seems closest to this: "Does it seem," you write, "odd that we are encouraged to recognize and credit 'radical transformations' in recent and contemporary art, however ephemeral they may be, but are discouraged from recognizing the ones that really mattered, had productive and even epochal outcomes, in the past? Not odd at all, I suppose, if one accepts the replacement of diachronic modes of understanding by synchronic ones, and all the rest." I think the problem is much larger, more abstract, and more insidious than diachronic and synchronic modes of organization. For that reason I also am unsatisfied by conversations about *Art in China* that note its gambit of talking about art that happened to be made in China (that move also came up in our Renaissance Theory roundtable, when people were talking about how to define the Renaissance): but this is enough, too much, and maybe the meaning of that assertion of Craig's can be a good place to take up next time.

So sorry for the long delay in writing, and best from Ireland (where we had a day of hailstorms, followed by a lovely clear cold evening),

Jim

3B. James Cahill to James Elkins

Vancouver, June 5, 2006

Dear Jim,

I've let my end of our correspondence go untended for too long, I'm afraid—I was, among other things, putting together a paper for the Wen Fong Festschrift, and it turned out to be longer and more absorbing than I had anticipated. Now that's finished and submitted, and the next really big project—getting back to my long-delayed book, after hearing (soon) from

Yale U. Press about some undecided aspects of it—is still a short way in the future. So it's a good time to get off a reply. I reread yours of April 9 this morning, and scribbled all over the margins of my printout with comments both admiring and argumentative.

This correspondence has been valuable for me, in making me clarify and articulate some of my long-held beliefs and arguments, and in letting me understand better, through your exegeses and analogies, the thinking behind the arguments of those I will call The Opposition. (Putting it that way suggests a Manichaean duality I don't really intend, but let me, for our present purpose, lump them together that way, while hoping you will realize that I'm not a lumper in practice.)

Once more I open with a minor protest. You write that I am "probably nearly alone among art historians" in writing about having the aesthetic experience without "feeling it also necessary to say something about your reflections on the historical conditions of your experience." Does my failure to mention these conditions every time I refer to the experience mean that I'm unaware of them? Has anyone written more than myself about how historical, social, economic, and other factors appear to have affected the ways people experienced (aesthetically and otherwise) Chinese paintings in different periods and situations? That's mostly, for instance, what the long last chapter of my *Painter's Practice* book was about, some of it rather Bourdieu-ish, at least in intent. Do you think I believe my own experiences to be timeless and universal? We respect each other's views enough, I hope, to not do the reductionist thing.

What I believe—and this is my quarrel with much of what you write (not all of it reflecting your own beliefs, of course)—is that any aesthetic experience or judgment, any human act or thought, is made/takes place in the context of a multiplicity of conditions and contingencies and factors that all affect it in varying degrees without any of them determining it absolutely.

When I talk or write about the circumstances surrounding the creation of a work of art, I sometimes invoke Baxandall's chapter on the design and building of the bridge over the Firth of Forth. Now, here is where we diverge: if the Rosalind Krauss faction is permitted to prevail, there won't be a bridge. (I use her as an example because you did.) This is because they argue as though the particular conditions they choose to emphasize among the great cluster of circumstances behind the creative act or critical judgment, the ones that best suit their particular political or other stance, somehow dissolve (or invalidate or neutralize—it's hard to state what appears to be the underlying assumption) that act or judgment. Krauss telling her followers back in 1971, as you summarize her argument, that art criticism isn't going to be about judgments any more, but about "the conditions under which judgments seem plausible," has that implication and has had that effect, for those who accept it: to the degree that it prevails, judgments have to be hedged around with so much baggage that they become all but impossible (cf. your complaint about the decline of criticism), and any judgment becomes, if one believes that way, as good as any other, since none can do more than "seem plausible." I may exaggerate, and in any case I don't mean to get into the cultural relativism problem as such.

I mentioned in an earlier letter a course in aesthetics that I sat in on at the University of Michigan in the 1950s, given by a UCLA philosophy professor named Abraham Kaplan, which I found enlightening. A section of it dealt with the circumstances behind an ideal aesthetic experience, which rendered critical judgments based on it more valuable than others: a full experience of the object (citing concert reviewers who weren't there when the piece was played), familiarity with related works, other factors in the prior experience of the critic, an attitude of objectivity (as much so as possible, not standing to benefit from one's appraisal), and so forth. And Kaplan ended up saying that the sum of judgments made under those conditions by the greatest number of critics/informed people might as well be accepted as the "right" judgment for its time—anything else is asking for a judgment from God. If someone had asked: Do historical and social/political factors affect those judgments? he would have replied: Of course they do. To a follow-up question, Are they the only ones that matter? he would have replied: Of course not, what a dumb idea. That taking account of these factors affecting the judgment should compromise the judgment itself to the point where we are obliged to shift our attention away from it to its context (Rosalind Krauss) wasn't even, so far as I know, a proposition with any currency then; nobody would have asked about it.

So, what lies behind the belief that the historical and social-political conditions are the only ones that matter? I remember some of our grad students in the 1980s–90s, including some of our best, saying: The only issues that matter now are race, class, and gender. (Or something like that.) One can't argue against that belief, any more than one can argue against assertions that nothing matters now except global warming, or the extinction of species, or spiritual salvation, or achieving world peace. If someone wants to read older literature only to detect traces of colonialist attitudes in it, they're welcome to do that. But that's a very limited enterprise within the larger study of literature, and becomes offensive when they begin urging or implying that we all are morally obligated to do the same.

Back to your letter. In your account of the "Renaissance Theory" roundtable, I wonder whether you are running the risk of misrepresenting the people you didn't invite with the assumption that they would be "interested mainly in facts, dates, styles, forms, and provenances"—as opposed, one assumes, to the concerns of the seven panelists you invited. The rejected ones might, that is, have concerns that go beyond the simple ones you attribute to them, but that also differ from those of yourself and your panelists? What you write after that brings up an old issue, much discussed in our previous correspondence, about "what it means to study the fifteenth century in the twenty-first." And its corollary: what it means for someone outside the culture to study the products of the culture and make pronouncements about them that differ from, even contradict, those of the "insiders." This problem has arisen throughout our correspondence, partly because it's central to your ideas about a global art history, partly because I myself am regularly charged with doing just that, and acknowledge freely having done it. I found some notes I'd made toward a response to that issue meant to be included, but not included, in one of the previous letters, and insert it here.

I was quite close to the late Wang Chi-ch'ien or C. C. Wang over the fifty years or so I knew him; we spent a lot of time together looking at paintings—in his collection, in the Freer, at the Palace Museum, etc.—and I came to understand, and respect, his kind of connoisseurship—I learned a lot from him. But in time I came to realize that there was a crucial disparity between his arguments and his practice. He argued that one should look only at the brushwork in a painting, the hand of the master, which he compared to the voice in an opera aria. The "scenery," the story, didn't really matter much. But in practice his judgments took into account the function of brushwork in depicting form, much more than he would admit: a painting with "good brushwork" but somehow clumsy or badly represented "scenery" didn't make it with him. He was impelled by a rhetorical position when he wrote or talked, but rose above it when he looked at a painting. Now, I would use this as an example of what I believe about Chinese theoretical arguments more generally: they are often driven by well-established rhetorical positions that have taken on the status of dogma, and these are repeated even when they don't correspond with the practice of those who repeat them. This is especially true of artists who give us the old formulae when they write or talk, while painting in far more interesting ways than their theoretical pronouncements would permit.

I made this point about Dong Qichang in the second of my Harvard (*Compelling Image*) lectures, and was told afterward that people were saying I was taking very "round-eyed" positions. And some Chinese reviewers have criticized the book rather heavily for this. But the prevalent view now seems to be that the book should be welcomed by Chinese readers for breaking away from received wisdom and thus providing a model and support for others who may want to do the same. Stephen Owen, the Harvard specialist in Chinese poetry and literary theory, has written brilliantly original books and essays in his field, on a higher level—I would be very happy to be judged as having accomplished for Chinese painting something approaching what he has for poetry. I haven't read Chinese responses to his writings, but I'm unaware that anyone has raised the issue of his being non-Chinese. (I suppose it's likely that someone has.)

When you add that we should consider also what it means "to write essays about the art that would have puzzled the original artists," you seem to imply a belief that the original artists must have articulated consciously whatever directions and stratagems we may find in their works, if our findings are to be valid. I think of that as the Buster Keaton argument: Buster would always scoff at the interpretations of his movies made by French and other critics, saying that he just used a lot of gags. Some of these interpretations do indeed seem over-intellectualized, but others seem convincing, and add to my enjoyment of his films. And I would assume that much of what I write about what Chinese painters were "up to" would indeed puzzle them, because they didn't consciously articulate their projects in those terms. (Baxandall again: "The intention to which I am committed is not an actual, particular psychological state or even a historical set of mental events inside the heads of Benjamin Baker or Picasso, in the light of which—if I knew them—I would interpret the Forth bridge or the Portrait of Kahnweiler. Rather, it is primarily a general condition of rational human action which I posit in the course of arranging my circumstantial facts or moving about on the triangle of re-enactment." *Patterns of Intention*, p. 41.)

Under "the nature of art" you write: "An aesthetic experience, if I want to say I had such a thing, would become, I suppose, an object of interest in its own right." And so forth. But here is the same old fallacious contention (sorry if I sound harsh): thinking about the factors and circumstances behind the experience prevents you from having it? Poor Jim, if that were true—sitting there listening to the last movement of Mozart's *Jupiter Symphony* (a recent intense aesthetic experience of mine) and thinking only of why it affects you that way. Max Beerbohm has a lovely moment in his *Christmas Garland* book, in his parody of Henry James, in which the Jamesian children sit before their presents on Christmas morning, unable to decide whether it's more pleasurable to open them or to prolong the delicious sense of anticipation over what they might contain. Not the same but related: the perils of dwelling too much in the once-removed.

The group of right-thinking scholars you conjure who wouldn't "insist on it [the aesthetic experience] in so many words, because to do so would be to present an entire history of political and social decisions . . . as if they were simply or merely true. . .": Straw horse: who says they are "simply true," who denies that there are political and social decisions, among others, behind the experience? But who with any sense would argue that to acknowledge this should prevent you or me from recounting and analyzing the experience itself, in whatever terms, and turning it to our purposes, whatever they may be?

I wish it were possible to say simply, "Yes, but the part doesn't equal the whole" and blow away the whole thing. Alas, no. But it seems to be self-destructing.

No doubt you have dealt with the argument I'm making in some theoretical/methodological writing of your own, since it's an obvious objection and must have been used by many others. And I will be interested to read how you meet it, if you give me a reference or copy it out or restate it. (It's probably discussed in your *Art History versus Aesthetics:* I should get a copy of that and read it. Some of it will of course be what you've already sent me.) But I'm inclined to think that in this letter I've said as much as I mean to on these big matters, and could only repeat myself if we continued. So I would suggest that this can be my last letter in the series, to which you can respond as you will—a statement of mine was the first in this series, as I recall. And then we will have a document that Jason can eventually publish or distribute in some form, if he thinks it warrants that.

The final pages of your letter, about why my old *Chinese Painting* book and Craig Clunas's *Art in China* are fundamentally different kinds of books is clear and perceptive, and will help others as it helped me, to realize what is involved in the distinction. And I continue to respect what Clunas and others are doing, and grant the validity of it as another, valuable way of thinking and writing about art. The only dispute I would have with what you write is with the seeming underlying assumption that the one has really killed off the other forever (cf. Rosalind Krauss's pronouncement on criticism, "from this moment on": the cultural critic as self-appointed deity) and that my (and others') accounts are "not somehow in his book as much as they are revealed as ruins by the book." (Your metaphor is a good one, not unrelated to mine in the complaint in my Princeton lecture that we may have "abandoned the practice of architecture before we have built our city." So my city is in ruins before it has even been built!)

But it's hard to tell, from what you write, how far you really believe in the would-be finality of all this. I can only say that someone who has lived eighty years, as I have, has watched quite a few such pronouncements of the demise of this or that be succeeded by a reappearance of whatever it was, in different but still recognizable form—music can no longer be composed with traditional harmony, the symphony (opera, whatever) is dead, no more easel painting, or representational painting at all, and so forth. You seem to be joining in the too-common practice of denying the possibilities of rebirth or revival when you write about how the "canon," once it has been "dissolved" by Bourdieu and others (see above for my opinion on that "dissolved" bit), can only seem to reappear, it isn't really reappearing. Advocates of that kind of thinking have a professional and emotional stake, I suppose, in believing that they are really killing off these pernicious old beliefs and practices (along with their older colleagues) once and for all: it's like saying "My side has prevailed, and will be followed by right-thinking people forever!" They need to believe that their way of thinking about art, or cultural formulations more generally, has made older ways ultimately untenable; that once we've realized the world is round we can't go back to seeing it as flat. But it isn't by any means that kind of irreversible change, it's a recent and different way of thinking that nobody is obliged to follow forever. Every now and then someone on the other side, like the Yale English Lit. Dept. chair I quoted in a note to my original essay, pronounces "the Age of Theory" to be over. Both sides want to see the end of the other; neither seems likely to die soon.

That, at least, is the way I would see it; you see it in a different way, finding more ultimate validity in Theory, New Cultural Criticism, whatever we call it. Alas, neither of us is likely to be able to say to the other, two or three or four decades from now, "See? I told you so." But my ghost will come back, believe me, to gloat a bit: "Look! writers on art are once again deeply concerned with 'aesthetic, formal, stylistic, and humanist significance' in art!" I will be very surprised, posthumously, if that isn't true. In fact, much of what I read on art and literature and music these days convinces me, comfortingly, that it's already true in a lot of writing that can't be so easily dismissed. The Yale chairman quoted above was reviewing Helen Vendler's latest book, and I could list lots of other examples. The critics I find most penetrating have never stopped being concerned with the qualities you would like to think are ruled out of responsible criticism.

And that brings me conveniently back to where I began, with a heartfelt argument for what I've found, in my long engagement in the field, to be really the best way to bring people to fuller and more gratifying understandings of the kinds of art we write about. At its best, it doesn't accept canons but it doesn't reject them altogether either; it remakes them (as I've been trying to do throughout the later decades of my career for Chinese painting, mostly in the direction of expansion, greater inclusiveness. It doesn't throw out "narratives" altogether, but tries to revise or replace old ones with new ones that better respond to, and illuminate, passages of art history according to the new understandings of them we have reached. In short, like the best of Chinese painting itself, it doesn't try to throw out the past but builds on it, rejects what no longer seems to work, incorporates what still does work into new and challenging formulations. (I cited a few examples of this—Stravinsky vs. Varèse, Hongren vs. Wang Shichang—in my second letter, in arguing that breaking the rules isn't in itself a sufficient criterion of value in art.) If this isn't the view of art history writing and teaching that prevails in the end—or at least comes back into a condition of being openly acknowledged as the most widely accepted goal—I will be very (posthumously) surprised. And disappointed. (Oh, restless spirit!)

Jim

P.S. We never did get back, really, to the global art history issues; but I didn't really have much to contribute to those, not being nearly so versed and engaged as you are in the proposals and the arguments behind them. The best I could do was raise objections to two of your proposals—not much help.

4A. James Elkins to James Cahill

[*James Elkins's note: This letter was written after I had just finished writing my response to an essay by Jonathan Hay that was to be published in* The Art Bulletin *("The Mottled Discourse of Chinese Studies," September 2007); that text is presupposed in what follows and should be read first.*]

Ithaca, New York, July 10, 2006

Dear Jim,

I'm sorry this is to be the last installment in our exchange. For me, the discussion is just starting. I have notes on how I wanted to open the issues, and we're only on point one out of five! I think what we're trying to do here is a very important kind of project—not to say that *these* letters are important, or that somehow we've discovered something momentous—because what normally happens in disciplines with rifts is that people on either side of the rift more or less ignore one another. I am so familiar with the kind of shrug, or sigh, that greets the name of some scholars. In Western art history, some people sigh, or shrug, when they hear a name like Michael Fried or Rosalind Krauss. The wordless response means something like, "Oh God, she's hopeless, but thank heavens there's no need to go into that subject now." Sometimes the sigh is accompanied by a knowing nod, which means, "Yes, right, we both know she's hopeless, and we're agreed there's no way to address the problems. We just have to live with that kind of thing."

My point isn't that people are rude—they are!—it's that when gulfs open within disciplines, or within specialties, people tend not to actively engage. People don't honestly, openly, address such differences: instead they learn to live with them. I'll tell you an odd story about that. Last month I was at a conference in London called "Beyond Mimesis and Nominalism," which was set up by an art historian (Matthew Hunter) and a philosopher of science (Roman Frigg); it was intended to address theories of representation that go beyond Gombrich and Goodman. The final plenary speech was by Catherine Elgin, an analytic philosopher from Harvard. She gave a paper about the forms of explanation, claiming that art historians sometimes deal with propositions in the form "*x is a y-representation as z.*" I won't give an example, because it's not pertinent, but as you can imagine, her talk was very abstract. Her claim was that art historians make many such propositions, in competition with one another, and that we sort them all out by arguing. She said her role, as philosopher, was just to show us what *form* our arguments take. In the question period, I said that I thought she was right about some of her abstract forms, but that art historians do not usually argue. We argue when it comes to particular cases—the *Riverbank* controversy, disagreements about the *Arnolfini Portrait* or the *Tempesta*—but in the vast majority of cases, we do not argue. What happens instead is that alternate theories just accumulate. Scholars pick and choose their favorites, but do not argue at length about previous interpretations. I think that is patently true of the great majority of art historical interpretations, and I think it can be proven by looking at specific cases. Piero della Francesca's *Flagellation,* for example, has had at least twenty interpretations, and none of them argue at any length with the preceding interpretations. They simply *propose* the new meaning, with glancing references to selected previous literature.[8] Catherine didn't say much at that point, but a few minutes later some PhD students from the Courtauld, who were in the audience, asked a question and one said in passing, "By the way, Elkins is wrong: art historians argue all the time." This was by way of informing the audience: the remark wasn't addressed to me. Afterward I wondered if I wanted to talk to them about their claim, but I realized I would be in the strange position of *arguing* that art historians don't argue!

That's a long-winded way of illustrating just how marginal argument is in art history. It *seems* prominent, because paintings like *Riverbank* or the *Flagellation* attract controversy, but I think that obscures the great mass of art historical writing that proceeds on its own way, with nothing more than a sigh or a nod in the direction of approaches that are significantly different. That is what is happening in Chinese studies, I think, between approaches in sympathy with Clunas, for example, or those in sympathy with you. (I'm sorely tempted to name the people whom I've heard sigh when either your name or Craig's come up in conversation: but I won't!) That's why this exchange of ours is potentially so important, aside from whatever we've managed to say: it keeps the conversation going, it substitutes words for sighs. (The closest I know is Jerome Silbergeld's lovely piece on your work, which you mentioned: that's the kind of example that for me proves the rule.[9])

So, how to respond, knowing this is the final letter? I won't try to open more specific issues—I had thought about concentrating on particular cases, such as the history of scholarship on Hongren or Zhao Mengfu. And I won't say much about the points you raise in your last letter: they are, as you suspect, slight misunderstandings. Briefly, point by point:

1. The Renaissance Theory roundtable participants (including my co-editor Bob Williams) were acutely aware of the concerns of people who weren't present. It's a complicated issue, which we hope we'll resolve in the book by inviting the kinds of people who wouldn't have wanted to join our conversation to write "Assessments" which will be published in the book.

2. You asked where I had written about that difference between "pure" practice and "pure" theory: yes, in the opening chapters of *Our Beautiful, Dry, and Distant Texts: Art History as*

Writing. As you say, it's hard to locate my own position in the opposition I set up between Rosalind Krauss's position against unqualified judgment, and the positions of critics whose business it is to judge. I agree with you that it shouldn't be necessary to articulate the social contexts that determine one's aesthetic judgments every time such a judgment is made. But *shouldn't* is the key there: for various reasons it has become necessary to demonstrate—sometimes repeatedly—one's distance from one's judgments, or else one's awareness of the historical contingency of one's judgments. This is a fascinating subject, really, because it isn't a question of philosophy but of disciplinary expectations.

3. On the subject of writing essays that would have puzzled the original artists, your objections are all correct: but I hadn't meant it in that way. I agree artists' own ideas about what they do is usually very far from the ideas that historians assign to them—the ideas that give artists their places in history often have virtually nothing to do with what the artists understood themselves to be doing. I meant something more general. Some artists have accrued mountains of literature, describing them in all sorts of ways—Lacanian, Marxist, semiotic—which would not have been known in their lifetimes. Sooner or later that imbalance has to become an issue in its own right, aside from the difference between the claims in the modern literature, on the one hand, and the artist's intentions and awareness, on the other. Sooner or later what we write and how we write have to become a problem for a historiographically reflective practice. What are we doing, producing thousands of books and hundreds of thousands of essays on artists whose practice was understood, both by them and by their contemporaries, in much simpler ways? I know this is a tricky kind of argument to make, because it keeps sounding as if I'm saying that art historians should always square their interpretive methodologies with the awarenesses of the artists and their contemporaneous critics. It isn't that: it's the sheer weirdness

of applying such huge amounts of analytic attention to practices that were articulated quite differently. Think of the difference between a Fortean or Schenkerian analysis of Liszt, and Liszt's own very poetic and metaphorical understandings of his own music. If you wrote an essay on Liszt these days, using his own late-Romantic prose-poem style of criticism, it would never be published. You don't need to worry about the fact that Liszt never knew Alan Forte to worry that the discourse we are producing is something wholly new. So I am concerned about the *strangeness* of what we write, not so much about the match between our claims and things the artists would have immediately recognized or understood.[10]

4. About my claim "An aesthetic experience, if I want to say I had such a thing, would become, I suppose, an object of interest in its own right": you're right to suspect I have aesthetic experiences! (Most recently, for me, Messaien's *Vingt regards,* which for me is an overwhelming piece.) But I wanted to put it that way because there are plenty of art historians who either would deny they have strong aesthetic experience, or would want to say those experiences have no connection to historical writing. That is a sobering lesson I learned when I was researching *Pictures and Tears,* my book about people who have cried in front of paintings. I wrote to a number of art historians, asking if they had had strong emotional reactions, including crying, in front of paintings, and the famous people who answered me all asked to be anonymous![11] So again that claim was a matter of trying to put things in a way that doesn't misrepresent people.

5. How much do I believe in the "would-be finality of all this"? Not at all, not even a little bit. But I'm interested in the current conditions of understanding of history and art. To be read, to be taken seriously, to participate in current debates, it's necessary to speak and write in approximation to certain models. For me, that's sometimes an unhelpful constraint, and then I go away for a while and write something "useless"

like *What Painting Is.* At other times the constraints appear as opportunities: after all, it sometimes happens that the language of postcolonial theory (even though Gayatri Spivak has declared she's finished with the concept of the subaltern) is the one in which the most interesting debates take place, and so it's necessary to take it seriously, and to learn it, like a language.

So, how to conclude? Instead of continuing, and talking about particular cases like Hongren or Dong Qichang (I'd especially like to talk about artists like Pan Tianshou or Xu Beihong—their critical fortunes seem to have more to say about differences in Chinese and Western scholarship than some older artists)—instead of doing that, I would like to move in the other direction, and with something *very* abstract.

My response to Jonathan Hay's essay in the *Art Bulletin* is apposite here. As you know, I have been writing people about the unpublished English version of *Chinese Landscape Painting as Western Art History* for nearly fifteen years now. It's been read by a large number of people in the field. Jonathan Hay is one of the very few people who declined to correspond with me simply because I am not a specialist. (And, directly as a consequence of that, I've never met him.) His essay in *The Art Bulletin* has all the characteristics of work done by a specialist with limited acquaintance with the wider landscape of art history. He picks and chooses a wide variety of Western theoretical sources, and brings them all into his account—that's why I called his text "mottled."

Now of course all of us do this to some degree, mixing usually Western theoretical sources with Chinese primary texts. Hay is an extreme case because he collects very different sources, which are arguably incompatible with one another—Ziarek, Luhmann, Badiou, Deleuze—and he considers them rapidly, one after the other. My essay was intended to argue that he really has only one Western theoretical source, Merleau-Ponty, but he hasn't realized it yet. His essay in *The*

Art Bulletin is a hasty, multicolored collage. Take Michael Fried as a contrasting case: he acknowledges his fundamental indebtedness to Merleau-Ponty, so that his theoretical sources are strongly unified. (Freud and Lacan hardly appear, for example, in the psychoanalytically-inflected *Courbet's Realism*.)

"Mottled discourses" are common, I think, when one specialty looks outside itself and tries to find points of connection. In Hay's case, I think the mottling is a symptom of his not having thought through his Western sources. But on the other hand, *all* art historical writing is "mottled" or at least mixed. Your work, Jim, is an example of a very coherent, mixture of some Western interests and Chinese material. Craig's is another, also very well thought through, and as coherent as it might be.

When I say that your work blends Western modernist formalism with Chinese sources, or that Craig's mixes Western postcolonial and political theory with Chinese sources, I am speaking metaphorically. "Blending" and "mixing" are inadequate words, but I don't think English has a good word for what I mean: Craig's writing is an *effect*, say, of a particular late twentieth-century English political education and the Chinese works it finds intriguing, problematic, or congenial. I am not exempting myself, of course. My own belief that I might have something to contribute as an outside observer of the specialty produces another kind of mixture, another "mottled" discourse.

My point in relation to Hay's essay was that a severely mottled collection of sources is a sign of a transitory stage in the encounter of specialties or disciplines. My point here is that all of us exhibit mixtures, and so a *study of mixtures* is a way to continue to talk across apparently unbridgeable rifts. I'm suggesting we can consider art historical texts of all sorts—but especially those that experiment with ways of interpreting non-Western material—as *pictures*. Texts with lots of footnotes to different sources, like Hay's essay in *The Art Bulletin*, are like collages; other pictures are more unified. The difficulty in describing differences between your work and Craig's is partly this relative unity. There are no bits and bobs to pick apart: the projects are strongly unified and very different.

That is my very abstract rumination. I think that paying attention to the *texture* of our writing—the shreds of imported discourses, the collage of Western theory and Chinese sources, the shards and lumps of unexpected citations in footnotes—is a way to continue to think about the *strangeness* of producing Western art historical interpretations of Chinese paintings in the twenty-first century. Our activity is much odder than we think, and it's a good idea to find ways of focusing our attention on the strangeness—the historical, political, literary, philosophic, geographic specificity—of what we produce under the name "art history."

It has been a real privilege to have this exchange. So few people are willing to find ways to talk: to me, an interest in thinking seriously about unbridgeable gaps is one of the best and rarest qualities in our discipline.

Best,
Jim

Notes

1 The reasons for that are explored at length in my *Stories of Art* (New York: Routledge, 2002), also translated into Korean (Seoul: Artbooks, 2005).

2 Hal Foster, Rosalind Krauss, Benjamin Buchloh, and Yve-Alain Bois, *Art Since 1900: Modernism, Antimodernism, Postmodernism* (London: Thames and Hudson, 2005).

3 *The Domain of Images* (Ithaca, N.Y.: Cornell University Press, 1999); *Master Narratives and Their Discontents,* with an introduction by Anna Arnar (Cork, Ireland: University College Cork Press; New York: Routledge, 2005).

4 *Master Narratives* (above, n. 3) is vol. 1 in a series called Theories of Modernism and Postmodernism in the Visual Arts.

5 (New York: Routledge, 2008). Ning's paper was one of six on verbal and visual ideas in different cultures.

6 James Cahill, "Some Thoughts on the History and Post-History of Chinese Painting," *Archives of Chinese Art* 55 (2005): 17–37; responses by Robert Harrist (35–37) and Jerome Silbergeld (39–52). I think also of the response of Richard Vinograd and others when I gave the lecture at Stanford. These are all good friends and respected colleagues, and I am not putting them down as wrong, only using them to exemplify a point in my argument.

7 Barry Gewen, "State of the Art," *New York Times,* December 11, 2005, book review section, 28–32.

8 This is argued with several examples in my *Our Beautiful, Dry, and Distant Texts: Art History as Writing,* 2nd ed. (New York: Routledge, 2000).

9 In *Archives of Chinese Art* 55 (2005): 39–52.

10 This is argued more articulately in my *Why Are Our Pictures Puzzles? On the Modern Origins of Pictorial Complexity* (New York: Routledge, 1999).

11 James Elkins, *Pictures and Tears: A History of People Who Have Cried in Front of Paintings* (New York: Routledge, 2001).

5

Narrative and Metanarrative in Chinese Painting

Richard Vinograd

Chinese painting studies and histories are shaped (like all art historical accounts) by a variety of narratives. Some are explicit story lines, others are unspoken but operate as shaping procedural or structural assumptions, and still others are metanarratives that have to do with overarching or underlying assumptions about the purposes, values, and significance of art and of art historical practice. I should clarify at the outset that this essay is focused on historiographic or art historical narratives, rather than pictorial narratives in the form of narrative or illustrative paintings and prints of historical, religious, or literary subjects, as interesting as those topics have become in recent scholarship.[1] I shall however have something to say about visual narratives in relation to textual or historiographic narratives. This discussion of narrative will be mostly descriptive and historical rather than theoretical, but there are some sporadically acknowledged theoretical horizons to it—supplied variously by Northrop Frye, Hayden White, Jean-François Lyotard, Gérard Gennette, and Tom Gunning (for properly visual narrative).

An account of Chinese painting studies over the past half century is thus to some degree a study of the field's overlaid and implicated narratives. This kind of self-conscious or self-reflexive enterprise is characteristic of a certain historiographic turn in ours as in many other academic fields. I think it can be useful and important to the extent that it doesn't result in a crippling self-absorption, as it has sometimes done. My account will be necessarily partial and somewhat arbitrary, but in the present context it makes sense to use James Cahill's *Chinese Painting* (1960) as a starting point, with Craig Clunas's *Pictures and Visuality in Early Modern China* (1997) as a more contemporary comparative foil, useful in part because it is so self-conscious and explicit about its approaches and methodologies.[2] I choose Cahill's book because his career is central to this volume; because it was and remains a widely read general account of Chinese painting that claims (if only implicitly) to represent that broad subject, and was certainly a signpost of Chinese painting studies in Postwar America; because the book's success depends substantially on the stories it tells and how they are told, as coherent, readable, absorbing, satisfying narratives; and not least because it was a very important book for my own formation. Of course we should recognize that there are many other writers who could be central to such a discussion, and that my focus on these two itself represents a narratological choice, inflected by this occasion and many other more deeply embedded factors.

It should be clear, though it will probably bear repeating, that the point of this exercise is not to judge which approach is in some sense better; the books belong to such different periods and environments and harbor such different agendas that any comparisons need to be elaborately qualified, and in any case I don't attempt a full analysis of either book. My intent most especially is not to critique some straw dog version of a canonical model—if only because Jim Cahill has continuously participated in reshaping his own and the field's narratives up to the present. Indeed, I might just as easily contrast the early Cahill of *Chinese Painting* with the later and present Cahill of *Three Alternative Histories*, *The Painter's Practice*, or "Paintings Done for Women in Ming–Qing China?"[3] In any case, *Chinese Painting* is its own best defense, still widely read, and amazingly readable and sound after nearly half a century. It is one of the foundational texts of our field, in large part because its narratives—both textual and visual, the latter embodied in choices of illustrated monuments—have been so persuasive. Rather, I want to juxtapose Cahill's text, which is structured so strongly around narrative practices in all the senses noted above, with Clunas's critiques of narrative or outright anti-narrative positions, to foreground these central historiographic issues for our field. I hope this account might be useful in assessing not only how far we've come since the 1950s, as intended by this volume, but also what has been gained and perhaps lost along the way.

Let me begin with a characterization—I hope not a caricature, though I will heighten the contrasts and perhaps gloss over some of the common ground—of the agendas and positions of each writer and text. Cahill (I mean primarily the Cahill of *Chinese Painting*) writes a general history of Chinese painting. Clunas (primarily in *Pictures and Visuality*, but also in *Art in China*, and other writings) questions the validity of general histories as a byproduct of nineteenth-century Hegelian historical practices, and questions also the meaningfulness of the categories "China" and "Chinese art."[4] Cahill focuses on scroll paintings made with brush, ink, and color, on paper or silk. Clunas discusses pictures: paintings, prints, lacquer and ceramic designs, textiles, and any medium with a picture on or in it. Cahill focuses on painting from the Han through the eighteenth century. Clunas's focus is on Ming (or early modern) pictorial culture.[5] Cahill emphasizes autograph works by artists of significant historical reputation. Clunas gives more or less equal attention to anonymous workshop paintings, lacquerware, and ceramic designs as he does to works by famous painters (although *Art in China* includes a good deal about notable calligraphers and painters). Cahill discusses famous individual paintings, masterpieces in the commonplace sense of the term. Clunas is concerned primarily with categories and types of objects with multiple instantiations. Cahill is interested in the artist's biography, temperament, and expression.

Clunas's interest in biography has primarily to do with social status, cultural roles, relationship networks, and social obligations. Cahill sees style as a carrier of expression and meaning. Clunas's attention to style is mostly categorical, as a marker of status, class origin and/or audience, or social distinction. Cahill highlights artistic technique and skill. Clunas is more concerned with standards of valuation and criticism. Cahill focuses on the artist's production and the viewer's response. Clunas attends more to systems of production and reproduction, and to social patterns of reception, consumption, and taste. Cahill is interested in transmission, of paintings, styles, and traditions. Clunas foregrounds a more open-ended circulation of objects, tastes, and values.

This is certainly far from an exhaustive list, but the contrasts in interests, values, and practices are sharp enough that we might question whether the two authors are really engaged in a common field, or a common enterprise—whether we call it the history of art, or painting studies on the one hand, or visual culture studies, or perhaps a critical history of art history, on the other.

There are nonetheless many commonalities, despite all the divergences. Both Cahill and Clunas come from curatorial backgrounds, and both know their way around objects extremely well, however they choose to manifest it. Both have been illuminating analysts of Chinese art texts in classical Chinese, though their approaches to those texts are rather different.[6] Both believe, though for different reasons and on different bases, that Chinese painting should be accessible to Western viewers and that it has many points of commonality with European painting. For Cahill, this is due to their common humanism, and some shared assumptions about the importance of the artist, personal style, human expression through formal means, and the like. For Clunas, this commonality is based (for the Ming) on a shared horizon of early modernity, mutual participation in an emerging world system, and comparable socioeconomic horizons of luxury consumption, status consciousness, and the deployment of taste and consumption patterns to claim social and cultural distinction. Both agree (despite Clunas's engagement with Hall and Ames's notions of distinctive world views, ontologies, and epistemologies) that Chinese painting functions in the same manner, and serves many of the same social and cultural functions as does Western painting.[7]

Cahill takes a knowledgeable insider's perspective, even in some ways a participant's perspective as a significant collector and connoisseur, who makes use of many historical approaches and techniques to understand and evaluate Chinese painting. Clunas takes more of an anthropologist's stance, taking nothing (including his own cultural and historical position) for granted, observing phenomena at the cultural and social levels and attempting to account for them. It might be said that Cahill is more visually centered in his analyses, and that Clunas takes text, theory, and discourse as focal concerns, but that's far from clear-cut—Clunas is deeply concerned with visuality, at the very least.

Explicit Narratives

What are some of the explicit narratives of *Chinese Painting*? First, that Chinese painting had a legible and more or less continuous history that began in some fashion around the Han dynasty and ended in the late eighteenth century. I say in some fashion because the beginning and ending points depend upon a certain conception of what Chinese painting comprises, as well as practical editorial considerations. That history had a structure, part chronological—organized around dynasties or parts of dynasties—and part spatial/geographical, organized around institutions or regional schools. Genre or subject classifications are also important to the structure of the early chapters of the book, though not to the same degree as are consistently operative historical categories. Within the larger horizon, there were two major, long-duration epochs: the period up through the end of Song, and post-Song painting, with the literati and Chan painters of the mid- to late Song bridging those two halves of the book and its account. Song and earlier painting is celebrated for its achievement of representational command, such that the viewer of a painting felt as if before the object (or place) itself, and culminating in an almost unsurpassable subtlety of atmospheric effects and refined brush techniques in the late Southern Song. Post-Song painting is represented as an alternative realm of values and qualities, newly recognized and explicated. These have to do with conveying the personal qualities of the artist, through independently expressive brush and ink forms. The trajectories of post-Song painting are much less clearly shaped than those of early painting, but they have to do with qualities of formal exploration and expressive intensity that seem richest during the Yuan (for formal exploration) and the seventeenth-century late Ming–early Qing era (for expressive intensity).

This is a bare-bones account, and there is a lot more going on in Cahill's text, but even this will be enough to occupy us for a good while. *Pictures and Visuality* is also a very rich account, but in a very different register. It disavows the ambition to continuous or seamless narrative history, and operates instead through a series of case studies, on topics such as print culture, Ming visuality and its anxieties, and cosmology and its pictorial counterparts. There are coherent accounts of particular topics like the *Gushi huapu* ("Master Gu's Pictorial Album") woodblock print compilation and an overarching concern with the status of pictures and paintings within Ming society, values, cultural practices, and material culture. The topic of narrative pictures is discussed, in terms of their status and popularity within Ming visual culture, and in regard to the circulation of narrative themes across media.[8] A fair number of specific historical anecdotes are also citied or quoted in Clunas's text.

Clunas, however, is wary of the apparatus and implications of much historical narrative: that it should presume some kind of unity and coherence of a historical field or era in which picturing occurs, and that it overlooks elements of contradiction and conflict within eras and artworks alike.[9] Clunas's accounts might be considered counter-narratives, in which print technologies, publishing economies, and discourses of visuality take on the roles of protagonists, or they might be seen as anti-narratives, that push against the narrativizing expectations of readers. Clunas tends to write in polylogues, keeping a number of theoretical, informational, and argumentative balls in the air at once, in a way that deliberately resists reduction to linear narrative. Without attempting to parse such questions too closely, I would only note that neither writing strategy is intrinsically more complete than the other, although Cahill casts his narrative net more evenly over the eras he discusses, and engages more of the internal historical signposts of artists and schools that emerged within the historical discourses of Chinese painting. On the other hand, Cahill disregards the non-painting pictorial media and many of the social strata that Clunas foregrounds. Both accounts can be seen as comparably rich and comparably deficient within the terms of their rough equivalence of length and numbers of illustrations. The degree to which those presences and gaps are considered significant, and whether more or less continuous and coherent narratives are preferred to those that emphasize fragmentation and discontinuity, are matters based on standards that are contingent byproducts of history writing and intellectual tastes.

The question of internalist versus externalist historical perspectives is of interest because neither writer takes an unmodulated position on the matter. Cahill assumes an insider's stance and substantially adopts the terms and categories that developed over the centuries he discusses. At the same time, the contemporary horizon is everywhere present in Cahill's authorial or narrative voice and point of view, though it is largely submerged within the narrative flow. The basic position is a contemporary overview of a stable historical past, receding back (and then flowing forward, in the narrative) from the late eighteenth century toward the more dimly understood Six Dynasties and Han. This is very deftly managed; aside from a few clearly anachronistic comments about modern artists and composers, all the interrogative, reconstructive, and hypothesizing dialogue with the past is subsumed within a unified narrative. This is part of the historian's art, or perhaps also a kind of ventriloquism: Cahill's distinctive authorial voice is everywhere present, yet the past seems to speak itself through its monuments. Clunas's narrative imbricates contemporary theory and methodological discussion with the historical in ongoing shifting configurations and counterpoints. All the stitching, gaps, and misfittings in the account show forth, and deliberately, so that the seductions of narrative can be disrupted and the status of history as contingent construct foregrounded. This apparently does not imply that the Ming historical past is unapproachable in its own discursive and cognitive terms—that effort of reconstructive historical understanding is explicitly avowed in Clunas's introduction.[10] Rather, this imbricated narrative is a product of a destabilized authorial position, where nothing about the contemporary scholar, author, or narrator (or reader or viewer) can be taken for granted, and everything has to be made a topic of analysis and interrogation—cultural position and identity, theoretical orientation, methodology and procedures, even the epistemological status of the observer. So for Clunas too, the contemporary horizon is everywhere present, and much more prominently foregrounded and announced than in Cahill, but it is a very different, let's say for convenience, postmodern or post-Structuralist present.

For all these reasons we should thus not expect much in the way of conventional art historical narratives in Clunas. What narratives there are tend to be historiographic stories, about the contours of art historical practice, rather than about the development of art. Indeed, it may be that the strongest narrative thread in *Pictures and Visuality* has not so much to do with the Ming, but instead concerns the history of art history and critical theory. In the introduction and throughout the text, references to the constructions of discourses about art and painting, and of art historical practices from the Ming down to the nineteenth- and late twentieth-century West, provide a chronological framing of the sort we might expect in explicit narrative. There is a framing argument, vigorously sustained, about the necessity of including Ming and other Chinese pictorial and visual practices in any adequate account of the history of art or visual modernity. Parallel arguments concern the importance of including all modes of painting and all pictorial media in accounts of the Ming/early modern era. A cast of characters is provided by contemporary critical historians and theorists like Bryson, Bhabha, Preziosi, and Appadurai, within an ongoing dialogue about method, as much as by Ming artists and writers.[11]

Embedded Narratives

Embedded narratives can include those intertextual concerns and agendas that may emerge in references, or asides, or more explicitly in footnotes and bibliographies, or at other times might need to be discerned by implication from a pattern of argument or attention. In some ways they are like backstories in narratology, or related to Gennette's paratexts—framing elements that undergird or thread through the explicit narrative, though I am pointing less to authorial framing than to deeper intellectual genealogies.[12] Embedded narratives in this sense involve also the preconditions and situations of writing, such as intellectual agendas, editorial constraints, and the rhetorical purposes of address to audiences. This notion of embedded narratives in art historical writing is quite parallel to our modes of approach to understanding artistic production: questions of the patronage situation and technical or economic constraints; the chain of stylistic, iconographic, and technical adoptions and appropriations that figure in and through the work; the decorum, rhetoric, and discursive forms that are appropriate to a given audience and artistic purpose. In these ways the work of art, or the work of art history, can appear like a palimpsest or tissue of motives drawn from multiple sources. *Chinese Painting* is by design an unfootnoted book, though accompanied by an interesting brief bibliography. The embedded narratives of *Pictures and Visuality* are more clearly signaled, but in any case the references are mostly to more recent intellectual currents and thus are probably familiar to students of the field. Because of that, and because a full unpacking of either text would yield a lengthy exposition, I'll just summarize a few concerns.

The sympathetic treatment of post-Song painting in Cahill's *Chinese Painting*, for example, which emerges as an explicit narrative by virtue of the extensive attention given it, takes place as a corrective or reaction against the dismissive attitude toward Ming–Qing painting displayed in Ludwig Bachhofer's *A Short History of Chinese Art* (1946) that still had some currency in 1960.[13] The positive attitude toward later Chinese painting in Cahill's book carried forward the proselytizing and perhaps market-making efforts of Jean-Pierre Dubosc in favor of Ming–Qing painting and Osvald Sirén's relatively catholic openness to the full range of pre-Song through Ming–Qing painting, at least from the point of view of a documentary history of biographies and texts.[14] Cahill's teacher Max Loehr's fundamental distinction between the representationally oriented painting of the Song era and the primary concern with style formation in post-Song painting may also be an embedded narrative structure, though Loehr's most notable formulations of the topic were published later.[15]

Thus there was a historical and situational embeddedness to *Chinese Painting*'s narratives, and a consequent agenda. Writers sympathetic to post-Song painting—Dubosc, Victoria Contag, Sirén, Aschwin Lippe, and Loehr—loom large in Cahill's bibliography, and others like C. C. Wang were perhaps more deeply embedded in his thinking through conversations and viewings.[16]

Cahill contributed to Sirén's bibliographies of Chinese catalogues and biographical sources, and to his "Annotated Lists," so Sirén's biographical focus, his ambition toward comprehensiveness in accounting for extant Chinese painting in a cataloguing and connoisseurial sense, and the Chinese sources he in turn relied on all shaped the agendas of Cahill's book in more than one dimension.[17] Sirén in a sense was a modern art historical conduit for the combined biographical, cataloguing, and connoisseurial/critical outlook of the mainstream classical Chinese painting sources. At the same time Sirén's project perhaps stimulated in Cahill a simultaneous emulation and rivalry—an ambition to be comprehensive though in a less encyclopedic way, and to display more acute critical and connoisseurial judgments. Sirén's work was a hybrid—part sourcebook, part encyclopedia, part reference work, and all monumental—more liable to be consulted than read through, at least in one sitting. Sirén's separation of his plates from his text was as symptomatic of his archival purpose as Cahill's integration of images and text was of his strategy of visual narrative.

Indeed one of the strongest embedded narratives in *Chinese Painting* is the connoisseurial-historical project of sorting out the authentic surviving monuments of Chinese painting and clarifying their interrelationships. This is largely unspoken in terms of its achievement, but the interplay of connoisseurial and historical judgments with the exposition of *Chinese Painting*'s chapters is everywhere present. The embedded narratives here are not only the attributions by historical Chinese scholars, emperors, and twentieth-century art historians alike that are variously corroborated, revised, or rejected, expressly or by implication, but also the ongoing linked accumulation of visual experience and art historical framework that contributed to those attributions. While the connoisseurial process isn't explicitly recounted, the properly visual narratives that run through the text are byproducts of that process. The exposition of representational and stylistic qualities of paintings in the text is also an exposition of connoisseurial standards of attribution and dating.

Another series of horizons for Cahill's *Chinese Painting* was established by the *Chinese Art Treasures* exhibition and catalogue project (also published by Skira, in 1961), in which Cahill was deeply involved.[18] He was a representative of the Freer Gallery of Art, instrumental and somewhat controversial in securing the photographic archive of the National Palace Museum and the National Central Museum in Taiwan for the University of Michigan Asian Art Photographic Distribution. In *Chinese Painting* nearly half of the color plates are from those museum collections. More deeply embedded historical horizons were shaped by the formation of the core of those museum collections by the Qianlong emperor in the eighteenth century, and by earlier imperial and private collections (many, like those of An Qi with their own textual apparatus) that had passed into the Qianlong court collection through inheritance, donation, or appropriation. I don't of course mean to suggest that Cahill was in any way channeling Qianlong, since the attributions and judgments of Qing and earlier scholars were as liable to his challenges as were those of modern scholars, but simply that a book like *Chinese Painting* that was so substantially composed of objects from the Qing imperial collection inevitably carried with it some tincture of the orthodox and the canonical as constructed by Qianlong.[19] There is also some cross-writing between *Chinese Art Treasures*—where Cahill was responsible for many of the painting entries—and *Chinese Painting*, having to do with imperial treasures, great masterworks, the orthodox tradition and the like so that some of the rhetoric of the one project infiltrates the other. There are of course many kinds of painting—the so-called Individualist masters and the Yangzhou eccentrics of the seventeenth and eighteenth centuries, and earlier Chan or Zen painting—prominent in *Chinese Painting* that were not significant components of the Palace collections or congenial to the interests and tastes of the Qianlong or other imperial collectors. This was in part an assertion of independence from orthodox Chinese art historiography on Cahill's part, and it also reflects the embedded narratives of Japanese taste and the viewpoints of art historians like Shūjirō Shimada and Yoshiho Yonezawa, who had, especially in the case of Shimada, impacted Cahill's outlook during his Fulbright years in Japan.

The absences in *Chinese Painting* are as interesting and revealing as what is included. In some ways curiously, court painting of the Qianlong era has almost no place in *Chinese Painting*, despite the strong shadow cast by Qianlong's collecting and cataloguing enterprises. This has to do with some other embedded or unspoken narratives operating in Cahill's book, narratives that convey by implication what does and doesn't count as Chinese painting. In this account, "painting" is overwhelmingly autograph brush painting, in scroll or album formats on paper and silk. Some anonymous paintings are included (though often within an implied horizon of solving identity and attribution questions), some Buddhist and Zen painting, but overall almost no archaeological material, mural/architectural painting, painted objects, hybrid Sino-Western court painting, or, obviously, given the chronological scope of the book, nineteenth-century or modern painting.

Some of these absences are shared by other histories from the same general era. Sirén's multivolume account, which does include abundant archaeological material, ends as Cahill's does with Luo Ping at the end of the eighteenth century, and both projects are improvements over the impoverished accounts of post-Song painting in Bachhofer and other earlier surveys. Even so, the congruence of Cahill and Sirén in this regard raises the question of why there should have been such a consensus. Some of these absences in Cahill's *Chinese Painting* could be partly accounted for as the byproducts of editorial constraints, and this may be as good a point as any to mention the embedded narratives of the publisher Albert Skira, and his Treasures of Asia series, of which *Chinese Painting* forms a part. In fact many of those narratives are not all that deeply embedded, and Jim Cahill has some wonderful stories about Skira and his controlling impulses which I will leave for him to tell. They are good stories, rich in incident, characterization, and humor, about vividly realized people and incidents. Those are also the literary qualities of *Chinese Painting*—for many readers it is as close to a satisfying novel as art history is likely to get. It is of some interest that one of those backstories is about Albert Skira's request for "fewer rocks and trees, Mr. Cahill" and more figures and stories, because even so, *Chinese Painting* has relatively few strongly narrative paintings in it. Among those that do appear are some that are what we might call literati narratives, in which nothing much happens or changes, other than the protagonist's feelings, or sensibilities—Lu Zhi's "Parting at Xunyang (Bo Juyi's Lute Song)" or Chen Hongshou's "Illustrations of the Homecoming Ode of Tao Yuanming" are of that kind.[20]

Skira's plan for the book and series clearly had much to do with the scope and rubric of *Chinese Painting*, with the length of its text, the number of color plates, and other prosaic but crucial parameters that inevitably shape art historical narratives. The imperatives for concision and consistency of subject matter and design, even to the look of the book, dominated by objects on paper and silk, could have had something to do with the absences in *Chinese Painting*. Archaeological material, much less abundantly and photographically well documented than it is today, may not have suited the editorially desired look of the book, especially in terms of the availability of color photography. Some of the most potent narratives of *Chinese Painting*, at any rate, were embedded in its full color illustrations, that lent even the many ink paintings included in the book a warmth and richness of tonality that gave real force to the notion of "the colors of ink." Against the background of available black-and-white illustrated histories of Chinese painting, moreover, in which the best-known types were Southern Song court paintings and their later iterations, celebrated precisely for their monochromatic subtlety, *Chinese Painting* was a revelation of a richly colorful pictorial tradition. Chinese painting, became, *tout a coup*, something less geographically and historically remote and archival and something more vividly present. There was an implication of modernity embedded in the medium of color photography itself, in an era of Technicolor films and emerging color television, that made the suggested commonalities with post-Impressionist and expressionist European modernisms more plausible.

The decision to end the account circa 1800 may have had to do in part with practical editorial concerns of length and the economics of printing, along with the then relatively undeveloped historiography of nineteenth century and twentieth century Chinese painting. But there are some patterns in those content choices that suggest other kinds of embedded narratives about what counted as authentic Chinese painting. Briefly, those choices imply that authentically Chinese painting should be scroll or album painting by named artists. Further, the category primarily includes self-referential and self-replenishing kinds of painting, and doesn't very well accommodate outspokenly hybrid Sino-Western styles, or modern idioms (similarly marked by Western programs and formal devices), or have very much room for archaeological material that had been long ignored or hidden. It's hard to avoid the sense of an unspoken assumption that authentic Chinese painting is something removed from the present and uncontaminated by intrusive foreign cultural elements, or by functionality (as is the case of tomb paintings or decorative pictures on objects). The geopolitics of American isolation from the People's Republic of China during the Cold War may also have had some underlying role in shaping those attitudes, encouraging a certain barriered distance in historical vision as well as in practical and political accessibility. That kind of practical accessibility of course had much to do with the contrastingly dominant presence of the Taiwan Palace and Central Museum collections, with all their consequent political implications. There was a parallel motivation on the part of the National Palace Museum authorities to construct a self-sufficient and historically distanced image of high Chinese culture, mostly walled off from the disorder, internal tensions, and conflicts of contemporary Chinese politics.

As with Qing court painting, so too "modern" Chinese painting was at once present in the conceptual horizons of Cahill's book and absent in explicit content. This is especially striking in that modern values of formalism and self-expression are so strongly foregrounded as narrative themes in Cahill's exposition. So it is not that Chinese painting can't be modern in its look or in its conceptual or aesthetic underpinnings, but that modern painting in some sense can't be fully Chinese. This view could be based on a belief that Chinese painting deployed modern values before they were manifested in the West, though Cahill argues this only in passing.[21] More likely it has to do with some mostly unarticulated sense of what is authentically Chinese, uncontaminated by other cultures. Modern Chinese painting, whether *guohua* or oil painting, with some stylistic features linked to European and American practices, and thoroughly infiltrated with modern Western political and aesthetic ideas, thus in some views might be disqualified as Chinese painting.

There are other embedded narratives in *Chinese Painting,* and a great many more could be identified in Clunas's *Pictures and Visuality*. In the interest of brevity I will mention just a few concerns in the latter book that thread through Clunas's other writings and his professional life, and which in some cases resonate with Cahill's themes. Clunas's framing narrative in *Pictures and Visuality* about integrating China's experience with pictorial culture, media, and visuality into the prevailing Eurocentric literature on printing, painting, and modernity is referenced also in his *Superfluous Things,* where he notes that his teaching experience in a history of design program jointly offered by the Victoria and Albert Museum and the Royal College of Art had a key role in forming his outlook on the question.[22] It is of passing interest that Cahill prefaces *Chinese Painting* with a somewhat parallel argument for the integration of the Chinese case into Malraux's imaginary *Museum Without Walls,* undistorted by the lens of Japonisme.[23] The Victoria and Albert Museum, where Clunas worked as a curator of the Far Eastern collections, was one of the institutions that took especially seriously the emerging critical literature on museological narratives and exhibitionary culture, and responded with displays that foregrounded the social and anthropological functions of art, rather than its historical development.[24] It was also a Chinese collection particularly rich in objects—ceramics, furniture, textiles, and the like—and much less so in autograph paintings. Each of those circumstances supported interests in objects, commodities, and consumption, theorized by Appadurai, Kopytoff, and others; these interests figure in *Pictures and Visuality* in the critique of a painting-centric historical discourse and in the foregrounding of images in prints and on objects of all kinds.[25]

Another prominent embedded narrative in Clunas's writing circulates around the idea of an early modernity in China, which replaces the standard historical Ming era in his titles. This resonates a bit with Cahill's identification of modern-looking and conceptually modern elements in Chinese painting. Cahill makes explicit comparisons of later Chinese painting with modern music and painting, a regime of abstract expression and feeling in which formal devices are ascendant over representational or descriptive ones—a modernity of sensibility and artistic practice for the most part.[26]

For Clunas, on the other hand, modernity in Ming pictorial art is part of a considered historical position, which takes Wallerstein's identification of an emergent "world system" in the "long" sixteenth-century as one point of departure.[27] This is centrally a political economy–centered mode of analysis, which sees the integration of world trade and monetary systems as driving forces with important cultural and economic effects: the rise of a money economy, but also the prominence of luxury consumption; international trade, but also the taste for exoticism and curiosities. There is a comparatist dimension to this agenda, but it also finds real commonalities between Renaissance and Baroque Europe and Ming China, in the primacy of markets, circulation, consumption, and commodities, all with more or less explicit references to projects by Appadurai and others.

Metanarratives

In literary theory metanarratives might refer to patterns of near-mythic generality, myths like Northrop Frye's modes—tragic, comic, romantic, ironic—archetypes for which specific narratives are instantiations.[28] Metanarratives might also be versions of master narratives, or *grands récits,* totalizing systems of thought and value like the Enlightenment narrative of the emancipation of reason and freedom, which postmodernists are expected resolutely to resist.[29] A certain complication arises from the obstinate persistence or attraction of totalizing and metanarrative tendencies, so that even those most critical of false historical continuities and totalizing systems, such as Foucault and Lyotard, have had metanarratives identified in their writing.[30] Another kind of metanarrative might be discipline-specific—for pictorial art, stories like the contest of Zeuxis and Parrhasius over realistic representation, or Medusa myths of looking, or, for China, Cang Jie and the invention of image writing, or the story of Wang Zhaojun and portrait making.[31] On a less mythic level, we might identify art historical master narratives, such as Wen Fong's postulation of era-specific structural principles of spatial representation, as an ongoing intellectual concern that runs through many of his specific writings.[32] Further, metanarratives might point to the assumptions, positions, and perhaps even worldviews that underlie specific narratives, operating somewhat like discursive systems in the Foucauldian sense.[33] In the present discussion I use the term broadly, without all the systematic implications of master narrative or discourse, to convey the guiding assumptions and positions of the authors, whether implicit or acknowledged.

The clearest metanarrative position in *Chinese Painting* circulates around the humanism that Cahill identifies as a central value in that artistic tradition.[34] *Humanism* is a term that, like *modernity*, has been so worn by use that its contours have become blurred, but the idea of the centrality of human ideas, feelings, or values over tradition, religion, or metaphysics is certainly visible in Cahill's understanding and use of the term. The precise contours of Cahill's concept of humanism are in any event less important to us than its narrative implications, which are many. Chinese painting is in this view a field of activity in which individual persons—painters, collectors, critics, and patrons—are important. Their biographies, sites of activity, associations, writings, and even momentary feelings are relevant topics. Painting is seen as a mode of meaningful communication between artists and viewers, who share basic capacities for understanding. Equally, art history is seen as a meaningful communication between writers and readers, on the same basis. The content of painting, beyond any representational or symbolic specifics, is primarily about human thoughts, feelings, and perceptions.

It is not that these communications are unproblematic. Cahill notes that China was "a humanistic civilization repeatedly beset by doubts about the validity of the humanist ideal" and artists such as Chen Hongshou exemplify complex, oblique modes of expression that require considerable cultural unpacking before the representational and expressive games he is playing can be recognized.[35] But the essential narrative position is that some coherent meaning and identity attaches to artist, painting, and viewer alike.

For Clunas (if I may do him the injustice of using him as a foil to Cahill, for my own narrative purposes) it's not that persons are mere postmodern subject positions, or posthumans, or whatever we have become nowadays, but that persons are of interest primarily in their social and economic engagements, operating within a discursive framework of language structures. People are in this view consumers, or educated elites, or seekers of social distinction first and primarily, constituted by their networks of friends, family, economic interdependency, and systems of value, more than by their individuality or personality.

Another large metanarrative assumption in Cahill's writing has to with the ascertainability of certain kinds of truth—most relevantly, truths about the authenticity of paintings, the identity of artistic hands, and the quality of paintings—matters of connoisseurship and art historical investigation. These sometimes surface as explicit reattributions (e.g., from Yan Wengui to Li Tang) or claims about the success or superiority of particular paintings, but they are often unspoken, underlying assumptions, on the part of the author and his readers, that the included paintings are authentic, high-quality examples, representative of their makers, schools, regions, and eras.[36] The conclusions do have a narrative presence, especially in the discussion of Song and earlier painting, where the criteria of authentication and attribution often figure as qualities of artistic purpose and style. They are not necessarily or explicitly canonical examples, though I think they have become so, more through the mechanisms of publication, academic inertia, and teaching practices than through any deliberate program. An interest in quality carries along with it other overarching assumptions—that particular instantiations are important, as are specific choices and formulations, even unique configurations (one understanding of the masterpiece, though not the one based on studio and guild practice in Europe). And all those components are part of larger metanarrative assumptions, that particular paintings fit into meaningful histories of eras, schools, and artists, and ultimately that Chinese painting is a valid historical category (even if one assigned by the publisher).

Again, it is not, I think, that Clunas would deny the possibility of making valid or truthful historical statements (if only that the images, objects, and texts he discusses are reliable products from the Ming/early modern era of some notional region called "China") but that those validities tend to be on the metalevel of social, economic, and discursive systems. For example, questions of authenticity, quality, and identity are historicized and problematized, and the topics of investigation are not particular pictures so much as systems, standards, and discourses of authentication, valuation, and identification. Thus one can analyze and reconstruct the system of valuations in *Superfluous Things*, but the authenticity, quality, and value of a particular object discussed in that text remains contingent.[37] Discourses and practices of copying, forgery, and plagiarism are of greater concern than particular cases of fakery. From this point of view, an anonymous design on a lacquer cosmetic box can be as useful an object of scholarly attention as is the sole surviving work from one of the famous masters that carries a huge apparatus of critical and catalogue literature trailing behind it. Clunas would note that textual retinue as an interesting historical phenomenon in its own right, and examine the notions of "canonicity," "great master," and "masterpiece" critically and historically, but wouldn't necessarily privilege that artist or painting in his narrative as a result. Moreover, categories like "China," "Chinese painting," schools, and even individual artists and paintings tend to be destabilized and opened up to diversification, hybridities, copies, impersonations, faking, and the like.[38]

The fundamental metanarrative assumptions that there are coherent categories of "China" and "Chinese painting," and that their history can be written, have been critiqued by Clunas. The contours and horizons of a stable idea of China are increasingly blurred by our attention to multiculturalism, the invention of tradition, and the projection of modern nationalisms back into the past. Likewise, what "Chinese painting" should comprehend seems increasingly unclear, or multifarious. Paintings, or pictures and prints? Pictures or pictorial ornaments and designs? Functional or art pictures? Pictographs and petroglyphs from within the territory of modern geographical China or pictures on paper or silk?[39] Modern and contemporary painting, prints, and perhaps photographs, or painting from imperial China? "Chinese" modes (however defined) or hybrid Sino-Western and export pictures? The practical writing strategies that are entailed by a very diverse view of Chinese painting or picturing requires casting a wider net, but not an indiscriminate one. Pictures are chosen to illustrate, demonstrate, or embody aspects of a diverse visual culture, and the question of where "Chinese" begins and ends is not abandoned totally, if addressed only by implication. It does seem fundamentally correct that "Chinese painting" is always a discursive construct, constituted by the institutional and literary practices of a community of interest—whether Ming critics or twenty-first-century academics—no more and no less. Wherever critics or academics of Chinese painting turn their attention is by definition Chinese painting.

Those choices of what to include in a text can be made, whether based on principle, editorial constraints, or taste, but the question of whether histories of Chinese painting should be written at all belongs to another order of concern. The questions are interrelated of course—if there is no stable notion of China, or Chinese art, or Chinese painting, it's hard to see how one could write a history of it. The objections to the writing of general histories operate both on higher principled levels and on more practical ones. On the level of metanarrative and narrative, general histories may encourage, if not demand, some reliance on chronotopic structures—chronological development within a notional space of activity, and may even encourage seeing a shape to that development of early, middle, and late, say, or plot lines of rise and fall, or of situation, complication/disequilibrium, and resolution; all the tropes of narrative presentation and what Hayden White calls historical "emplotment" that lurk temptingly in the background of exposition.[40] There is some of that in *Chinese Painting*—not heroes and villains to be sure, though indeed the "bad" paintings are marked by exclusion—but at the very least, there is a pull toward transitional passages (such as the chapter on late Song literati and Chan painting) that link Song and earlier representational painting with personally expressive kinds from the Yuan and after.[41] From a certain point of view we might say that the historical validity of such an episode is almost less important than its narrative necessity. And the grandest (or alternatively the most insidious) metanarrative structure is simply the assumption that narratives hang together somehow—that everything belongs to and plays a part in a story. Unity and coherence on many levels are implicit in narrative structures, and they can overshadow or exclude instances of aberration, fragmentation, negation, dead-ends, contradiction, and the like.

Metanarratives, in the sense of underlying narrative structures and assumptions, are hard to escape. This essay, for example, employs at times a narrative of comparison, so that there is a nearly unavoidable expectation of contrast, of greater and lesser presence and absence, threaded through it. I began my talk by disavowing any intent to contrast an older Cahillianism with a newfangled Clunasology—and that was based on expectations we might hold of chronological or developmental metanarratives, with structural plot lines of old-fashioned versus up-to-date (or, alternatively perhaps, solidly traditional versus meretriciously contemporary). But a comparatist metanarrative about narrativity runs an equal risk of casting Clunas into the narrative-deficient role.

This would be specifically unfair because at several points Clunas is critical of a narrative project, even in a general book like *Art in China*, which, like some other very useful books, is organized primarily around topical, or functional, rather than chronological rubrics. Clunas's anti-narrative position is in part based on a principled avoidance of nineteenth-century and particularly Hegelian historiographic practices, a concern that any notion of space-time continuum carries along with it specific notions of historical development or historical teleologies. He is specifically wary about metanarratives like the master narrative that sees Ming painting as a move away from mimesis or representation.[42] It is possible, without being perverse or unfair, to restore Clunas's principled anti-narrative position to the status of a metanarrative, since it enfolds his writing choices and his views of the operations of culture. I would also note that in a culture with a foundational art text like *Lidai minghua ji* [Record of Famous Painters of All the Dynasties] by Zhang Yanyuan (active ca. 847), where notions of linked succession of legitimate dynasties (linked as eras of some coherent, political-cultural entity, though certainly not "China" in the modern sense), famous (i.e., high quality, even canonical?) paintings (and painters), historical record-keeping, and period-differentiated accounts of the valuation and development of genres are all very much in evidence, that more than nineteenth century historiographic projection is in play, or at work.[43] Clunas acknowledges the indigenous sources of discourses of preference for self-referential scholar painting over mimetic art, or for the valorization of painting and calligraphy over decorative arts, but in his view we shouldn't be constrained by those historical structures, since they embody the values and claims to authority of particular and partial social classes or interest-groups, whether in early modern China or in the modern West.[44] The metanarrative assumptions of a ground of historical continuity and differentiated chronological development are perhaps of another order of generality, bound up with questions of cultural identity and agency in representation. In any case, the proof is in the writing, and Clunas's alternate accounts, organized variously around functional, topical, discursive, and case-study or microhistorical logics, are easily as rich in historical texture and critical judgment as are any more continuous and legibly patterned narratives.

Visual Metanarratives

Most of the narratives that we have considered so far, at whatever level—explicit, embedded, or metanarratives—have been textual narratives, either writing narratives or reading narratives, what the reader discerns or assumes from the texts. We should also consider visual or looking narratives. Visual narratives might also be textually based, as illustrations of literature, or of religious or historical texts. But instead of addressing those, or the question of textual versus visual approaches to Chinese art history (see, e.g., Chapter 2 of this volume), I want briefly to turn to visual narratives centrally involving form, insight, or perception—visual rather than textual matters.[45]

Clunas is interested primarily in visuality—social, cultural, and psychological practices of looking, attitudes toward looking, and valuations of looking; "seeing as social fact."[46]

Visuality involves the visual both above and below the level of physiological seeing and representational recognition and interpretation. Thus Clunas is concerned with anxieties and fears about looking; or with social functions and contexts of looking, as in appropriate subjects for birthday and congratulatory pictures. This kind of interest engages a good deal of narrative content, which can be about the erotic or auspicious narratives that are represented in those cultural contexts, or about the cultural reception or valuation of looking, or about specific kinds of representations. We can find narratives about visuality and visual theory, which certainly might qualify as a kind of visual metanarrative that frames accounts of vision and looking. At the same time Clunas does relatively little close analysis of particular visual objects.

Cahill's visual narratives often begin with formal description, analysis, and interpretation, and so might be considered a kind of formal analysis or formalism. There is a certain logic to this; Cahill emphasizes the centrality of the formal basis of expression in post-Song painting (and painting theory) in particular, and often draws comparisons between painting and relatively non-representational art forms like music and abstract painting. Moreover, the philosophical aesthetics of Susanne Langer was an important point of reference for Cahill and for his advisor at Michigan, Max Loehr—more embedded narratives to be sure.[47] When this kind of procedure results in an account or interpretation of a picture we have an example of a visually based narrative, and to the extent that a philosophical aesthetics like Langer's shapes those procedures it might be identified as a visual or formal metanarrative.

In both cases, however, we are routed back to the textual level of art historical interpretation or philosophical writing. Other kinds of narratives that operate in Cahill's book are more properly and fully visual, although of course they are often couched in language as much as images. The implied or embedded narratives conveyed by the selection of illustrations, and by the color plates themselves, have already been mentioned. They embody narratives of representational or stylistic affinities and development, and a certain congeniality with the visual qualities of modernity, which are part of the explicit narrative account. At the same time, they reference embedded narratives of connoisseurial judgment and historiographic categorization, by Cahill and a long line of earlier writers, collectors, and critics.

On a different plane, Cahill's writing around and through his images evokes visual qualities that thread through the image and the textual account, and seem to inhere equally in the painting and in the viewer's encounter. These might be narratives of perceptual subtlety or heightening, for example, or of disclosure or hiding, or of illumination, revelation, or penetrating discovery. Elsewhere they could be connoisseurial dramas of discernment, recognition, and insight; or narratives of production, such as the working out of some representational or compositional problem. These have analytical and historical dimensions, and they might be open to the critique that they embody selective attention, blind spots, or historical projections. In the most persuasive formulations, these qualities seem embodied in visual relations, with the metanarrative implication that the perception or discovery inheres in the painting not as hidden meanings but as potentials or capacities that await necessary activation by the viewer or critic. These qualify as visual metanarratives in that they convey something about how paintings work, and equally how viewing and art historical construction works.

I conclude with a brief excerpt of this kind from *Chinese Painting* (85–87):

> The future of Chinese painting lay outside the Academy; but the direction it was to take is accurately forecast in another small signed work by Ma Lin, one that reveals him as a still more enigmatic figure. Titled

> *The Fragrance of Spring: Clearing after Rain*, it is a picture of trees, bamboos, and briers growing in disorderly profusion on the banks of a stream. Mists drift over the marshy ground and among the trees. An aged and twisted plum tree, growing from between rocks, puts forth new buds; the exuberant regeneration of plants in spring is revealed as an unruly force, and no effort is made to idealize it. On the further shore of the stream, a splintered tree stump stands as just the stark memorial to death and decay that all standard landscapes of the school had diligently excluded. From the pleasure parks of orthodox Ma–Hsia [Ma–Xia] landscape (including most of Ma Lin's own) we are brought back suddenly to the real, unkempt world. Much of the school manner is preserved—the rocks are Ma Yuan's, and the trees are obviously by the same hand that drew those in the *Waiting for Guests by Lamplight*, but it is applied to a composition in which the canons of the Academy are violated, and turned to the excitation of feelings quite outside the fairly narrow range of the Academy taste. The painting thus anticipates developments in the Yüan and later dynasties, when there was no longer to be any fixed relation between a style and the expressive uses to which it was put.

That's 263 words, and a lot going on: some description, some interpretation—"stark memorial to death and decay"—some connoisseurial stylistic categorization of trees and rocks, some school-based art history (Ma–Xia school), some narrative transition, from early to later Chinese painting, and some art historical metanarrative—the overarching move from representational to expressive art. One could argue with some parts of it, from the characterizations to the art historical framework, but it would be hard to match its concision and evocatively rich content. It's a characteristic passage from *Chinese Painting*, which above all looks *into* paintings, and works out from them into its larger narratives. Part of the agenda of this volume is to see how far we've come in Chinese painting studies over the last half-century. Certainly there has been added to the agenda of art history or visual studies a lot that is absent in this passage, but there is as well a certain amount present that has been lost in contemporary practice (even Jim Cahill's own), and I must say I rather miss it.

Notes

1 See Julia Murray's many studies of narrative paintings and prints, including "What Is Chinese Narrative Illustration?" *The Art Bulletin* (December 1998): 602–15.

2 James Cahill, *Chinese Painting* (Geneva: Editions d'Art Albert Skira, 1960); Craig Clunas, *Pictures and Visuality in Early Modern China* (Princeton: Princeton University Press, 1997).

3 James Cahill, *Three Alternative Histories of Chinese Painting*, The Franklin D. Murphy Lectures 9 (Lawrence, Kans.: Spencer Museum of Art, 1988); *The Painter's Practice: How Artists Lived and Worked in Traditional China* (New York: Columbia University Press, 1994); "Paintings Done for Women in Ming–Qing China?" *Nan Nü* 8, no. 1 (2006): 1–54.

4 Craig Clunas, *Art in China* (Oxford and New York: Oxford University Press, 1997), 9.

5 *Art in China*, however, which is more comparable in its historical scope to *Chinese Painting* than is *Pictures and Visuality*, does have a good deal of linked chronological narrative, including elite calligraphy and paintings of the Song through Qing.

6 James Cahill, "The Six Laws and How to Read Them," *Ars Orientalis* 4 (1961): 372–81. Craig Clunas, *Superfluous Things: Material Culture and Social Status in Early Modern China* (Cambridge: Cambridge University Press, 1991).

7 See Clunas, *Pictures and Visuality*, 133 for Hall and Ames on "knowing": cf. p. 13 on commonalities between Europe and China in the status of painting.

8 Ibid., 41–49, on "Iconic Circuits."

9 Ibid., 23 (citing Preziosi).

10 Ibid., 11.

11 Ibid., 12–23.

12 Gérard Gennette, *Paratexts: Thresholds of Interpretation* (Cambridge: Cambridge University Press, 1997).

13 (New York: Pantheon, 1946). In a forty-page discussion of Chinese painting, the "sixteenth–eighteenth" centuries are afforded three pages, with no mention of anything beyond the mid-sixteenth century.

14 Jean-Pierre Dubosc, "A New Approach to Chinese Painting," *Oriental Art*, n.s., 3 (1950): 50–57; Osvald Sirén, *Chinese Painting: Leading Masters and Principles*, 7 vols. (London: Lund Humphries, 1956).

15 Max Loehr, "Chinese Painting after Sung" (Yale University Art Gallery Ryerson Lecture, March 2, 1967). Cahill notes on p. 7 of *Chinese Painting* that Loehr read and critiqued the manuscript of the book.

16 Cahill, *Chinese Painting* (above, n. 2), 199–200.

17 See Sirén, *Chinese Painting*, vol. 2, p. 5 of the separately paginated "Annotated Lists of Paintings and Reproductions of Paintings by Chinese Artists"; see also vol. 4, p. ix for Sirén's acknowledgment of Cahill's contributions.

18 National Palace Museum and National Central Museum, eds., *Chinese Art Treasures* (Geneva: Editions d'Art Albert Skira, 1961).

19 Ibid., 15.

20 For the Skira quote, I am indebted to a personal communication from Jim Cahill. For the Lu Zhi and Chen Hongshou paintings, see Cahill, *Chinese Painting*, 133, 157.

21 *Chinese Painting*, 91.

22 *Superfluous Things* (above, n. 6), 3–4.

23 See Cahill, *Chinese Painting*, 5.

24 See Rose Kerr, ed., *Chinese Art and Design The T. T. Tsui Gallery of Chinese Art* (London: Victoria and Albert Museum, 1991), with texts by Kerr, Clunas, and Verity Wilson.

25 Clunas, *Superfluous Things*, 2.

26 Cahill, *Chinese Painting*, 101, 156, 167.

27 Ibid., 172; cf. Immanuel Wallerstein, "The Rise and Demise of the Capitalist System," in *The Essential Wallerstein* (New York: New Press, 2000), 71–105.

28 Northrop Frye, *Anatomy of Criticism: Four Essays* (Princeton: Princeton University Press, 1971). For a specialized use of metanarrative or metadiegesis in narratological studies as second-degree narrative, which contains or comments upon the first narrative, see Anastasios D. Nikolopoulos, *Ovidius Polytropos: Metanarrative in Ovid's Metamorphoses*, Spudasmata 98 (Zurich and New York: Georg Olms Verlag, 2004), 31–37.

29 Jean-François Lyotard, *The Post-Modern Condition: A Report on Knowledge* (Minneapolis: University of Minnesota Press, 1984).

30 See Hayden White, "Foucault Decoded: Notes from Underground," in *Tropics of Discourse: Essays in Cultural Criticism* (Baltimore and London: The Johns Hopkins University Press, 1978), 230–60, esp. 251–55. On Lyotard see, for example, Shaun Gallagher, "Conversations in Postmodern Hermeneutics," in *Lyotard: Philosophy, Poetics, and the Sublime*, ed. Hugh J. Silverman (New York and London: Routledge, 2002), 56.

31 Norman Bryson, *Vision and Painting: The Logic of the Gaze* (New Haven and London: Yale University Press, 1983), 1, 3, 160, where the Zeuxis story is seen as a myth or metanarrative of painting and art history alike. For Cang Jie, see, for convenience, Clunas, *Pictures and Visuality*, 109.

32 Wen Fong et al., *Images of the Mind: Selections from the Edward L. Elliott Family and John B. Elliott Collections of Chinese Calligraphy and Painting at the Art Museum, Princeton University* (Princeton, N.J.: The Art Museum, Princeton University in association with Princeton University Press, 1984), 9–11 for structural analysis, and 2–73 for its application to an account of figural and landscape painting.

33 See Francis Barker and Peter Hulme, "'Nymphs and Reapers Heavily Vanish': The Discursive Con-Texts of *The Tempest*," in *New Historicism and Cultural Materialism: A Reader*, ed. Kiernan Ryan (London: Arnold, 1996), 130–31.

34 *Chinese Painting*, 5–6.

35 Ibid., 5, 156–58.

36 See ibid., 40, or the discussion of the "Han Palace" on p. 79. See also the interesting discussion of the Gao Keming "Clearing after Snow on the River" handscroll, which seems to foreshadow some misgivings about the attribution. It is of interest for the present discussion that in his recent "Paintings Done for Women?" (above, n. 3), 49–50, Cahill argues for the irrelevance of criteria of authenticity for certain kinds of functional paintings.

37 See for example, Clunas, *Superfluous Things*, 125.

38 Clunas, *Pictures and Visuality* (above, n. 2), 170.

39 Richard Barnhart et al., *Three Thousand Years of Chinese Painting* (New Haven and London: Yale University Press, 1997), embodies in its project a very expansive scope of Chinese painting, but still perhaps not as inclusive as that implied by Clunas's notion of iconic circuits.

40 Hayden White, "Interpretation in History," in *Tropics of Discourse* (above, n. 30), 51–80.

41 Cahill, *Chinese Painting*, 89–98.

42 Clunas, *Pictures and Visuality*, 18–23.

43 See the translated excerpts in Susan Bush and Hsio-yen Shih, comps. and eds., *Early Chinese Texts on Painting* (Cambridge, Mass. and London: Harvard University Press, 1985), 52–55, 60–62.

44 Clunas, *Pictures and Visuality*, 14–15, acknowledges the indigenous sources of a historical-critical discourse of elite literati painting.

45 For general discussion of the distinction between textual and visual narrative, and the interplay of telling and showing, focused on film and photography, see Tom Gunning, "Theory and History: Narrative Discourse and the Narrator System," ch. 1 in his *D. W. Griffith and the Origins of American Narrative Film: The Early Years at Biograph* (Urbana and Chicago: University of Illinois Press, 1994), 10–30.

46 Clunas, *Pictures and Visuality*, 10 quoting Hal Foster; see also 111–33, 149–71.

47 See Susanne K. Langer, *Feeling and Form: A Theory of Art* (London and Henley: Routledge & Keegan Paul Limited, 1953), 82–83 for a discussion of the visual "forms of human feeling."

6

Authenticity, Style, and Art History: Wen C. Fong and Studies of Chinese Art History

Harold Mok

Writings on traditional Chinese painting come in an impressively dazzling array. Yu Shaosong (1885–1949), for one, recorded more than 860 titles of such writings datable before the Republican period in his *Explanation of Publications of Painting and Calligraphy* [*Shuhua shulu jieti*]. The works are grouped by nature under ten categories, namely, histories and biographies, execution, discussions, classification, inscriptions and eulogies, catalogues, miscellaneous writings, collectanea, fakes, and lost writings, all of which are further divided into subcategories. Despite their volume, these traditional writings on painting, especially painting history, could no longer serve modern studies of Chinese art history and satisfy the stringent requirements of modern scholarship as the discipline became increasingly specialized in the twentieth century. To the modern scholar, the traditional biographical approach that characterizes these writings can provide at best limited description of and information on the development of painting. At worst, such an approach may compromise scholarly understanding of art history.

These limitations became even more obvious in light of intellectual developments in the West. While diverse approaches focusing on stylistic analysis, iconographical studies, social or cultural dimensions, and psychological analysis have sprung up since scientific theories began to influence Western art in the late nineteenth to early twentieth century, similar methodologies for studies of Chinese art history were practically nonexistent in the early twentieth century. As can be seen in Pan Tianshou's *History of Chinese Painting* [*Zhongguo huihua shi*], Yu Jianhua's *History of Chinese Painting* [*Zhongguo huihua shi*], and Teng Gu's *History of Tang and Song Painting* [*Tang Song huihua shi*], the approach was then very traditional and void of innovation.

Wen C. Fong has contributed a great deal to the study of Chinese painting history. Having engaged in scholarly studies for long years in the United States, he fully grasps approaches to art history adopted in the West. With his profound knowledge, keen perception, and broad vision, he has opened a new door for the study of Chinese painting by establishing a scientific theory and approach that has paved the way for Chinese painting history to become truly a discipline. Fong's contribution to the study of Chinese painting history is herein discussed in the context of painting authenticity, style, and history.

Authentication Based on Real Objects: The Starting Point for Studying Chinese Painting History

Traditional writings on Chinese painting history can be traced all the way back to *Record of Famous Painters of All the Dynasties* [*Lidai minghua ji*] written by Zhang Yanyuan (active ca. 847) of the Tang Dynasty. Comprehensive in coverage, the book invaluably informs on pre-Tang painting and offers enlightening insights into the development of painting. The format follows the conventions of historical writings and centers around individual painters, presenting each of them chronologically in biographical form.[1] Such an approach typified later writings on painting history. Culturally, this presentation attests to the importance Chinese historians attached to personal achievements. Great masters were thus portrayed as makers of history who propelled the development of Chinese art through their innovative endeavors. Unfortunately, the actual works of painting, or the very bulk that makes up the history of painting, were deprived of any objective and scientific examination. With an inundation of copies, imitations and fakes of Chinese painting widely circulated through the ages, authentication became difficult. The history of painting, were reconstruction possible, was built on quicksand since authenticity, dating, and authorship remained elusive, and all that was known about the painters was based on inadequate or faulty understanding.

Having immersed himself in Western art theories, Fong analyzed in the 1950s the painting *Five Hundred Lohans*, housed in the Buddhist temple Daitokuji, and presented his research in his PhD dissertation, which won praises from Erwin Panofsky, the giant of iconographical studies.[2] He then proceeded to address the limitations of traditional Chinese painting history with his fundamental theories about methodology. He believed every study of Chinese painting history should begin with the objects if authenticity was to be resolved and the history of painting to be reconstructed. In an article published in 1960 on the Yuan painter Qian Xuan (ca. 1235–ca. 1307), he gave a detailed stylistic analysis of the painting *Sparrow on an Apple Branch* (fig. 1), housed in the Art Museum of Princeton University, and attributed it to Qian Xuan or his contemporary.[3] In using stylistic analysis to arrive at new dates for some other works attributed to the same painter, the article demonstrated his new approach. Fong further pointed out that stylistic analysis is the first step to clear the path to the study of Chinese painting and to interpreting the objects in the light of literature and artistic tradition. What he meant by "style" is the structural and representational characteristics of a particular piece of work. Establishing style is the prerequisite for rebuilding a reliable history of styles, which is essential for properly distinguishing works by great masters from those by ordinary painters or even from imitations.[4] More than an exercise in authenticating extant works, the article effectively demonstrates a model for reconstructing the history of Chinese painting.

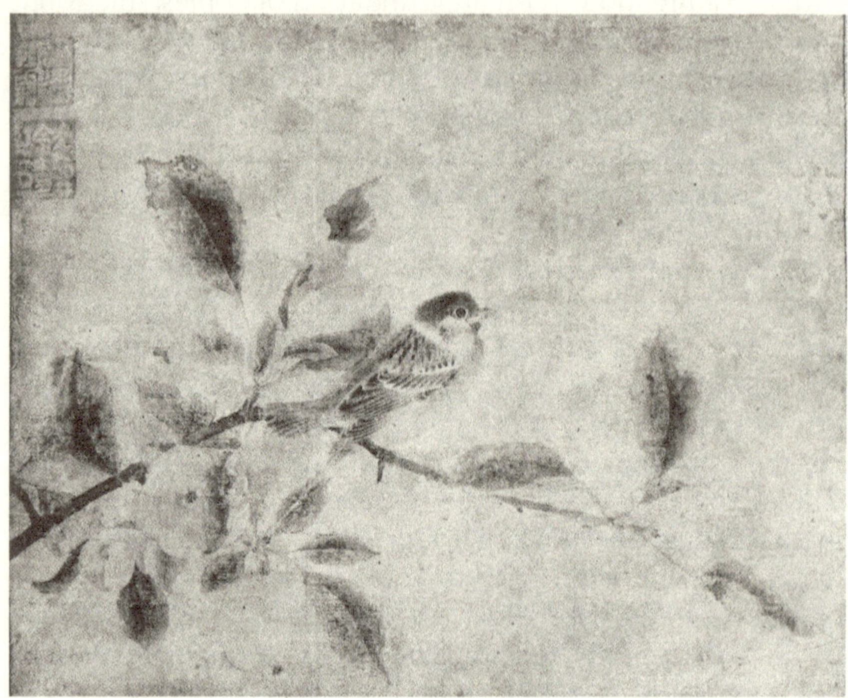

Figure 1. Qian Xuan, *Sparrow on an Apple Branch*. Princeton, Art Museum. After *The Art Bulletin* 42 (September 1960): 185.

In 1962 Fong published an article on the authenticity of Chinese painting and discussed in detail the issues of copies, imitations, and fakes.[5] The urgency of authentication was reiterated in another article of his about methodology for studying Chinese painting published in the following year.[6] The examples cited were three landscapes in the Palace Museum collection, namely, *Mountains Seen from a River Bank* (fig. 2), *Rongxi Studio* (fig. 3), and *Mountain Scenery with a River Lodge* (fig. 4), all of which had been displayed in London between 1935 and 1936. Then invariably attributed to Ni Zan (1306–1374) of the Yuan period, the works are similar in theme and brushwork and were traditionally believed to be characteristic of the great master. Fong, however, argued that the similarities could not be counted as stylistic characteristics. He explained that in the morphological approach, there is an organic relationship among the leaves, branches, mosses, and rocks throughout *Rongxi Studio* whereas the representations in the other two works are relatively patternistic and decorative and hence incongruent with it both visually and structurally. His conclusion was that the three paintings could not be contemporary with one another, let alone produced by the same painter. Thus, authentication was a pressing problem if the history of painting was to be reconstructed. When works attributed to Ni Zan are in fact not entirely so, there is no way to understand properly the style of the Yuan painter, or the history of painting for that matter.

Detailed stylistic analysis of objects calls for both analytical and linguistic skills. According to Meyer Schapiro, "style" is tripartite, comprising form elements or motifs, form relationships, and quality.[7] Although form elements and quality are addressed in traditional Chinese discussions of painting, the relationship between the two (the second of Schapiro's three parts) is often neglected. The economy of traditional rhetoric further eclipses in-depth stylistic analysis. In a departure from such traditional treatment, Fong based his stylistic analyses of Qian Xuan and Ni Zan on Shapiro's definition.[8] By stressing the form relationships on top of form elements and quality, he succeeded in offering a complete stylistic narrative.

As far as Fong's methodology, Heinrich Wölfflin must not be overlooked. Wölfflin is best respected for expressing in words the systematic stylistic interpretation of objects based on visual observation. He demonstrated how the "history of styles" can be reconstructed through five pairs of stylistic terms, namely "linear mode" versus "painterly mode," "plane" versus "recession," "closed form" versus "open form," "multiplicity" versus "unity," and "clearness" versus "unclearness."[9]

Although Fong explicitly referred to Wölfflin's method, he was aware that the approach could not fully account for the stylistic changes seen in the history of Chinese painting. To trace the pattern underlying such changes, a viable option was wanting.

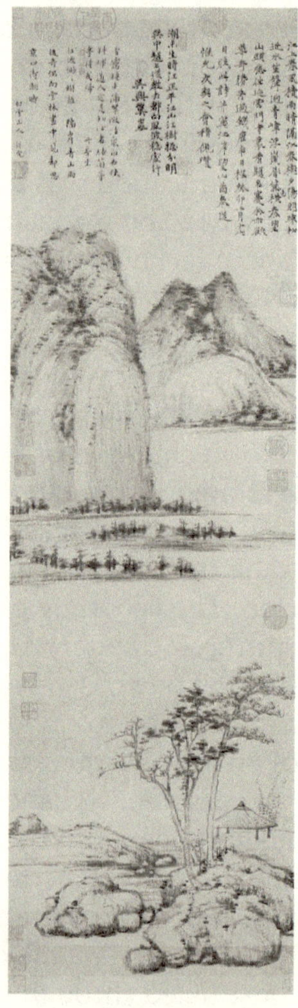

Figure 2. Ni Zan, *Mountain Seen from a River Bank*. National Palace Museum, Taipei. After *A Panorama of Paintings in the Collection of the National Palace Museum* (Taipei: National Palace Museum, 1993–95), 3:118.

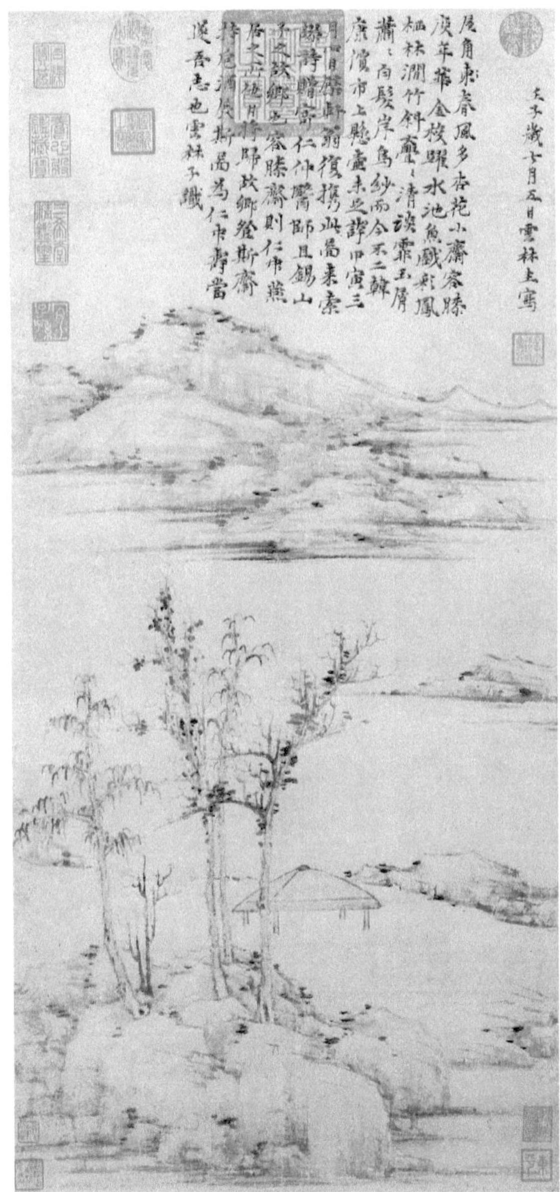

Figure 3. Ni Zan, *Rongxi Studio*. National Palace Museum, Taipei. After *A Panorama of Paintings in the Collection of the National Palace Museum* (Taipei: National Palace Museum, 1993–95), 3:128.

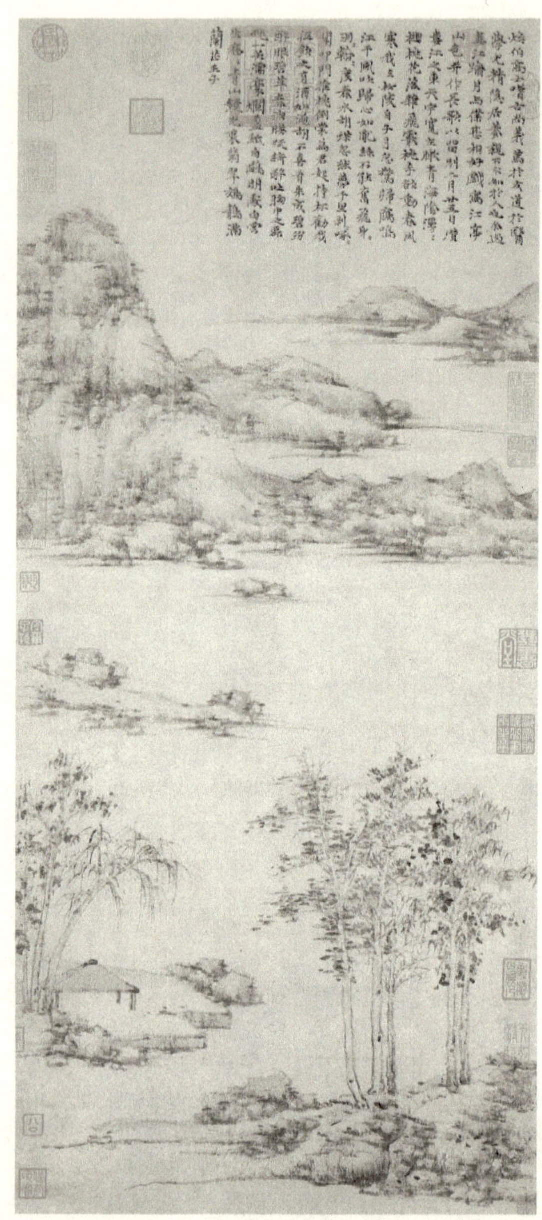

Figure 4. Ni Zan, *Mountain Scenery with a River Lodge*. National Palace Museum, Taipei. After *A Panorama of Paintings in the Collection of the National Palace Museum* (Taipei: National Palace Museum, 1993–95), 3:132.

Structural Analysis of Chinese Landscape Painting: The Birth of a Methodology

Chinese connoisseurial tradition has given rise to a profusion of authenticating methods. Yet the traditional way of judging the authenticity of a painting by its "spirit" depends heavily on an individual's experience and fails to offer a reliable foundation for reconstructing the history of styles. Although in the 1960s Li Lincan (1913–1999) proposed a systematic approach consisting in examining six aspects of the material—technique, contemporary practices, personal style, inscriptions and seals, transmission, and written records—stylistic dating remained more or less an unresolved problem.[10]

Before the 1960s Western scholars had attempted to apply the stylistic analysis of Western art history to Chinese painting. Sherman Lee, for one, used stylistic analysis to divide Song painting styles into the "fine," "realistic," "lyric," and "rough" periods,[11] whereas George Rowley, who taught at Princeton in the 1950s, preferred dating in accordance with the intrinsic development of form, or "seeing." A student of Rowley's, Fong was greatly inspired and was thus initiated into the realm of stylistic analysis.[12]

Enlightened by both his contemporaries and predecessors, Fong dedicated himself as early as the 1950s to the dating of Chinese painting. In 1955, in *Streams and Mountains without End*, co-authored with Sherman Lee, he dated the eponymous painting to the first quarter of the twelfth century.[13] Derived from Western art history and modified to suit the special circumstances of Chinese painting, their methodology was a far cry from the time-honored institutional and experiential approach, and was an improvement on Western stylistic analysis, which did not take into consideration the presence of fakes and imitations. Later, in the 1960s, Fong divided his attention between reiterating the importance of stylistic analysis for dating and devising a pragmatic approach for observing stylistic transformation in Chinese painting. Believing that formal relationships change with time, despite constancy in theme or technique, he put forward a structural approach. His 1969 article on structural analysis of landscape paintings represents further progress in this area.[14]

Although not necessarily of the highest artistic order, archeological finds, with their confirmed dating, are reliable guides to the structure of landscape paintings from a certain period. Affirming this belief, Fong discovered that Chinese landscape painting underwent a number of stages from the pre-Tang to the early Yuan, establishing this from his close observation of Tang pieces in the collection of the Shōsōin in Nara, the Tang silk banner in the British Museum; the mural *Autumn Landscape* excavated from the eleventh-century Eastern Mausoleum at Qingling; fragments of thirteenth-century landscape sketches unearthed from Khara-khoto, Inner Mongolia; and the thirteenth-century wall painting from the Tomb of Feng Daozhen in Datong, Shansi. First, in the pre-Tang period, there were the overlapping triangular mountain motifs. And then, between the seventh and eighth centuries, there emerged the fixed compositional schemas of "high-distance," "flat-distance," and "deep-distance." Space was compartmentalized with individual additive motifs right down to the early Song. In the thirteenth century spatial continuity developed and fragmented mountain masses originally united by mists now gave way to integration of landscape elements through a consistent ground-plane. In the succeeding Ming and Qing periods, landscape painting was characterized by their "decorative" and "abstract" qualities respectively.[15] Although falling short of accounting for the contributions made by individual painting masters, the structural analysis Fong gives provides benchmarks for dating paintings by style. Fong hoped that by complementing his approach with historical and literary records, artistic treatises, and attributed works, the complete history of painting could be reconstructed.

In view of the wide circulation of copies and stylistic affinities, which make it difficult to arrive at a complete and reliable dating scheme using Wöfflin's stylistic analysis or Panofsky's iconographical approaches, Fong turned his attention to George Kubler's theory, believing that the idea of "formal sequences" and "linked solution" could lend itself to sequencing stylistically similar works for further study. Under this theory, when the original work and its closest copies are examined for signs of successive replication and transformation, the development of a stylistic tradition through different periods presents itself.[16] Thus Fong took the significant step toward resolving the problem of dating in Chinese painting, through modifying the Wöfflinian model with Kubler's theory.

In his subsequent writings Fong continued to apply, reiterate, and perfect such structural analysis of Chinese landscape painting. The effectiveness of his analysis is best demonstrated in his study of *Summer Mountains* published in 1975, in which he concluded the probable artist to be Qu Ding (active ca. 1023–ca. 1050) of the Northern Song, by dating the painting through both structural analysis and literary evidence.[17] This was followed by the elaborate account of the stylistic development of Chinese landscape painting given in his major work *Images of the Mind* (fig. 5), published in 1984.[18] Building on previous structural analyses and employing diagrams, the book explains the three transformational stages of Chinese landscape painting from 700 A.D. through 1400 A.D. in terms of structure. In the first stage, the period between Tang and early Northern Song, space was suggested by overlapping triangular mountain motifs distributed from the front to the back in a compartmentalized manner. In the following late Northern Song to the Southern Song, the triangular mountain forms were arranged from the front to the back in a continuous sequence, unified by surrounding mists at their bases. Finally, during the Yuan period, the landscape elements shared a common ground-plane to conjure a three-dimensional physical environment. To provide more evidence, the latest archeological finds like the silk painting *Landscape* unearthed in Yemaotai, Faku, Liaoning, are cited to show that space is indeed compartmentalized in landscape painting from the tenth century. Fong then assigns new dates to extant early masterpieces, including *Mount Kuanglu,* attributed to Jing Hao; *Autumn Mountains at Dusk* and *Waiting to Cross a Mountain Stream,* attributed to Guan Tong; *Wintry Groves and Layered Banks* and *Xiao and Xiang Rivers,* attributed to Dong Yuan; *Seeking the Dao in Autumn Mountains* and *Xiao Yi Seizing the* Lanting *by Trickery,* attributed to Juran; *A Buddhist Temple amid Clearing Peaks,* attributed to Li Cheng; and *Sitting Alone by the Stream,* attributed to Fan Kuan. In addition to providing a key to understanding early Chinese landscape painting through resolving the dating of these works, the book also demonstrates how Kubler's approach can be employed to unravel the stylistic transformation of a painting tradition. When discussing Fan Kuan's landscapes, Fong illustrates how the texture dotting technique seen in the great painter's authentic work *Travelers among Streams and Mountains* gradually developed into the schematic archaizing formula of the mid-thirteenth century through the stylistic sequence discernible from five related big hanging scrolls, namely, *Sitting Alone by the Stream and Waiting to Cross a Mountain Stream* (in the National Palace Museum, Taipei), *Landscape in the Style of Fan Kuan* (in The Metropolitan Museum of Art, New York), *Landscape in the Style of Fan Kuan* (in the Art Museum, Princeton University), and *Landscape in the Style of Fan Kuan* (in the Freer Gallery of Art, Washington, D.C.).

In blending together an objectivity based on real objects and the importance of stylistic characteristics, Fong's structural analysis has proved to be a reliable tool for establishing

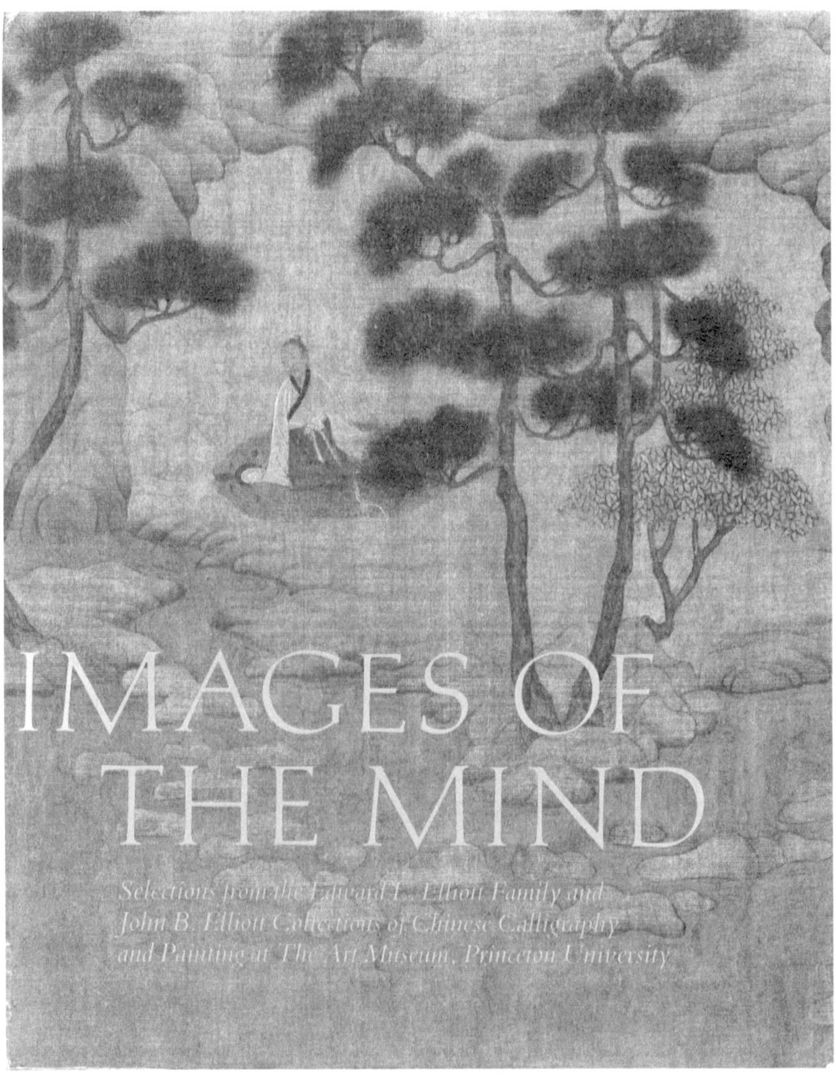

Figure 5. Book cover of *Images of the Mind*.

the dating of Chinese painting. The analysis contributed significantly to the dating of *Riverbank*, attributed to Dong Yuan, when the authenticity of the painting stirred quite some debate in the academic community in 1999. In his discussion, Fong made full use of his analysis of the work's visual structure and determined the painting to be from the tenth century.[19] Among the diverse views expressed in the course of the debate, with some going so far as to suggest it to be a forgery by Zhang Daqian (Chang Dai-chien, 1899–1983), there is no denying that Fong has offered the argument by far the most convincing for its objectivity and analysis.

Cross-cultural Exploration: Reconstructed Chinese Painting History and Contemporary Art

When he first put forward his structural analysis, Fong pointed out that it could help shed light only on the general stylistic development of Chinese painting rather than on the complex circumstances surrounding the thoughts and creations of individual painters. He believed that for stylistic analysis to be effective, the form and content of a painting have to be described concurrently so that the macro-analysis of visual structure could be united with micro-examination of personal events and happenings.[20] In other words, the reconstruction of painting history should be a comprehensive survey also dependent on historical and literary records as well as the relationship between painting and Chinese culture. This is exactly what Fong has practiced all along. In addition to examining a painter's life, thoughts, and background, he has equally emphasized the value of historical and literary records. Despite taking stylistic analysis of a painting as the cornerstone for reconstructing art history, *Images of the Mind* gives due attention to cultural context as well, and hence the recurrent reference to the artist's creative idea and frame of mind. His 1987 essay on Zhu Da (Bada Shanren, 1626–1705) serves as yet another typical example. The fact that the life and artistic career of this painter, active in the late Ming and early Qing, are presented by phases in accordance with literature and extant works and that due reference is made to his time, thoughts, and feelings fully testifies to the importance Fong placed on extant works in the study of painting history as well as the mutually complementary roles played by literary research and stylistic analysis.[21] The year 1992 saw the publication of *Beyond Representation* (fig. 6), another voluminous work similar to *Images of the Mind*. Focusing on the collection of The Metropolitan Museum of Art, the book traces the development of Chinese painting and calligraphy from the eighth to the fourteenth century. Stylistically analyzed, Chinese painting and calligraphy are also discussed through culture, in the light of political, social and ideological factors, promptly pointing to the inseparability of painting and calligraphy on the one hand and the artist's life and inner world on the other.[22]

Fong divides the history of Chinese landscape painting into the major transformational phases of pictorial representation of the Song through the calligraphic self-expression of the Yuan and the revivalism of the Ming down to the synthesis of early Qing. He points out the correspondence of transformations in art with fundamental changes in China's cultural history. He believes that several issues that merit attention, namely, the relationships between painting and calligraphy, words and images, nature and art, representational and self-expression, and revival and synthesis.[23] The transition from pictorial representation of the Song, which emphasizes the rationality of nature, to calligraphic self-expression of the Yuan, which emphasizes the emotionality of the painter, was a visual extension of the transition from the School of Principles of the Song to the School of the Mind of the Ming. Such dual emphases on both the outside world and the inner world explains why there is an interdependence between painting and calligraphy, words and image, and nature and art. As far as the antithesis between representational and self-expression, and that between revival and synthesis, the unique philosophical and historical perspectives differ from that found in Western painting. It can be said that tackling these issues will culminate in understanding not just the cultural context of Chinese painting but also the very nature of Chinese painting in a global perspective.

The book *Possessing the Past*, published in 1996, represents Fong's macro-examination of the cultural phenomena of Chinese painting or even Chinese art as a whole.[24] To understand how Chinese art moved from reflecting the political and cultural environment to expressing the self, Fong suggests considering a number of aspects, including different modes of pictorial representation, period styles, Confucian beliefs in art, and the pursuit of antiquity. All these aspects are then dealt with in the contexts of traditional Chinese philosophy, literature, political history, social conditions, and cultural heritage, to facilitate a deeper understanding of Chinese art history and to highlight the cultural uniqueness of Chinese art. To cite an example, when comparing Eastern and Western perceptions and uses of the past, he says, "Thus Chinese archaism, as opposed to Western classicism, is historical and relativistic rather than idealistic and absolutist, paradoxically serving what appear to be contradictory impulses: both tradition and innovation, orthodoxy and rebellion."[25] And then, when he talks about the close link between the inclination toward revivalism in Chinese art and sociopolitical development, he says, "In the late thirteenth century, under Mongol rule, calligraphers and painters recalled the Chinese cultural heritage by creating new styles based on ancient sources. And following the Ming restoration in 1368, political repression again led scholar-artists to turn to the study of the past in their search for an alternative life, away from the imperial court. To curry favor with the educated and propertied classes, however, the court would inevitably co-opt the scholarly style. In the mid-seventeenth century, for example, the Manchu emperors of the early Qing dynasty, eager to establish their own legitimacy, quickly supported the revival of Sung and Yuan painting idioms, an act of political expediency."[26] In these discussions, culture invariably serves as the backdrop since art history is about not just styles but also cultural or cross-cultural phenomena in macro-perspective.

The significance of historical study lies not just in establishing historical truth but also in providing references for the present and the future. The same applies to the study of art history. In his more recent writings, Fong voices his opinion about contemporary art. As an art historian, Fong bases his views on in-depth studies of Chinese art rather than pure subjectivity. In summarizing the characteristics of post-Song painting, he thinks that the Chinese painter is trying to understand the outside world with his heart while at the same time remaining faithful to the graphic vocabulary that he has inherited from the past. These characteristics are not only favorable for the contemporary Chinese artist but also inspiring to the Western one. The advice he offers is: "The Chinese artist today, for whom the future of Chinese painting is necessarily bound up with the modern international styles, has yet to come to terms with his past, something he must do in order to forge and define his own modernity."[27] In an optimistic tone, he reiterates, "For a while longer, the struggle in the Chinese academies between traditionalists and Westernizers will rage on. But as security and confidence return to Chinese life, I hope traditionalists and rebels alike will feel free to study and imitate a multitude of models, from China's own past as well as from the West, and liberally re-invent themselves."[28] In his eyes, traditional Chinese art still holds immense value as a source of reference, since the rich cultural resources of traditional Chinese art and history will converge with our modern life with the new visions of the twentieth century.[29] He is confident that the pictorial vocabulary and structure in the Chinese tradition will become a powerful language of art in the modern world.[30] The artistry of Chinese painting will evolve to allow unrestrained expression of the self, since the West will eventually realize, when all other artistic languages are depreciating with precipitation, that the fine Chinese tradition of availing of both words and images will benefit its artists.[31] Invocation of the past for transformation and innovation has stood the test of time as a efficacious means to preserve and perpetuate cultural heritage, so the Chinese example of cyclical rather than linear development, as in the West, will be looked upon as a viable and exciting option for reintegrating the disintegrated, restoring the collapsed, and transcending the transformed.[32] As for the prospects of Chinese painting, he ventures to predict as an art historian that modern Chinese painting will eventually evolve into a new synthesis while perpetuating the past.[33]

Fong is unmatched for his contribution to the transformation of Chinese art history from its biographical beginnings into an academic discipline in the past decades. With a history of styles that draws from historical records and ancient theories properly reconstructed, Chinese art history can now be viewed and studied objectively in both historical and cultural perspectives. In the course of this development, Fong has played a leading role establishing methodologies, putting theories into practice, and encouraging further studies. Naturally, the picture would be incomplete if his contribution to museums and tertiary education were to be omitted. With Fong at the helm, The Metropolitan Museum of Art has distinguished itself with a remarkable collection of Asian art, additional galleries for their display, modernization of art conservation, organization of significant thematic exhibitions, and numerous publications and educational programs. While at Princeton, in addition to expanding the collection and scope of studies undertaken by the university museum, he devoted himself to the training of art historians. Many of his students now occupy key positions in museums and academic circles both in the West and in Asia. All in all, Fong deserves the highest respect for his contributions in bringing the professional study of Chinese art history to the next level and thus gaining increasing attention from a bigger audience in the West. There is no doubt that his legacy will continue to be felt for a long time in the study of Chinese art history.

Notes

An earlier version of this essay was published in Chinese in *Wenyi yanjiu* 4 (2004): 115–22.

1 For a discussion of the *Record of Famous Painters of All the Dynasties* and traditional writings of Chinese painting history, see Shi Shouqian "Gudai shiji de huashi yu zhulu," in *Zhongguo gudai huihua mingpin*, Shi Shouqian et al. (Taipei: Xiongshi, 1986), 148–52.

2 Wen Fong, "Five Hundred Lohans at the Daitokuji" (PhD dissertation, Princeton University, 1956).

3 Wen Fong, "The Problem of Ch'ien Hsuan," *The Art Bulletin* 42 (September 1960): 173–89.

4 Ibid., 188.

5 Wen Fong, "The Problem of Forgeries in Chinese Painting: Part One," *Artibus Asiae* 25, nos. 2–3 (1962): 95–140.

6 Wen Fong, "Chinese Painting: A Statement of Method," *Oriental Art*, n.s., 9, no. 2 (summer 1963): 73–78.

7 Meyer Schapiro, "Style," in *Anthropology Today: An Encyclopedic Inventory*, ed. A. L. Kroeber (Chicago: University of Chicago Press, 1953), 287–312.

8 Wen C. Fong, "Toward a Structural Analysis of Chinese Landscape Painting," *Art Journal* 28, no. 4 (Summer 1969): 390, n. 6.

9 Heinrich Wölfflin, *Principles of Art History: The Problem of the Development of Style in Later Art*, trans. M. D. Hottinger (New York: Dover, reprint of 1950 edition).

10 Li Lincan, "Zhongguo hua duandai yanjiu li," in *Qingzhu Dong Zhuobin xiansheng liushiwusui lunwenji*, ed. Zhongyang yanjiuyuan lishi yuyan yanjiusuo (Taipei: Zhongyang yanjiuyuan lishi yuyan yanjiusuo, 1961–62), 1:551–82.

11 Sherman E. Lee, "The Story of Chinese Painting," *Art Quarterly* 11, no. 1 (1948). For a discussion of the studies of Chinese painting in the United States, see Xue Yongnian, "Meiguo yanjiu Zhongguo shuhuashi fangfa lüeshu," in *Shuhua shilun conggao* (Chengdu: Sichuan jiaoyu chubanshe, 1992), 473–89.

12 Wen Fong, "Xifang de Zhongguo hua yanjiu," trans. Shi Shouqian, *Gugong wenwu yuekan* 4, no. 9 (December 1986): 49.

13 *Streams and Mountains without End: A Northern Sung Handscroll and Its Significance in the History of Early Chinese Painting*, Artibus Asiae Suppl. 14, 2nd ed. (Ascona: Artibus Asiae Publishers, 1967).

14 "Toward a Structural Analysis" (above, n. 8), 388–97.

15 Ibid.

16 George Kubler, *The Shape of Time: Remarks on the History of Things* (New Haven and London: Yale University Press, 1962), 33–39.

17 Wen C. Fong, *Summer Mountains: The Timeless Landscape* (New York: Metropolitan Museum of Art, 1975.)

18 *Images of the Mind: Selections from the Edward L. Elliott Family and John B. Elliott Collections of Chinese Calligraphy and Painting at the Art Museum, Princeton University* (Princeton, N.J.: The Art Museum, Princeton University in association with Princeton University Press, 1984).

19 Wen C. Fong, "*Riverbank*," in *Along the Riverbank: Chinese Paintings from the C. C. Wong Family Collection*, Maxwell K. Hearn and Wen C. Fong (New York: Metropolitan Museum of Art, 1999), 2–57; idem, "*Riverbank*: From Connoisseurship to Art History," in *Issues of Authenticity in Chinese Painting*, ed. Judith G. Smith and Wen C. Fong (New York: The Metropolitan Museum of Art, 1999), 259–91; idem, "A Reply to James Cahill's Queries about the Authenticity of *Riverbank*," *Orientations* 31, no. 3 (March 2000): 95–140. See also below, chap. 7, n. 3 and Jason C. Kuo, ed., *Perspectives on Connoisseurship of Chinese Painting* (Washington, D.C.: New Academia, 2008).

20 Fong, "Xifang de Zhongguo hua yanjiu" (n. 12 above), 54.

21 Wen C. Fong, "Stages in the Life and Art of Chu Ta (A.D. 1626–1705)," *Archives of Asian Art* 40 (1987): 7–23.

22 Wen C. Fong, *Beyond Representation: Chinese Painting and Calligraphy, 8th–14th Century* (New York: The Metropolitan Museum of Art, 1992).

23 Wen C. Fong, "Modern Art Criticism and Chinese Painting History," in *Tradition and Creativity: Essays on East Asian Civilization*, ed. Ching-I Tu (New Brunswick: Rutgers, State University of New Jersey, 1987), 98–108.

24 Wen C. Fong, "Chinese Art and Cross-Cultural Understanding," in *Possessing the Past: Treasures from the National Palace Museum, Taipei*, Wen C. Fong and James C. Y. Watt (New York: The Metropolitan Museum of Art; Taipei: National Palace Museum, 1996), 27–35.

25 Ibid., 35.

26 Ibid., 36.

27 Ibid.

28 Wen C. Fong, "The Modern Chinese Art Debate," *Artibus Asiae*, 53, nos. 1–2 (1993): 304.

29 Wen C. Fong, *Between Two Cultures: Late-Nineteenth- and Twentieth Century Chinese Paintings from the Robert H. Ellsworth Collection in the*

Metropolitan Museum of Art (New York: The Metropolitan Museum of Art; New Haven and London: Yale University Press, 2001), 259.

30 Fong, "Xifang de Zhongguo hua yanjiu" (n. 12 above), 56.

31 Ibid.

32 Ibid.

33 Ibid.

7

A Tale of Two Scholars:

Cahill and Fong on Chinese Painting

Jason C. Kuo

Words move, music moves
Only in time; but that which is only living
Can only die. Words, after speech, reach
Into the silence. Only by the form, the pattern,
Can words or music reach
The stillness, as a Chinese jar still
Moves perpetually in its stillness.

—*T. S. Eliot,* "Burnt Norton"

The most recent impetus for this essay came from James Cahill's opening remarks at the symposium "A Bridge to Heaven," in honor of Wen C. Fong at Princeton University in April 2006. Cahill had this to say about his long-standing rival Fong and himself:

> [In the late 1950s] a new high-powered young specialist in Chinese painting had appeared on the scene, teaching at Princeton, who was setting out to revolutionize the study of Chinese painting. No one who was himself [i.e., Cahill] meaning to do just that could hear this news without a shiver: how will we two get along? Will we be adversaries and enemies, in the pattern established by the generation before us, like [Max] Loehr and [Bernard] Karlgren, or [Aschwin] Lippe and [Allan] Priest, or [Osvald] Sirén and everybody

> else? Again, disaster was averted; it turned out that we liked and respected each other, even as we argued and fought, and we have gone on doing that now for more than fifty years.[1]

On the other hand, in his 2006 autobiographical "Reflections on Chinese Art History: An Interview with Jerome Silbergeld," Fong characterized Cahill and himself as "the best friends, indeed comrades-in-arms, in making Chinese painting more accessible to the Western scholarly community and the public at large. . . . I have profound respect and admiration of Cahill's natural talent for writing directly and fluently about what he sees. For over half a century, Cahill has been a barometer of the increasing appreciation of later Chinese painting in the Western world."[2] Yet, over the years, we have also witnessed many disagreements in their public discussions. These public discussions highlighted important aspects of the historiography of Chinese painting studies in Postwar America.[3] Mindful of how scholarly writing is a social practice, not dissimilar to the nature of painting in China as explicated in Cahill's *Painter's Practice: How Artists Lived and Worked in Traditional China,*[4] I have written this essay in the same genre, to engage the work of living colleagues and to honor their scholarship by description and critique.[5] I do not intend to rank one above the other; such an argument would serve no purpose to the field.

Another impetus for this essay has been my interest in the historiography of Chinese painting studies in the "West."[6] Since the early 1990s, I have been working on a sort of archaeology of the history of Chinese painting scholarship in the United States. I organized a panel titled "Four Decades of Studies on Chinese Painting" at the College Art Association annual conference in Washington, D.C. in 1991.[7] At about the same time, I embarked on an oral history project and conducted interviews, either in person or on paper, with a number of American art historians about their life and work. The results of the project were first published in 2000 in *Discovering Chinese Painting: Dialogues with American Art Historians*.[8] The expanded and revised edition of the book, published in 2006 and retitled *Discovering Chinese Painting: Dialogues with Art Historians*, includes additional contributions from art historians working outside the United States as well as an art historian who is not a Chinese art specialist.[9] Cahill has contributed to both projects, but Fong, like many others, has not participated in the dialogues for various reasons.[10] My experience during these two projects, however, has convinced me that it would be useful to compare these two scholars' approaches to the study of Chinese painting.

My interest in the historiography of Chinese painting studies has naturally led me to offer several undergraduate and graduate courses on the topic. In the fall of 2003, for instance, I taught a graduate seminar at the University of Maryland titled "Orientalism, Scholarship, and the Western Image of Chinese Painting: Towards a Critical Historiography of Chinese Painting." The aim of the course was, through critical readings of major texts written by leading Western art historians of Chinese painting in general and scholars of Chinese painting in Postwar America in particular, to examine critically the historiography of the field of Chinese painting, to assess what achievements have been made, and to understand what and how personal backgrounds of scholars and institutional constraints (academia, museums, and technology, for example) may have affected various practices in the field. In the fall of 2005, furthermore, I taught a seminar, "Discourse, Power, Art Historical Knowledge, and the Making of a Postwar American Historian of Chinese Painting" at the University of Maryland. In many ways, this essay has been inspired by these graduate courses, because my encounters there with the history of American scholarship on Chinese painting in the Postwar period have made me increasingly aware of the different approaches to the field and the need to examine them critically.

A third impetus for this essay came from my participation in a panel titled "The Middle Path? Style and Cultural History in Chinese Painting Scholarship," organized by Kathleen Ryor and Jennifer Purtle for the annual conference of the College Art Association in February 2007 in New York City. In their call for papers, they wrote, "In the last decade, scholarship of the history of Chinese painting has begun to absorb the mandate of the New Art History to move past questions of style. While these approaches have given new direction to the field, they have also created tension, posited at the intersection of Sinology and art history, between a logocentric, literary Chinese-derived contextual history of Chinese painting and an imagecentric, visual approach to Chinese painting history."[11] Discussion at the panel further persuaded me to look at the contexts in which Cahill and Fong have undertaken their scholarship since the 1950s and to examine the nuanced differences between them.

Over the past fifty years, Cahill and Fong have, each in his own way, contributed tremendously to the field of Chinese painting. Both of them, although of different backgrounds, education, and temperament, have shaped the understanding of Chinese painting in the West.[12] Of course, each generation of art historians builds on the work of the preceding one. Cahill paid homage to his formative influences at the 1991 College Art Association panel "Four Decades of Studies on Chinese Painting," mentioned above. Throughout their development in the field, Cahill and Fong have established friendship as well as scholarly rivalry; at the same time, this intellectual engagement attests to their differences. They often attended the same symposia to present their scholarship (such as the 1970 International Symposium on Chinese Painting in Taipei, the 1984 International Conference on the Huangshan [Mount Huang] School of Painting in Hefei, the 1992 International

Symposium on Dong Qichang in Kansas City, and the 2002 Conference on the History of Painting in East Asia in Taipei); Fong often invited Cahill to participate in conferences he himself organized (such as the conferences "Words and Images" in 1985 and "Issues of Authenticity in Chinese Painting" in 1999, both at The Metropolitan Museum of Art).[13] And while they have both promoted the study of Chinese painting, their methods differ greatly.

Born in Fort Bragg, California, in 1926, Cahill studied in the Department of Oriental Languages at the University of California in Berkeley and received his B.A. in 1950; at that time the department's teachers included some of the most eminent sinologists, such as Peter A. Boodberg, Edward Schafer, Ch'en Shih-hsiang, the linguist Chao Yuen-ren, the historian Otto John Maenchen-Helfen, and the anthropologist Wolfram Eberhard. These teachers were of diverse backgrounds: Ch'en Shih-hsiang and Chao Yuen-ren came from China, Boodberg from Russia, Maenchen-Helfen from Austria (but trained in Leipzig), and Eberhard from Germany.[14] During his graduate studies in art history at the University of Michigan, he studied with Max Loehr (from Germany) from 1951 to 1953.[15] During his sojourn as a Fulbright student in 1954–55 in Japan, he studied with Shimada, then curator at the Kyoto National Museum. Then, in 1955–56, he worked with Osvald Sirén in Sweden on the annotated list of Chinese paintings in world collections for Sirén's seven-volume *Chinese Painting: Leading Masters and Principles*.[16] Thus, during his formative years, Cahill learned a rich array of approaches from his many teachers. In his paper, "Five Notable Figures in the Early Period of Chinese Painting Studies," he reflected on his experience with five pioneering scholars of diverse national and cultural backgrounds (Archibald Wenly, Osvald Sirén, Laurence Sickman, Shūjirō Shimada, and Max Loehr) who taught him, formally or informally, and helped him find his own niche in the scholarly world. Cahill's career path reminds us that scholars mature through their personal and educational experience. In 1958 he completed his doctoral dissertation at Michigan on the fourteenth-century painter Wu Zhen; after serving from 1957 to 1965 on the curatorial staff at the Freer Gallery of Art in Washington, D.C., he accepted a professorship in 1965 at Berkeley, where he retired in 1994.

There are many milestones in Cahill's academic career, but only a few can be mentioned here.[17] From 1976 to 1982, Cahill published three volumes of his projected five-volume *A History of Later Chinese Painting, 1279–1950*: *Hills Beyond a River: Chinese Painting of the Yuan Dynasty*; *Parting at the Shore: Chinese Painting of the Early and Middle Ming Dynasty, 1368–1580*; and *The Distant Mountains: Chinese Painting of the Late Ming Dynasty, 1570–1644*.[18] These three volumes have, generally speaking, superseded the treatment of the same periods in Sirén's equally ambitious seven-volume *Chinese Painting: Leading Masters and Principles*. In 1978–79, Cahill delivered the Charles Eliot Norton Lectures at Harvard University. The Eliot Professorship of Poetry has become one of America's most distinguished guest lectureships since 1925; other lectures in the series were given by such luminaries as Leonard Bernstein, Harold Bloom, John Cage, Aaron Copland, e. e. cummings, Umberto Eco, T. S. Eliot, Robert Frost, Leo Steinberg, Frank Stella, Igor Stravinsky, Lionel Trilling, and Meyer Schapiro. His lectures were published in 1982 as *The Compelling Image: Nature and Style in Seventeenth-Century Chinese Painting*. The book was awarded the College Art Association's Morey Prize for the best art history book of 1982. A comparison of *The Compelling Image* with Laurence Binyon's 1933–34 Norton Lectures, *The Spirit of Man in Asian Art* easily reveals how much Western understanding of Chinese painting changed in the half century that separates the two works.[19] Although Cahill's award-winning book has received criticism from some of his colleagues, it has been instrumental in establishing Chinese painting of the seventeenth century as a subfield in Chinese art history.[20] More specifically, whatever issues with the book one may raise (such as the extent to which European influences can be ascertained in specific works of art), his dialectical approach successfully invites critical reflection. The book puts into practice his own desideratum for art history, expressed in his earlier 1976 essay "Style as Idea in Ming and Ch'ing Painting": to examine "the human significance of style."[21] In the essay he also looks carefully at different painters' "conscious responses" to the tradition in which they worked, in the manner advocated by the intellectual historian Benjamin Schwartz.[22]

A series of other distinguished lectureships firmly established Cahill's eminence as an American scholar of Chinese and Japanese painting. His Bampton Lectures at Columbia University in 1991 were published in 1994 under the title *The Painter's Practice: How Artists Lived and Worked in Traditional China*. He gave the Reischauer Lectures at Harvard University in 1993; these lectures appeared as a book in 1996 under the title *The Lyric Journey: Poetic Painting in China and Japan.* He received the College Art Association's Distinguished Teaching of Art History Award in 1995. Recognizing "a time of great methodological shifts in the field" and a need to foster a "dialogue within and among the different generations of art historians," the College Art Association saluted him as its Distinguished Scholar at its annual convention in 2004. In 2007, he received the Distinguished Lifetime Achievement Award for Writing on Art from the College Art Association; the award jury explains in its citation: "Though scholarship on this vast subject has a long and distinguished past, Cahill has spent his career remaking the study of Chinese painting for [a] new generation of students. He is widely praised for his sensitive incorporation of innovative methodologies from European art history, many derived from distinguished colleagues at Berkeley, which he sensitively modifies and translates for use in their appropriate context for China. The combination of a curator's eye and an academic's methodological range has continued to inform Cahill's scholarship. . . ."[23]

Fong was born in Shanghai in 1930.[24] While still a youth, Fong began to study calligraphy; at the age of twelve, his calligraphy was exhibited in public. One of his early teachers was the calligrapher Li Jian (1882–1956; figs. 1–6); he later studied with another calligrapher, Wang Juchang (1900–1991; figs. 7–8) at Jiaotong University in Shanghai, before enrolling as a sophomore at Princeton.[25] Fong attributes most of his early training on art and history to Li. Fong explains how Li taught him "how to look, touch, and 'feel' art objects: works of calligraphy, brush paintings, seal carvings, and fine woodblock-printed books." Li also taught Fong to copy ancient calligraphy. This process instilled in him the importance of looking at the technical aspects of an artist's work. On this approach to art, Fong states, "I discovered that this way of copying—harmonizing and synthesizing ancient styles—was analytically modern and original, rather than mere slavish imitation. It explains why in traditional Chinese arts and crafts the impetus for innovation derived not from new technical or formal inventions (or the notion of 'progress'), but from the artist's intensive search for his individual Self."[26] Because Li Juiqing (1867–1920), the uncle and teacher of Li Jian, was also Zhang Daqian's teacher, Fong had over the years a special relationship with Zhang, calling him his "Uncle Teacher," in accordance with traditional Chinese practice. Naturally, Fong could write on the life and work of Zhang through firsthand experience; indeed, any in-depth study on Fong's scholarship must consider this relationship.[27] Looking at Fong's early educational experience, for instance, we should not be surprised at his emphasis on calligraphy in Chinese painting.

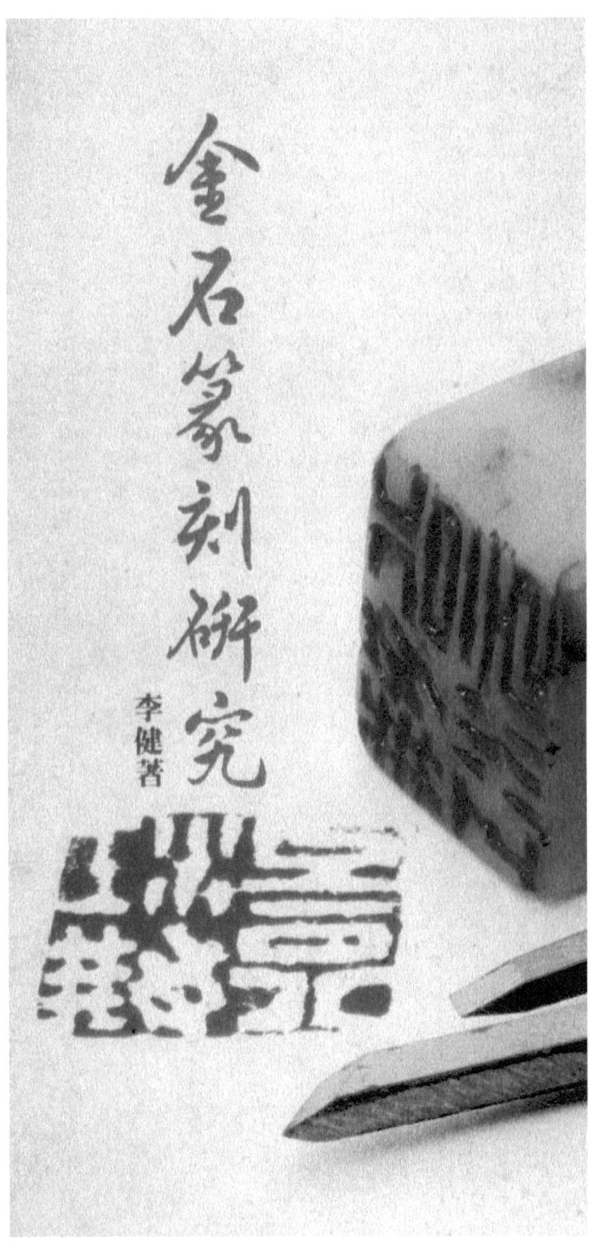

Figure 1. Cover of *Jinshi zhuanke yanjiu* by Li Jian (Hong Kong: Shangwu yinshuguan, 1964).

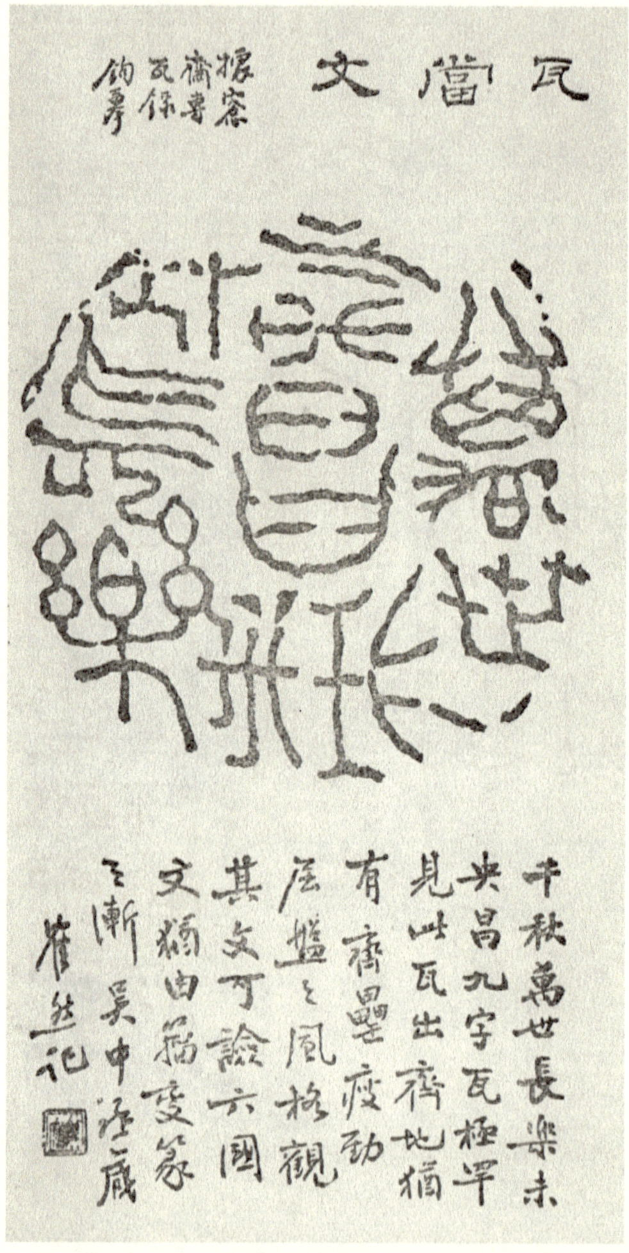

Figure 2. Li Jian, transcription of inscription on a tile terminal; published in his *Jinshi zhuanke yanjiu* (Hong Kong: Shangwu yinshuguan, 1964), 44.

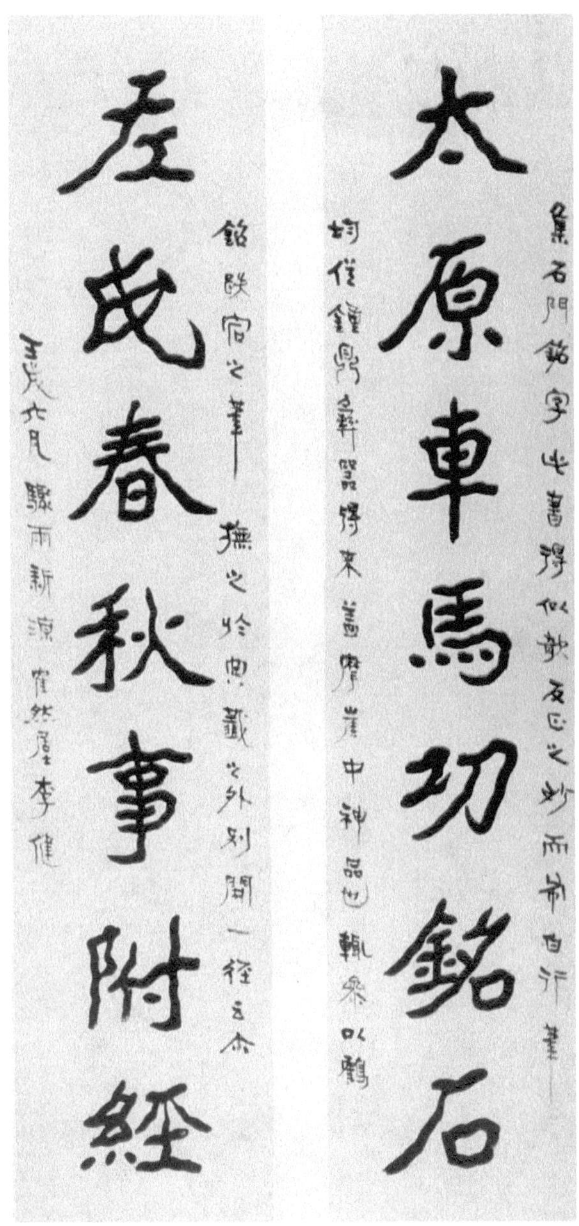

Figure 3. Li Jian, calligraphy couplet, pair of hanging scrolls, 1922; published in Wang Chaobin, ed., *Minguo shufa* (Zhengzhou: Henan meishu chubanshe, 1989), 152.

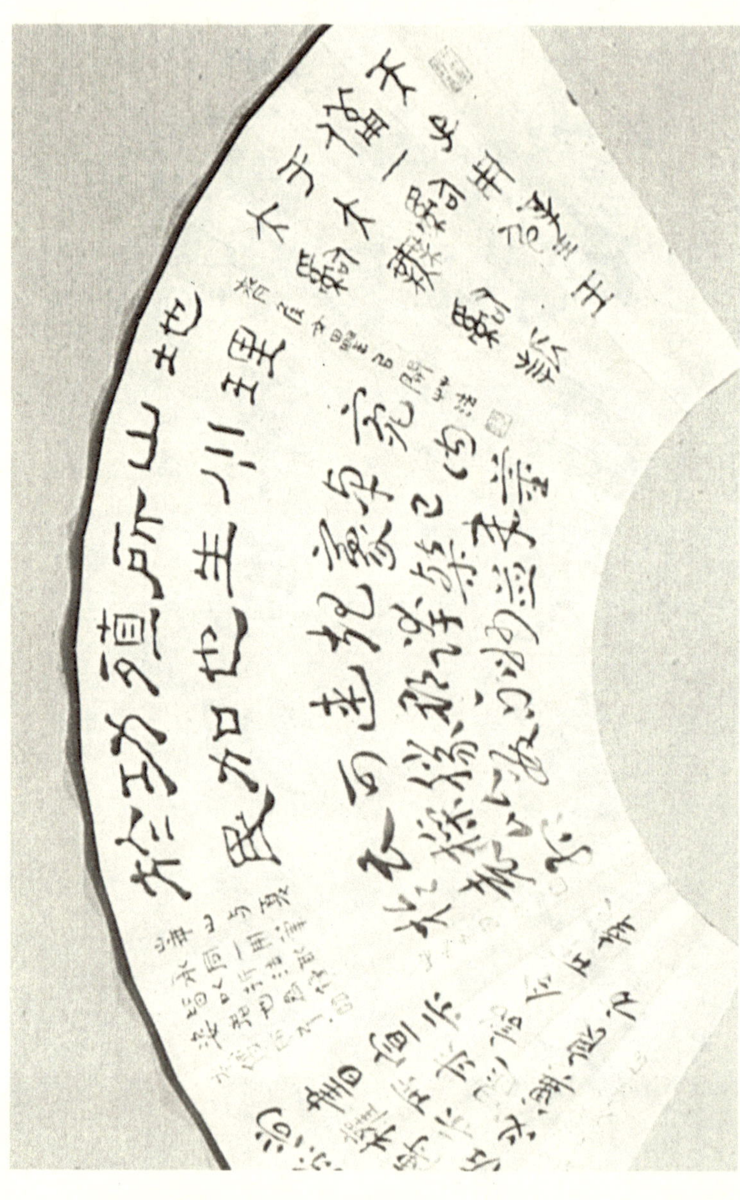

Figure 4. Li Jian, *Calligraphy in Four Ancient Styles* (private collection); published in Wen C. Fong, "Remembering Chang Dai-chien (1899–1983)," in *The International Conference on the Poetry, Calligraphy, and Painting of Chang Dai-chien and Pu Hsin-yu* (Taipei: National Palace Museum, 1994), 31.

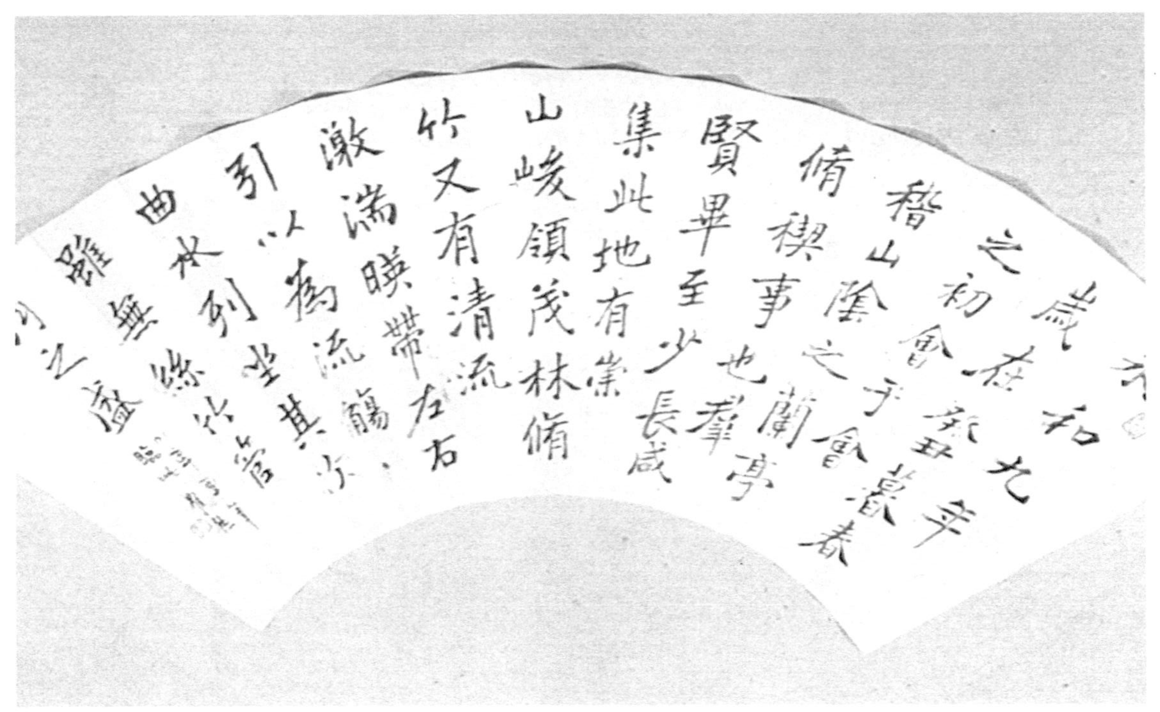

Figure 5. Li Jian, *Lanting by Ouyang Xun* (private collection); published in Wen C. Fong, "Remembering Chang Dai-chien (1899–1983)," in *The International Conference on the Poetry, Calligraphy, and Painting of Chang Dai-chien and Pu Hsin-yu* (Taipei: National Palace Museum, 1994), 32.

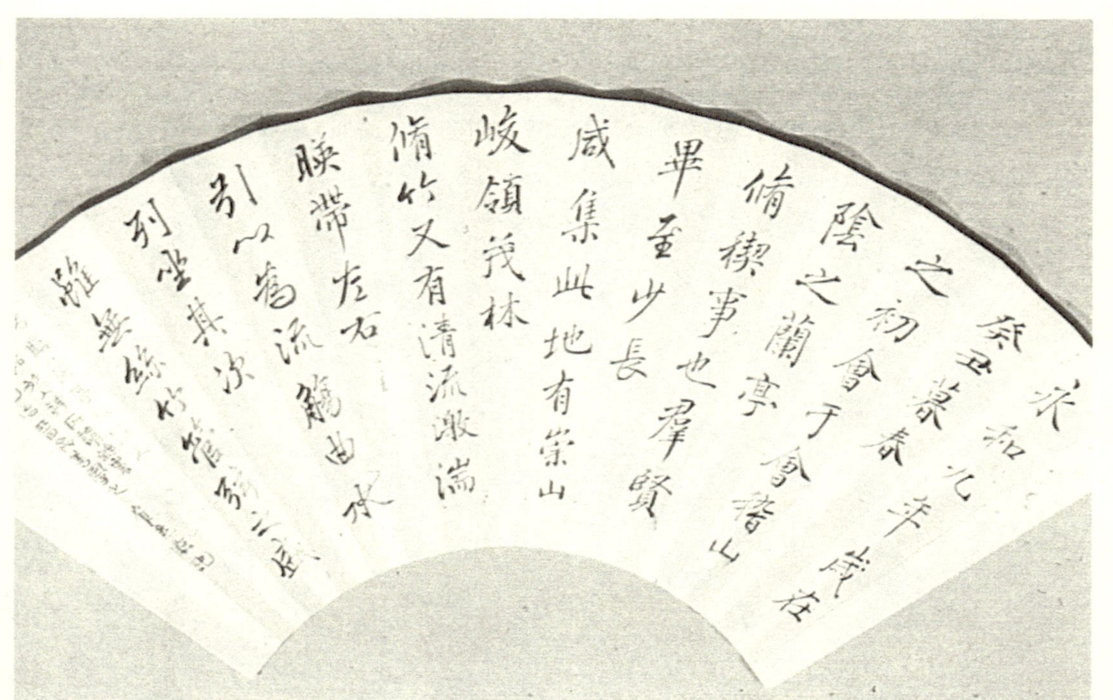

Figure 6. Li Jian, *Lanting by Chu Suliang* (private collection); published in Wen C. Fong, "Remembering Chang Dai-chien (1899–1983)," in *The International Conference on the Poetry, Calligraphy, and Painting of Chang Dai-chien and Pu Hsin-yu* (Taipei: National Palace Museum, 1994), 33.

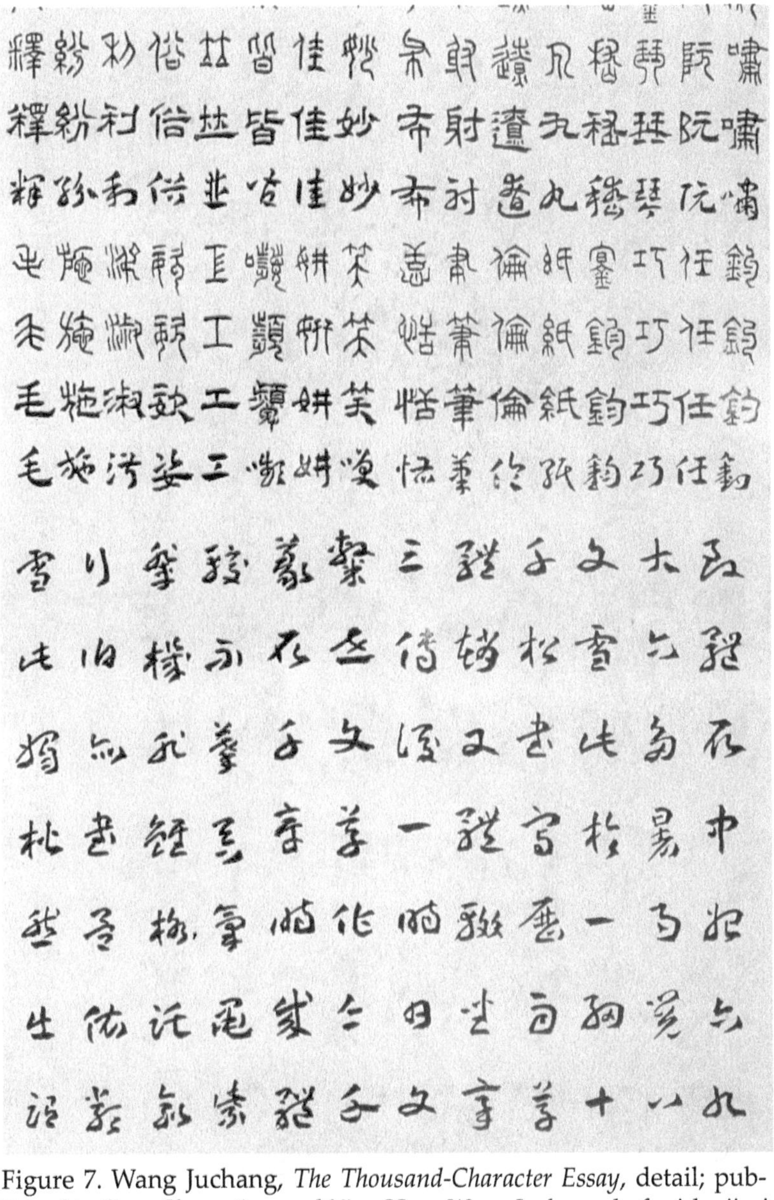

Figure 7. Wang Juchang, *The Thousand-Character Essay*, detail; published in Tang Shengtian and Xiao Hua, *Wang Juchang shufa yishu jiexi* (Nanjing: Jiangshu meishu chubanshe, 2001), 35.

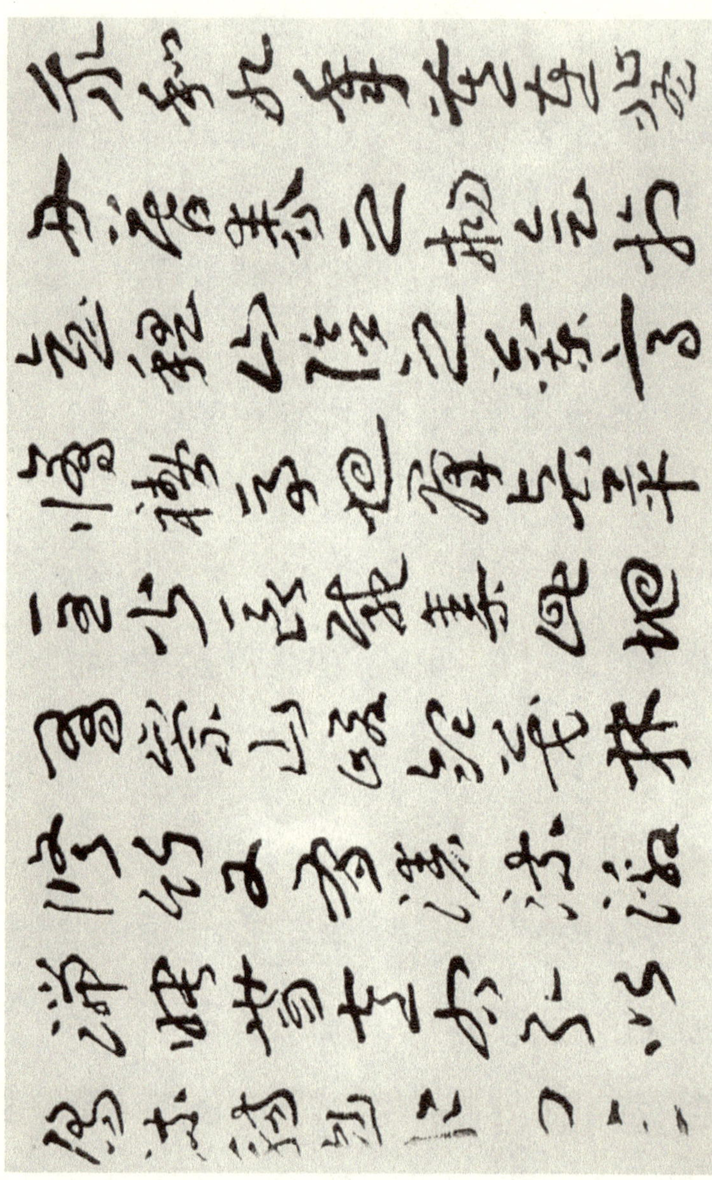

Figure 8. Wang Juchang, *Lanting*, detail; published in Tang Shengtian and Xiao Hua, *Wang Juchang shufa yishu jiexi* (Nanjing: Jiangshu chubanshe, 2001), 50.

Fong received his PhD from Princeton University in 1958; among his teachers were Kurt Weitzmann and George Rowley, both trained primarily in European medieval art history. Except for brief appointments at the Cleveland Museum of Art and the Yale University Art Gallery, he taught at Princeton most of his life until his retirement in 1999. He established in 1959 the first PhD program in Chinese art and archaeology in this country. While continuing his teaching at Princeton, he joined The Metropolitan Museum of Art as a special consultant in 1971 and became Consultative Chairman of the Department of Asian Art in 1990. In 1992 he was elected a member of the American Philosophical Society; in the same year, he was elected a member of the Academia Sinica in Taiwan and became the only art historian to be elected to that distinguished learned society. For his scholarship and profound influence on his students, he was named the College Art Association Art History Teacher of the Year in 1997. He was instrumental in making the collection of Chinese calligraphy and painting at The Metropolitan Museum of Art one of the most important in the United States. Over the last forty-five years, Fong has authored, co-authored, edited, and co-edited many books and catalogues, as well as numerous articles for journals and bulletins in Asian art.[28] In 2008, he was awarded an honorary Doctors of Arts degree from Harvard University at its 375th commencement. The citation reads: "Opening the eyes of the West to the art of the East, in the painter's hand he sees the heart's desire, and in the beauty of brushstrokes the breath of life."[29]

The 1950s is commonly viewed as a defining shift in Western Chinese art historical scholarship. In my conversations with them, American art historians have acknowledged this pivotal point, and added their own perception. James Cahill, discussing the state of the field at the time he first took it up, said:

> The field was being dominated by people like [Berthold] Laufer, who was an anthropologist and ethnologist who also wrote about certain aspects of Chinese art, of course, and people like [Paul] Pelliot himself who would occasionally venture into the field of art. This was considered to be the respectable way to do it. In other words, art history was something that people whose main field was something else did not in their spare time exactly, but sort of moved over into. . . . I have said recently that in the early phase of our studies we were so pleased at being able to read Chinese, and translate and use Chinese texts and use Chinese reference books, that we tended to write and think as though the ultimate truth was there in the text, if only we could dig it out and somehow apply it to the paintings—as though all the wisdom were somehow there in the ancient Chinese texts. Indeed we learned an enormous amount from them . . . . This idea of applying Chinese critical ideas to surviving works of art was very attractive and very good."[30]

It is important to point out here that many American scholars (such as George Rowley and Benjamin Rowland) who wrote on Chinese painting and who taught the generation of Fong and others were trained primarily in European art history before they took up Asian art; furthermore, some scholars (such as Chu-tsing Li and Sherman E. Lee) who became active in the field of Chinese painting at about the same time as Fong and Cahill were also trained as doctoral students in European and American art history.[31]

Scholars of Chinese painting in the late 1950s shared a common interest in getting rid of the "Orientalizing" in writings on Chinese art published in the West. For instance, in 1957 Fong published a scathing review of Amos Ih Tiao Chang's book *The Existence of Intangible Content in Architectonic Form*

Based upon the Practicality of Laotzu's Philosophy. In the review, Fong maintains that Chang's understanding of the Daoist classic *Daode jing* or *Tao Te Ching* was shallow and his interpretation of the text in relation to Chinese architecture misleading. On the other hand, the philosopher Wing-tsit Chan published a more sympathetic review, in which he concludes: "Chang has performed a unique and challenging service" in bringing Daoism and modern architecture together.[32] In 1957 and 1959 Cahill published two book reviews of Mai-mai Sze's *The Tao of Painting*.[33] He writes in his later, much longer, and more critical review, "The growing popular fascination with Chinese and Japanese painting concentrates more and more on an ill-defined *mystique* which is supposed to underlie this art . . . maintaining that the paintings are only to be properly understood in relation to Chan's Buddhism, to Taoism, to the cosmology of the *Book of Changes*."[34] In an earlier draft of the review, he writes, "Let us aim at clarity, not at the perpetuation of obscurity. In the face of a widespread public demand for assurance that the truth of Far Eastern art is so abstruse as to be virtually ineffable, let us try to offer instead lucid and intelligible discussions, however unwelcome they may be."[35] Urging "less *Tao*, please, more painting," Cahill asks his professional colleagues to avoid this kind of approach and let others, such as those in philosophy and religion and "the pseudo-mystics among our contemporary poets and painters," deal with it.[36] About the same time, in the introduction to his 1960 book *Chinese Painting*, Cahill writes:

> The "Japanism" is fading, as we become aware of how profoundly our view of Chinese painting was affected by Japanese ideas and attitudes during the pioneering stage of our studies, and set about to replace these with the more highly developed and pertinent ideas of the Chinese, as well as with some of our own.... Where Chinese painting once was insufficiently understood

> because of its supposed strangeness, it is now in danger of being misunderstood and distorted by those who feel it is not, in its true character, strange enough. The temptation is to see it as mysterious and therefore exciting.[37]

In the 1960s, both Cahill and Fong, like several of their colleagues, found it necessary to explicate the meaning of key terms in ancient Chinese texts on painting. Fong published three articles on Hsieh Ho's "Liu-fa" [Six Laws] between 1963 and 1966.[38] Cahill published in 1960 his "Confucian Elements in the Theory of Painting" on the basis primarily of written texts, and in 1961 "The Six Laws and How to Read Them."[39] The essay "Confucian Elements in the Theory of Painting" was written originally for one of a series of symposia sponsored by the Committee on Chinese Thought of the Association for Asian Studies, devoted to "the principal traditions of Chinese thought as these have influenced the cultural life and institutional development of China."[40] It was one of Cahill's major early scholarly articles and has been quite influential on both specialists (such as Susan Bush) and non-specialists (such as John Steadman, a Milton scholar) on Chinese painting.[41]

Similarly, it was also necessary for Fong, Cahill, and their contemporaries in the Postwar era to establish a core group of "monuments" of Chinese paintings. Fong co-authored with Sherman Lee a monograph on a single handscroll in the Cleveland Museum of Art; *Streams and Mountains without End* was published in 1955.[42] Fong then completed his PhD dissertation, "Five Hundred Lohans at the Daitokuji," at Princeton in 1956. During the research for his dissertation, he identified, among the treasures in the Freer Gallery of Art in Washington, D.C., two of the paintings originally owned by the Daitokuji and sold to a private collector at the turn of the twentieth century; in 1958, the Freer Gallery published his discovery in a small volume.[43]

In 1950, Cahill began graduate studies at the University of Michigan, under a newly formed concentration in Chinese painting studies. Cahill studied under the direction of Max Loehr, one of the first scholars of Chinese art history in the United States who was trained both in sinology and art history. While studying at Michigan, Cahill worked at the Freer Gallery of Art in Washington, D.C. In 1956, Cahill took a full-time position with the Freer and soon found himself spending "a lot of time going through old paintings, studying them, making judgments and comparisons, going through reproduction books and trying to find other things by the same artists."[44] This was the first stage in Cahill's development as a connoisseur. Cahill later explains, "You build certain sensitivities into the mind so that when a certain pattern or characteristic of style recurs, you are able to attach a name, or maybe even a date to it."[45] The sensitivities for patterns that Cahill speaks of are foundations for the practice of connoisseurship. Among his contributions to the field during his tenure at the Freer was the reattribution of many paintings, previously attributed to famous artists from the Song Dynasty (960–1279), to an artist of the Zhe School in the Ming Dynasty (1368–1644). As Richard Barnhart has pointed out, "In the United States, James Cahill has been particularly active and effective for many years in pursuing this work. As a case study, we can examine the collection in which Cahill conducted much of his work, that of the Freer Gallery of Art in Washington, D.C."[46] Building on the work of his predecessor J. E. Lodge from the 1920s, Cahill contributed tremendously to the rewriting of the history of Chinese painting during his Freer years. As Barnhart has put it, "Beginning anew in the late 1950s, James Cahill, fresh from study of the superb Zhe School and Ming academy collections in Japan, began a systematic assessment of the Freer painting, and in many cases associated them with specific masters, styles, or schools."[47]

Cahill's work was continued by his successors at the Freer, such as Thomas Lawton and Shen C. Y. Fu.

While Cahill was working at the Freer Gallery, he came into contact with Wang Jiqian (Chi-chien Wang or C. C. Wang [1907–2003], as he was commonly known in the field of Chinese painting). Having looked at a large number of paintings with Wang, Cahill acknowledged Wang's formative influence on him.[48] Wang was a painter, calligrapher, and connoisseur who studied painting and connoisseurship with Gu Linshi (1865–1933) and Wu Hufan (1894–1968) in China. In 1949, Wang moved to the United States and began to promote the study of Chinese painting, and soon found himself giving lectures at various universities and becoming a liaison to the major museums and collectors at that time. Cahill recalled his experience with Wang at the Freer and said how Wang would "glance at something and say oh, yes, that's really a work by so-and-so."[49] Once Wang attributed a painting to Lu Yüan, but Cahill had to admit that at the time he "had never heard of Lu Yüan."[50]

In his foreword to "A Definition of Brushwork-Oriented Criteria in Chinese Literati Painting," a series of interviews with C. C. Wang conducted by Joan Stanley-Baker in the 1970s, Cahill expresses his profound admiration for Wang as a connoisseur and for Wang's explication of brushwork or "brush-wielding" and the "central preoccupation of Chinese painters and critics at least during the past seven centuries or so." As Wang puts it in the introduction to the interviews, the criterion of brushwork "is unique to the Far East where it is an essential part of an artist's technique. In China it serves a dual function. Aside from being the basic pictorial ingredient, brushwork serves to reveal the quality of the artist as a person, in particular his mental, spiritual cultivation." Wang maintains that brushwork as a criterion in connoisseurship is "peculiar to Chinese painting" and that "Westerners are not the only ones unused to the study of brushwork, of *bimo*.

Even the majority of Chinese do not understand it. For here is something which is addressed to the specialists (the person of like-caliber cultivation)." In the same foreword, however, Cahill, while praising Wang's accomplishments as belonging to one of the most distinguished connoisseurs of Chinese panting, cautions against "over-reading some of Wang's assertion on the importance of brushwork, or failing to balance them against other statements he makes." Consistent with his tendency to cast a skeptical eye on traditional Chinese ways of connoisseurship or writing about Chinese painting, Cahill writes, "Brushwork is a crucial criterion, but only one criterion, in the Chinese connoisseur's judgment. It can be the deciding factor in judgments of *authenticity*, where the distinction between original and copy may depend principally on a recognition of the 'hand' of the master. In judgments of *quality*, on the other hand, brushwork is the smallest—or, if you will, basic—component in what may be an unbroken series of strengths and strong relationships, from the single brushstroke through the forms and structures of form that the brushstrokes build, up to the whole composition, if the painting is to succeed completely."[51]

Wang was a major contributor to the permanent collections of Chinese calligraphy and paintings that are now in the major museums in the United States. Wang supported Fong's acquisitions of paintings from the Wang family collection and elsewhere for the University Art Museum at Princeton and The Metropolitan Museum of Art. Fong has written of Wang as the "heir to a long tradition of great private Chinese collectors, such as Hsiang Yuan-pien [Xiang Yuanbian] (1525–1590), Liang Ch'ing-piao [Liang Qingbiao] (1620–1691), Kao Shih-ch'i [Gao Shiqi] (1645–1704), and An Ch'i [An Qi] (1683–after 1742)."[52] Wang, however, was not the instrumental factor in Fong's connoisseurship training that he was to Cahill; Fong's experience with Chinese art began many years before his encounter with Wang, but clearly, his engagements with Wang over the years contributed greatly to his role as a curator-scholar-teacher. As Fong himself puts it, "Over the years C. C. [Wang] and I may have had disagreements about paintings, but we never once wrangled or struggled over any business dealings. We remained the easiest and best of friends."[53] Any in-depth study of Fong's scholarship will have to take this relationship into consideration.

In his important 1962 article "The Problems of Forgeries in Chinese Painting: Part One," Fong articulates the fundamental procedures in the authentication and dating of Chinese painting.[54] Following Panofsky's idea of an "organic circle," Fong is keenly aware of the methodological issues in connoisseurship, both in general and of Chinese painting in particular. As he told his audience at a symposium organized by the Asian Conservation Laboratory in 1963, "The question of authenticity, that is, the question of determining the date and origin of individual objects, raises many methodological problems.... The familiar paradox of the general versus the specific indeed broadens out and turns into an inevitable methodological circle when we attempt to define the style of an undated work in terms of a history of style or styles, while the latter can only be built on the basis of individual works . . . the question of the applicability of the Western art historical method to non-Western art is not easily answered."[55] Combining Western connoisseurship with traditional Chinese approaches, Fong convinced many of his dating and authentication. But he sometimes refrained from publishing the results of his research because, as he put it, "the subject has too much—and sometimes nothing but—sensational appeal."[56] As Warren I. Cohen puts it, "for evidence of Wen Fong's disruptive role in the late 1950s and early 1960s, ask the curator of Chinese art at any major museum."[57] At the same time, Fong's connoisseurship attracted a number of new collectors (such as Earl Morse and John B. Elliot) who often sought his advice in building their collections from scratch. For instance,

Morse gave us this account of how he and his family began their collecting adventure: "We did not expand our collection of painting further, until after our accidental meeting in 1964 with Dr. Wen Fong. . . . Professor Fong was writing a study of Wang Hui and wanted to see examples in our collection. Unfortunately, some years earlier, little realizing its historic and artistic value, I had been persuaded to sell our 1660 painting to a close friend of mine who had much admired it. When Professor Fong saw this picture at my friend's apartment, he insisted that I must have it back, and luckily, the sale was reversed (plus a handsome Ming painting as a bonus to my understanding friend)."[58] Several controversies concerned with acquisitions made by Fong during his groundbreaking tenure at The Metropolitan Museum of Art are fascinating topics for future research but are beyond the scope of this essay, because they require close examination, both of the documents on these acquisitions and of the long-term personal and professional relationships among Fong and two of the best-known twentieth-century Chinese artist-connoisseurs-dealers, Zhang Daqian, and C. C. Wang.

For his part, Cahill, when he was Curator of Chinese Art at the Freer Gallery, organized a symposium in New York in 1961 on the great "Chinese Art Treasures" exhibition from the National Palace Museum in Taiwan; the exhibition, which toured several major cities in the United States, was instrumental in attracting many future American historians of Chinese art. As Cahill put it, the symposium was "variously termed 'the Palace Museum Exhibition Post-mortem Symposium, the First International Convocation of Painting-worms, and the Conference for the Fragmentation of Chinese Painting Studies." It was attended by almost everyone studying or teaching Chinese painting (including Fong and Loehr) and some thirty graduate students from Harvard, Princeton, Michigan, Chicago, New York University, Columbia, and other universities. The opinions of the experts at the symposium on the dating and authenticity of many of the paintings in the exhibition were so different that one person was reported to have said, "I should think the graduate students present would be strongly tempted to turn to government service."[59] Cahill did not give up. He continued his wide-ranging connoisseurship of Chinese painting even after he left the Freer to take a professorship at Berkeley in 1965. In addition to his earlier efforts in putting his connoisseurship to use by helping Sirén prepare the famous (but now outdated) "Annotated Lists of Chinese Paintings,"[60] he published many of his new assessments of a vast number of paintings in collections around the world in *An Index of Early Chinese Painters and Paintings: T'ang, Sung, and Yuan* (1980) and continued his project on Ming and Qing paintings.[61] His curatorial experience at the Freer and his experience as a private collector have undoubtedly deepened his connoisseurship and at the same time contributed to his scholarship and teaching.[62]

Fong has long presented himself as an "insider," one who intimately understands Chinese culture and is well qualified to explain it to others. In several of his publications since the 1960s, Fong seems to have attempted to explain Chinese painting in terms of *Tao* or "spirit." For instance, in his major essay "Chinese Painting: A Statement of Method," he writes:

> As the real objective of the Chinese Painter was the "spirit" rather than the mere physical appearance of the thing, visible improvements in representational skill in the history of Chinese art were looked upon as mere incidental changes. . . . In fact, in Chinese art criticism, the importance of representational problems has been consistently played down, since the greatness of a painter was measured solely according to his success in attaining the fixed ideal of *chen*, the "real," which, in representing, in the last analysis, nothing other than the eternal Tao, or the "Way" of the universe, appears

> rather remote from the mere mechanics of picture-making.[63]

In his 1971 essay "How to Understand Chinese Painting" he asserts: "A Chinese looks at Chinese painting as one from within a continuous, self-renewing tradition. The use of the past is an integral part of every artistic activity. Since the Tao of painting is considered eternal and unchanging, it follows that being is more important than merely new ways of doing things."[64] Toward the end of the essay, he reiterates, "Since the Tao of painting was considered unchanging, for as long as traditional Chinese culture remains intact, ancient form-types proved to be effective means for creative transformations."[65]

Fong's approach is evident especially in his many statements on the relation between Chinese painting and calligraphy as well as in what he has written on calligraphy itself.

In his preface to *Calligraphy and the East Asian Book*, published on the occasion of an exhibition at the Art Museum at Princeton University, the late Frederick W. Mote (a sinologist who worked closely with Fong at Princeton and was instrumental in establishing the very first American doctoral program devoted exclusively to Chinese art) explained that Chinese calligraphy as an art form owes its special character to the nature of the Chinese script itself. He wrote, "Its forms are capable of a vast range of extension and variation; subject to the discipline of tradition and the inventiveness of personal style, for which alphabetic scripts in the Western tradition offer no counterpart."[66] "Calligraphy" (< Gk. *kalligraphia* < *kalos* beautiful + *graphein* to write) is actually a misnomer in reference to Chinese, because Chinese writing does not involve a simple alphabet of a few dozen symbols; it embraces some 60,000 distinct glyphs, giving it a diversity and complexity far greater than what is found in any other modern writing system. Sinologists have used the familiar term "calligraphy" simply to create a convenient English-language equivalent to the art of writing Chinese characters. The Chinese writing system is such a deep part of Chinese culture that there have been violent political movements associated with some historical attempts to standardize it. On the basis of reliable early texts on the art of calligraphy, it is evident that Chinese calligraphers, at least among the elites, experienced the challenge of an art in which "style" often functioned as "idea" about one millennium earlier than painters experienced it, as Cahill argues in his 1976 essay "Style as Idea in Ming-Ch'ing Painting."[67] Writing has also undergirded Chinese literati painting for more than a thousand years, because both calligraphy and painting are traditionally done with the same kind of brush and similar kinds of line production; Chinese paintings sometimes even incorporate writing into the composition. In China, at least among the classically educated elite class, calligraphy is often regarded as the most important and demanding in the hierarchy of the visual arts. Moreover, calligraphy, poetry, and painting are often mentioned together by Chinese literati as the *sanjue* or "Three Perfections" in Chinese cultural and artistic discourse.[68] Traditionally, the ideal of the Chinese literati has been to integrate all visual and verbal representations into individual works of art.

While Fong has wholeheartedly embraced this traditional Chinese concept, Cahill has on several occasions expressed considerable skepticism. For instance, he maintains that if we are ever to talk about the relationship between word and image in Chinese painting, we can not start by repeating the cliché that paintings are soundless poems and poems are painting in silence.[69] He also argues that, in general, in a Chinese painting the inscription or colophon (if it does not merely name the object depicted or record the circumstances of its creation) tends to superimpose meanings on the object that are not inherent in it, eroding its simple status as a useful or beautiful thing.[70] Cahill's position is similar to that of the modern Chinese scholar Qian Zhongshu, who, in an insightful essay titled "Chinese Poetry and Chinese Painting," first published about sixty years ago, argued convincingly that traditional Chinese poetry and painting have quite different criteria and that scholars must try to explain the difference.[71] Cahill's reservation about the traditional Chinese view of the affinity between painting and poetry, however, has not prevented him from devoting himself to exploring this fascinating aspect of Chinese cultural history, as seen in his book *The Lyric Journey* and several essays. On the other hand, Fong seems to have little, if any, reservation against the traditional Chinese view of the affinity between poetry and painting, and indeed has endeavored to explicate its various manifestations in several of his publications.[72]

There is no doubt that the study of Chinese art and cultural history should be enhanced by a deeper understanding of the history and aesthetics of Chinese calligraphy as a high art. For a long time, however, Chinese calligraphy was neglected by art historians in the West. In the Postwar United States, the cultural, scholarly, and artistic importance of the art of Chinese calligraphy has been featured in several major exhibitions, organized respectively by the Philadelphia Museum of Art and curated by Tseng Yu-ho Ecke (1971), the Yale University Art Gallery and curated by Shen C. Y. Fu and others (1977), and the Princeton University Art Museum and curated by Robert E. Harrist, Jr. and others (1999); both Fu and Harrist were Fong's students at Princeton.[73] In fact, under Fong's tutelage, his students at Princeton have completed many doctoral dissertations and articles on Chinese calligraphy.[74] The exhibitions, however, focused on the history of the art of pre-Modern Chinese calligraphy. Precisely because the aesthetic content of Chinese calligraphy lies beyond nature, though derived from it, Chinese calligraphy since the late nineteenth century has been less subject to criticism from reformers who sought to revitalize Chinese painting by means of importing "scientific realism" from the West. On the other hand, modern Chinese calligraphy, like modern Chinese painting, has undergone its own kind of transformation and demonstrated the vitality of the calligraphic traditions as well as the potential for their renewal. Modern Chinese calligraphers, like many of their contemporaries in painting, were confronted with an important challenge: to be creative while remaining true and responsive to the past. Compared with modern Chinese painting, which has only recently been getting the scholarly attention it deserves after its long neglect, modern Chinese calligraphy is an almost nonexistent field of research outside China. One promising approach would be to examine the extent to which modern Chinese calligraphy and painting developed together.

Fong's writings on the relationship between calligraphy and painting are extensive. For instance, in *Image of the Mind,* Fong writes:

> The common tool for both Chinese writing and painting is a brush tapering to a point.... Pliant yet resilient and capable of infinite shades of subtlety, the brush became a potent instrument in the hand of a master...at once a physical extension of the artist's arm and a magic wand that gives him access to the powers of creation. The very simplicity of the instrument, as well as the physical nature of its application, inevitably determined the characterization of its function in Chinese cosmogonic terms: the blank wall, silk, or paper came to represent an undifferentiated oneness; the first stroke establishes a primary *yin* and *yang* relationship; the second stroke combines with the first to create all kinds of new *yin* and *yang* situations, each successive combination begetting stroke after stroke, until the multitudinous are reconciled and reunited into a harmonious whole.[75]

Clearly Fong's early training in calligraphy has had a tremendous impact on his scholarly approach and on his teaching. For instance, he writes in his 1963 essay on method, mentioned above, "The close alliance between painting and calligraphy, both in theory and in practice, apparently conditioned the Chinese visualization from the very start. Imitation of nature always played a decidedly secondary role to the suggestion of life-rhythm, which is a quality both desired and attainable in the writing of the ideo-pictographic script as well as in the drawing of the conceptualized pictorial images."[76] He has continued to argue for the unchanging oneness of calligraphy and painting in Chinese art. Further, he wrote in 1993 in an essay titled "The Modern Chinese Art Debate": "Both Chinese writing and painting are based on a system of signifying graphic conventions. In Chinese painting, natural forms are expressed in graphic formulas, and a holistic vision is preserved: there is total interdependence and communicability between nature and art, representation and self-expression, words and images."[77] Indeed, calligraphy becomes, for Fong, an aspect of Chinese painting that is both essential to its understanding and a formidable roadblock to those who are uninitiated, especially the Westerner: "The key to Chinese painting lies in its calligraphic brushwork and its potential to express the individuality of the artist. Calligraphic expression as a subject of art history—how it works in Chinese painting and the belief that painting and calligraphy are the same—is not, however, easily understood by the Western viewers. The problem is that it appears not to meet the analytic requirement to situate art-historical phenomena within a material and socioeconomic contexts."[78] Fong's interpretation of post-Yuan literati painting in terms of calligraphy is exemplified in his discussion of Dong Qichang's mature landscapes, such as his *In the Shade of Summer Tree* from about 1635, now in the National Palace Museum:

> [It] displays a stylistic synthesis of the Tung Yüan [Dong Yuan] and Huang Kung-wang [Huang Gongwang] idioms. A bold and complex exercise in the study of rock and tree forms rendered *calligraphically,* the painting is conceived as the integration of abstract, cubic, dynamically expressive masses, achieved by the unifying breath of the artist's physical movements. The volumetric, three-dimensional masses are placed against a flat, two-dimensional picture surface. Thrusting boulders, twisting overhangs, and richly fused patterns of dense foliage rise and fall in a symphony of kinesthetic movement.... In his [Dong Qichang's] paintings, forms jumping backward and forward are melded into a single animated mass; elements of near, middle, and far distance collapse into one another, fusing together. Tung conceived landscape composition *calligraphically,* as massive abstract elements constructed like characters, with sweeping brush movements and carefully balanced architectonic units. Circulating through the interconnecting landscape forms, the artist's breath-momentum is the integrating principle—the principal that, in projecting the kinesthetic energies of the artist, would open the way for a new *abstract-expressionist* style in landscape painting [emphasis added].[79]

In *Between Two Cultures*, one of his most recent publications, Fong attempts to relate modern Chinese painting to Chinese calligraphy through copious examples of the works of calligraphers who painted and painters who were also well versed in calligraphy. This contrasts greatly with Cahill's most extensive treatment of modern Chinese painting, an extended essay "Wu Changshi and Qi Baishi," published so far only in Japanese translation, in which only cursory references to the importance of calligraphy to these modern painters can be found.[80] Given their different trainings and outlooks on

Chinese art in general, it is perhaps not surprising that Fong and Cahill would approach modern Chinese painting so differently.

Modern Chinese painting embodies the heroic story of constant renewal and reinvigoration of Chinese civilization amid rebellions, reforms, and revolutions, even if the process may appear confusing and bewildering. It also demonstrates the persistence of tradition and the limits of continuity and change in modern Chinese culture. Indeed, the history of Chinese painting and the writing of that history, both by Chinese scholars and by scholars working outside China, provide fertile ground for considering many issues in modern Chinese art history: "tradition" versus "modernization"; cultural nationalism and cultural politics in *guohua* or "national painting"; Chinese responses to Western art; Japanese influences on modern Chinese art; Chinese influences on modern Japanese art; and diverse paths taken by painters living under different political and economic conditions in the second half of the twentieth century (mainland China, Taiwan, Hong Kong). Unlike pioneering scholars on Chinese painting such as Michael Sullivan and Chu-tsing Li, Cahill's attitude toward modern Chinese painting can be characterized perhaps as ambivalent.[81] As mentioned above, he has written about modern Chinese painting; in addition to the extended essay "The Art of Wu Changshi and Qi Baishi," he has also published articles on the Shanghai School of Painting in general and Ren Xiong in particular and has contributed several essays or occasional exhibition brochures in support of several contemporary Chinese painters (such as Zhang Daqian, C. C. Wang, Chen Qikuan, Wu Guanzhong, and Liu Guosong, among others).[82] He expresses considerable reservation or ambivalence about the value of Chinese painting after the eighteenth century. In his introduction to *The Lyrical Journey*, Cahill explains why the book does not discuss Chinese painting after the eighteenth century: "I have sometimes found myself trying to explain to students or colleagues, why Japanese painting of recent centuries seems to me, on the whole, more interesting and original than Chinese painting of the same periods—why, for instance, no Chinese contemporary of Yosa Buson can match the freshness and emotional appeal of his best."[83] He further asserts: "Two recent exhibitions of eighteenth- and nineteenth-century painting, excellent as they have been as scholarly projects and well chosen as exhibitions, seem to me nevertheless only to confirm this view, containing some outstanding works but in the end unable to present the painting of these late periods as exhibiting levels of originality and other strengths equal to those of earlier periods."[84] In contrast, even though I am not aware of any writings by Fong concerning living Chinese painters, his book *Between Two Cultures* is clearly sympathetic toward modern Chinese painting and is optimistic about the future of Chinese painting.

But if Cahill has so far not paid as much attention as Fong has to Chinese calligraphy in his body of writing (even though he has not totally ignored calligraphy or brushwork in his writings on Chinese painting), he has often used analogies to musical performance to help his reader understand Chinese painting. For instance, he comments on the seventeenth-century artist Chen Hongshou:

> But of all the late Ming masters who manipulate the past in complex ways, Chen Hongshou is the most sensitive and sophisticated. Typically, his paintings are bitter-sweet evocations of old themes, themes that prove to be as moving as ever, even while Chen regards them a bit distantly and ironically. This bitter-sweet flavor distinguishes his variety of archaism from Lan Ying's deadpan imitations or Wu Bin's deformations of established landscape types. It is the same flavor one finds, perhaps, in some of the music of Ravel and Poulenc

> that plays similarly on rococo or romantic style, evoking feelings in the old way while establishing an emotional distance from them with astringent twists on the familiar harmonies.[85]

Cahill has often used episodes in music history to explain broader transitions in the history of Chinese painting. For instance, he maintains that the way early Yuan Dynasty literati artists reacted against the style of their predecessors, the artists in the imperial painting academy in the Southern Song Dynasty, is similar to how some early twentieth-century Western composers (such as Stravinsky) reacted against the overly romantic style of earlier composers such as Tchaikovsky. As he puts it, "My intension is to draw on familiar materials in the minds of many readers to sensitize them to familiar passages in unfamiliar materials, Chinese painting. . . . I know from my own experience, and from the responses of others, that this kind of analogy has 'worked' for a great many people, And, as with all such allusive writing, using such allusions can (if they aren't too hackneyed, or obscure, or other wise objectionable) work toward a sense of affinity between writer and reader: we are both people who are sensitive to *this*, now let's go on to *this*."[86] There is no doubt that Cahill's lifelong enthusiasm for music performance and his passion as a record collector have inspired the musical analogies in his writings on Chinese painting.

Working in the Postwar era in the United States in a relatively recent subfield of art history, Chinese painting scholars such as Fong and Cahill often feel compelled, consciously or unconsciously, to justify the importance of the study of Chinese painting. For instance, Fong often argued that Chinese painting history *anticipated* what happened in the West during the Modernist or Postmodernist periods. In his "Modern Chinese Art Debate" he writes, "Modern psychology, in exploring the unconscious and the subconscious, unseated the optical criteria in Western representation—that is, art as a mirror of external reality—and replaced these standards with mental ones.... It was at this juncture that the West began to think about the East. The mystic tradition of Zen Buddhism suggests a common need to break through the veil of appearances to a higher truth. From Kandinsky to Jackson Pollock, modern Western artists have talked about 'inner necessity' and spontaneous self-expression. Similar statements have long been made by ancient Chinese calligrapher-painters."[87] Fong's position is rather similar to that of Feng Zikai (1898–1975), who argued in an essay, published in 1930, for the "triumph" (*shengli*) of Chinese art in the "modern" (*xiandai*) era.[88] Quoting approvingly from Clement Greenberg's much-anthologized 1960 essay "Modernist Painting,"[89] Fong said to his audience at a meeting of the American Philosophical Society in 1998, "Chinese landscape painting of the fourteenth century finds a parallel in Western painting of the twentieth. . . . In his use of calligraphic brushwork, the Yuan landscapist, like the modernist painter in the West, created free-flowing rhythms on a flat picture surface, using not only brush and ink but the movement of his own body as a medium of expression."[90] And in an essay written in 2006, Fong still argues for the importance of Chinese art history to world art historical scholarship: "The study of visual structure—of lines, planes, and parallel perspective schemas—of Chinese art offers an example for art historians [in the West?] now seeking alternative visualities, which they consider crucial to modern art-historical studies."[91]

Another recurring idea in Fong's writing concerns the uses of Chinese art for world art history. It can be seen in his essay "Why Chinese Painting is History."[92] In it, he quotes Gombrich, Danto, and Foucault, and says, "What strikes us as the crucial point, with profound implications, is the 'end' of mimetic representation in art history both East and West. What comes after the 'end,' whether it be the seemingly limitless experimentation that we see in Western art or the continuing exploration of cyclical change and historical revival that we see in post-Song Chinese art, makes the history of art a totally different structure."[93] On the other hand, he seems uncomfortable with developments of multiculturalism and postmodernism in much of contemporary American culture: "The current debate on the ideas of 'culture' is, however troubled on the one hand by the ultimate nihilism of post-modernism, and on the other hand, by multicultural identity politics. My own view is that cross-cultural understanding must base itself on the rational universalism of sound and enlightened scholarship."[94]

American scholars of Chinese painting often compare Chinese painting and Western painting. Perhaps unconsciously following the examples of his predecessors and contemporaries, such as Jean Pierre Dubosc, Laurence Sickman, and Sherman Lee,[95] Cahill, in his 1960 book *Chinese Painting*, not only draws several general parallels between Chinese painting and Western art, but also agrees with Dubosc, who argued that Wang Yuanqi (1642–1715) shared with Cézanne a common approach to nature and painting. Cahill writes:

> Like Cézanne, Wang protested always that his art was founded in nature, and recommended constant observation of real scenery to his pupils; but also like Cézanne, he was absorbed with problems not so much representational as abstract—with, in his own words, "that which is produced by an interaction of the empty and the solid," with erecting new structures in a new space, with an intellectual reordering of the physical world. He was *not* interested in descriptive color (his use of simple warm and cool tones is another link with Cézanne), or in characterizing individual trees or rocks, or in effects of weather, season, light or shade, excepting a few perfunctory indications. It is important to realize

> all this in approaching Wang's works or those of a great many other literati painters; to stand before them and continue to talk, in the accepted manner, about the Chinese artist's profound penetration of nature, is much like maintaining that Cézanne's primary aim was to reveal the inner essence of his apples."[96]

By the time he wrote the 1967 catalog *Fantastics and Eccentrics in Chinese Painting* for a show he organized at the Asia House Gallery in New York City, he began to compare specific Western art styles or artists with seventeenth- and eighteenth-century Chinese painting. Following Lee, he characterized Mei Qing's style as "Rococo."[97] Toward the end of his essay, Cahill writes, "It is left to the reader now to assess the validity of the statement made at the beginning: that later Chinese painting, especially the kinds treated here, offers what may be the best parallel in the whole of world art to recent developments in Occidental painting."[98] To argue for the art historical and cultural significance of the transition from the Song to the Yuan Dynasties, Fong points out a similarity between that transition and what Foucault wrote about European history. As Fong puts it, "This shift from mimetic representation [after the end of the Southern Song Dynasty (1127–1279)] to calligraphic self-expression in fourteenth-century Yuan China bears a striking resemblance to the displacement of the representative by the expressive in Western modernism."[99] These comparisons, although they can be useful as pedagogical tools for ordinary American museum-goers, should be read with caution.

All art historians and most museum curators, however, must write. Panofsky, in his 1940 essay "The History of Art as a Humanistic Discipline," compares the connoisseur and the art historian: "The connoisseur might thus be defined as a laconic art historian, and the art historian as a loquacious connoisseur."[100] He then cautiously but somewhat optimistically prescribes the job of the art historian: "Because of the fact that the objects of art history come into being by a process of re-creative aesthetic synthesis, the art historian finds himself in a peculiar difficulty when trying to characterize what might be called the stylistic structure of the works with which he is concerned."[101] As Linda Seidel points out, "In his preface to the English translation of Max Friedländer's *Early Netherlandish Painting,* Panofsky remarked that 'The very object of the art historian's analysis and interpretation, much as he may strive for objectivity, comes into being in a process of subjective recreation.' Panofsky was speaking of Friedländer; is it possible to imagine that the distinguished scholar knew at the end that he was also writing about himself?"[102] Writing art history, apart from simply doing research in art history, raises a number of issues important for the discipline itself, as Paul Barolsky, David Carrier, and Ivan Gaskell have recently argued.[103] Furthermore, as David Summers has also reminded us in several recent essays, the language of art historical description is highly problematic.[104]

If description of art objects in an art historian's writings is by necessity interpretative, it makes sense for us now to turn to a comparison of their writing styles. Cahill is very proud of the critical reception of his 1960 book *Chinese Painting* (fig. 9) and values the comment that it reads like a novel.[105] As a matter of fact, *Chinese Painting* has inspired some of its readers (such as Martin Powers) to enter the academic field of Chinese art and Chinese painting.[106] Cahill's description of a painting by Ma Yuan (ca. 1190–1230) titled *Walking on a Mountain Path in Spring* (in the National Palace Museum in Taipei; fig. 10) very richly shows the painting: "In delicate gradations of ink tone, he opens behind the sharply drawn foreground group a middle distance bounded by the dim silhouettes of leafy trees, and a limitless void beyond that. The gaze of the viewer is inevitably drawn back into this void, moving from the material world to one without substance; and the universal human proneness to associate space with spirituality gives to the experience a touch of the mystical."[107] Cahill describes the emotional experience that the viewer feels while looking at the painting—how the painting affects the viewer. His use and placement of adjectives helps justify Cahill's reputation for writing like a novelist. Cahill is aware that his writing has been subject to criticism, that he would push his materials around a little "to make them neater and to give them a certain dramatic force and continuity." Cahill admits that he "was always, from the beginning, meant to be a writer." To defend his approach, Cahill explains that his style makes his writing readable, and "if people can read it easily, it means that you can reach a lot of people you couldn't reach otherwise."[108]

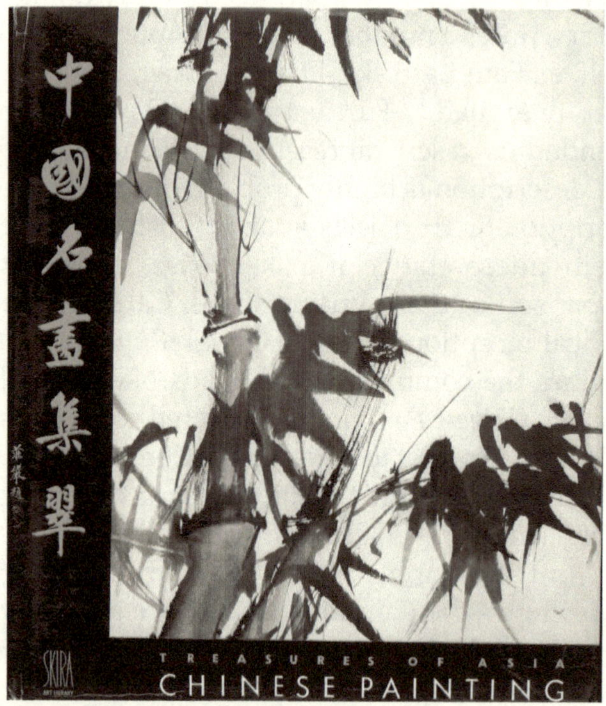

Figure 9. Cover of *Chinese Painting* by James Cahill (Geneva: Editions d'Art Albert Skira, 1960).

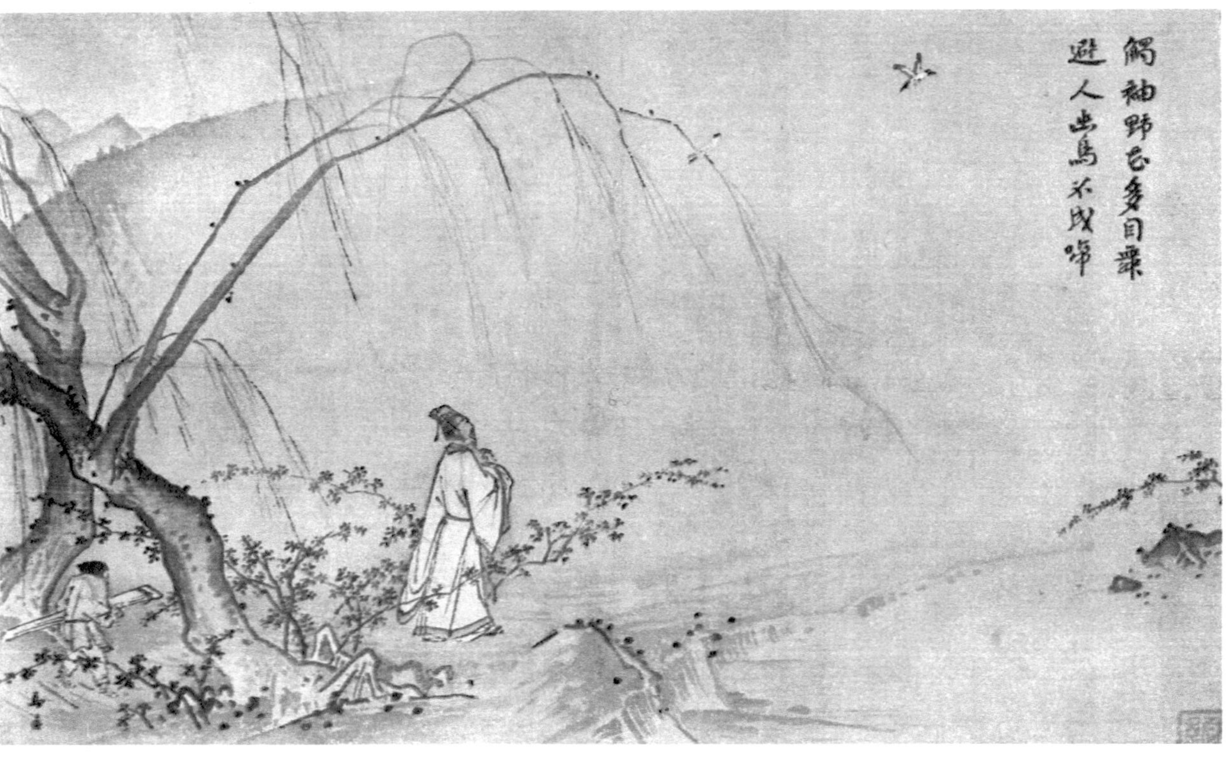

Figure 10. Ma Yuan (ca. 1190–1230), *Walking on a Mountain Path in Spring*, album leaf. National Palace Museum, Taipei.

Cahill's elegance can be seen again in his writings on Yuan painting in the 1976 book *Hills Beyond a River: Chinese Painting of the Yuan Dynasty, 1279–1368.* Cahill gracefully describes a fan painting on silk by Zhu Derun (1294–1365), a follower of the Li–Guo (Li Cheng and Guo Xi) tradition, by taking the reader on vivid journey through the painting: "The foreground plane is marked clearly by sharply silhouetted trees; other trees, drawn in dimmer ink stone, occupy a plane that is slightly more distant; the foggy region beyond is indicated only by a stream that flows out of it, dropping through a succession of shallow-stepped pools."[109] Again, Cahill's use of adjectives to describe the painting puts the reader into it, and conducts the viewer along a tour.

Calling Fan Kuan's *Travelers among Streams and Mountains* (in the National Palace Museum in Taipei; fig. 11) a "conceptual vision of the macrocosmic universe," Fong describes the painting in a compositional manner, illustrating how the artist renders the piece. Fong provides the reader with a structural analysis of this painting; he explains, "Although these great mountain forms are simple, generalized triangular masses with enveloping parallel folds, the depiction, with its pointillistic 'raindrop' texture pattern and scrubby foliage on the peaks, vividly captures the landscape peculiarities of Shanxi in northwest China."[110] In this sentence, we see Fong's knowledge of painting composition and his appreciation for technique in his description of the texture. Fong show us again his attention to composition and analysis when he explains how the painting's "vertical composition proceeds from front to back in three separate stages—the foreground with its minute human figures, the middle distance with massive trees, and the background with towering mountains."[111] Fong's explanation of the form of the painting is produced very technically, dividing the aspects of perspective that the artist incorporates into the painting.

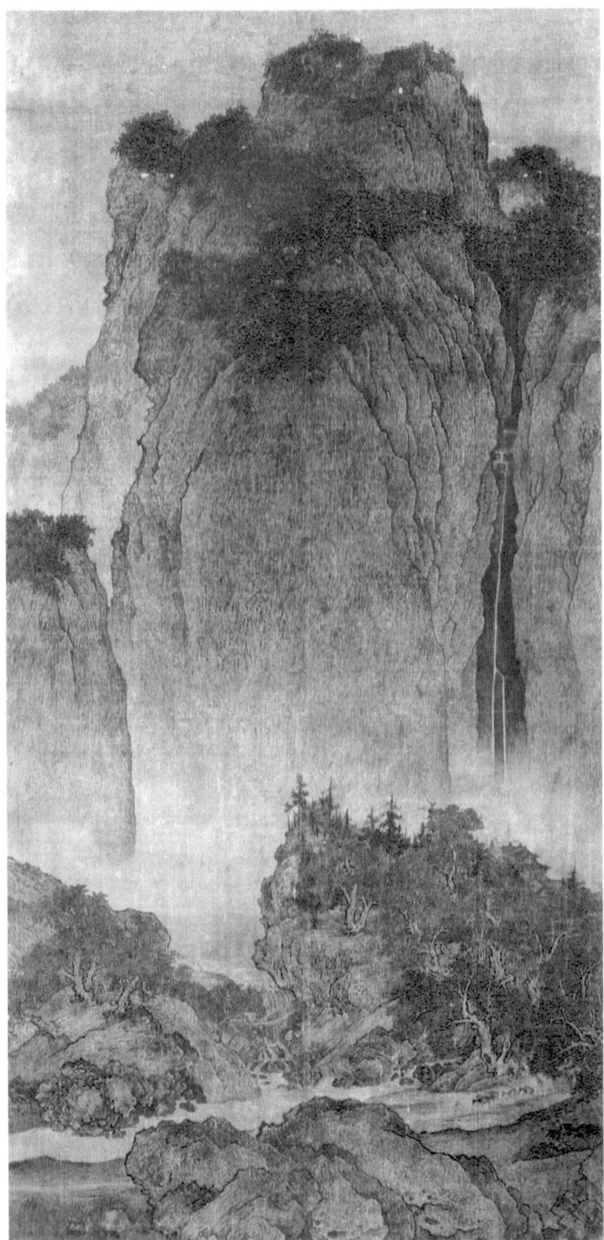

Figure 11. Fan Kuan (early eleventh century), *Travelers among Streams and Mountains*, hanging scroll. National Palace Museum, Taipei.

Cahill's narrative on the painting and its structure is written in a different manner than that of Fong. He begins his passage on the painting by implying its heroic manner, stating: "It is a vision so compelling that questions of subjectivity or objectivity, pursuit of likeness or the rejection of it, become irrelevant; the world of the painting seems neither to reflect faithfully the physical universe nor to overlay it with a human interpretation, but to have an absolute existence in itself."[112] Cahill has already impressed the majestic presence of the piece in the reader, highlighting a quality that Fong summarized in one sentence. He moves the viewer through the painting, describing the "dark, mysterious cleft, a waterfall drops as a thin streak of white." Cahill goes on further to detail how the "mists thrown up at its base drift through the valley, adding a further impression of soaring height to the cliff by obscuring its base."[113] While Cahill may overemphasize the qualities of the painting, it brings a flow to his words; he explains the majesty and significance of the piece and takes the reader into the painting, narrating his way through the image and producing the idealized concept of what the artist is depicting.

Cahill conducts the viewer into the world of Guo Xi's masterwork *Early Spring* (dated 1072; fig. 12), in the National Palace Museum in Taipei, by first calling attention to its opulence and then by leading the reader through the sections of the painting. Once Cahill moves past the lavishness of the painting, he explains how the "earth forms, swollen to exaggerated rotundity, fuse and interpenetrate like parts of a vast organism."[114] This sentence and Cahill's use of adjectives to illustrate the painting is his trademark. His novel-like evocation inculcates empathy in his audience.

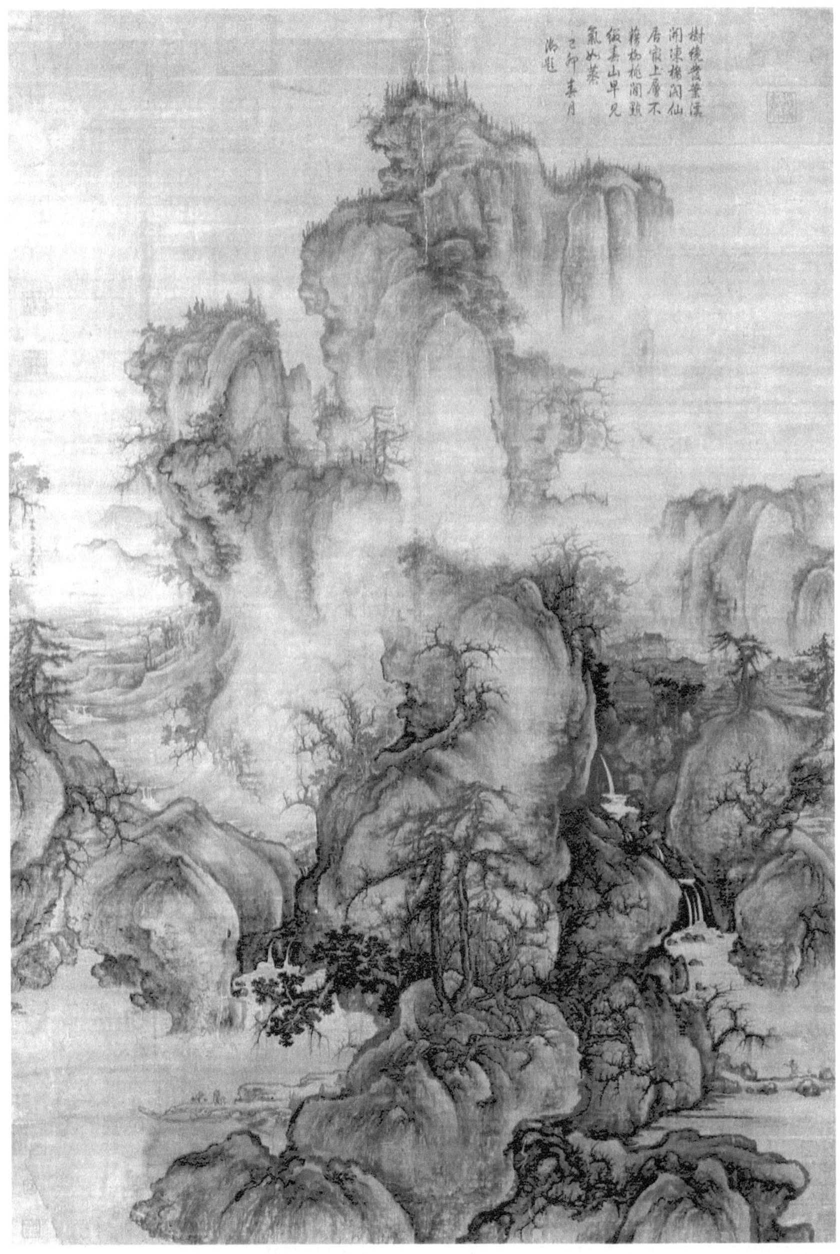

Figure 12. Guo Xi, *Early Spring*, dated 1072, hanging scroll. National Palace Museum, Taipei.

Fong also approaches this painting in a unique style. Fong does not attempt to fascinate the reader with the opulence of the painting, as Cahill does. As noted above, Fong's interpretations rely on his conscious effort to employ technique and structural analysis. Fong depicts the painting much more simply: "*Early Spring* . . . with its wildly twisting, turning peaks, is a landscape of the imagination. The brush technique and use of ink are rich and extravagant, as Kuo Hsi [Guo Xi] boldly casts aside precision of expression in favor of a dramatic interpenetration of solids and voids, the landscape elements simultaneously emerging from and receding behind dense, wafting mists. A highly complex landscape, *Early Spring,* though it suggests great depth remains a composite of compartmentalized pockets of space."[115]

Here we see Fong explain that the painting is a "landscape of the imagination"; end of sentence. He does not overamplify the painting's idea of majesty, but recognizes the piece's genius. He does however imply that the strongest aspects of the painting are its techniques in brushwork and its compositional form. In doing so, Fong again points out details that the connoisseur would notice in production, by stating the subtle nuances that make this work uniquely Guo Xi's. In his description of Northern Song landscape paintings, Fong further breaks down the technical aspects that are produced in the works of Guo Xi. Fong explains that "In Kuo Hsi's [Guo Xi's] mountain forms, outlines, interior texture strokes, and modeling ink washes are thoroughly fused; thickening and thinning brushstrokes, in a whole range of ink tones from charcoal black to transparent gray, are applied simultaneously, so that the different tones of ink run into each other to create the wet and blurry effects of the mist."[116] Fong describes not only how the artist creates his forms with his brushwork but also the way the artist infuses his color schemes, and the effect of this procedure on the painting.

In Fong's account of the painting *Cloudy Mountains* by Fang Congyi in The Metropolitan Museum of Art, we see first-hand his role as connoisseur. Fong associates Fang's style in this piece with another artist, describing how "Fang Ts'ung-i [Fang Congyi] combines Fan Kuan's raindrop texture pattern with round Mi-dots and wet ink wash."[117] The comparison shows how Fong has trained his eye, how he can distinguish in one master's style the works of another.

Fong develops the comparison further: "Fang Ts'ung-i [Fang Congyi] in this remarkable handscroll uses very few of the round, horizontal brush-dots that characterize the Mi [Mi Fu and Mi Youren] idiom."[118] Thus, Fong is clearly attuned to the style of these artists. He recognizes their similarity, but also differentiates their styles, the distinctive aspects of their craft. Fong explains in detail how "Fang's secret in making the mountains appear to levitate lies in the kinesthetic brush-strokes that, wound up as if in a revolving rhythm, give the mountains an expressive liveliness that almost defies their physical structure."[119] Fong describes to the reader what the artist did in his painting to make the painting more alive, an attribution that could be made only if one were highly trained in the visual analysis of a painting and had familiarity with how the brush works.

Cahill describes the same painting in a greatly different fashion. Cahill structures adjectives and analogies to carry the reader through the painting, somewhat romanticizing how the artist created his work: "Almost immediately, however, the artist carries us back to distant hills, of which only the tops can be seen above a fog; and then, with a sudden wrenching of space, as if through a badly misused zoom lens, pulls us forward again to the middle ground, where a ridge rises abruptly from the water. On its crest, extending over most of the rest of the scroll, are projections, jagged in outline, which take part in a free vertical movement, more like clouds blown by wind than solid matter."[120]

Obviously, they did not have zoom lenses in the fourteenth century, but Cahill's description allows the reader to envision the approach of the artist and the painting's illusionistic qualities. Cahill refers to the artist's use of perspective when he talks about how the artist carries the viewer into the background of the hills, not in the way the artist used a linear development for this purpose, but in the way that Fang's painting created the illusion of distance.

In contrast to Fong's persistent emphasis on the uniqueness of Chinese painting, especially in its use of calligraphy, an explication often informed by his familiarity with the theories and practices in Western art historical enterprise, Cahill has in recently years taken a quite different direction. "Today . . . I would argue in the other direction, that maybe the time has come to be a bit more critical of Chinese ideas, to realize that they are limited historically, that they have their own contexts and the people who espouse them or express them have their own reasons for doing so: it's not something that happens purely in a vacuum. And that we should not take them as the final truth, in other words."[121] Indeed, since the 1980s, he has moved away from his teacher Loehr and espoused a more contextual "alternative" approach. At a panel at the College Art Association annual conference in 1985, he said:

> By "alternative" I mean: other than the standard ways with which we are familiar, from a great many articles, dissertations, etc.: tracing sources of style, and influences; seeing styles in developmental sequences; writing about the expressive value of a style—that is, what the artist appears to be expressing by creating or adopting this style (always thinking of it as reflecting something the artist is feeling—style as a medium of personal expression). In the purest state of the enterprise, style becomes an element in the closed system we call style history. My teacher Max Loehr does this

> on the highest level. . . . To take the stands that I think some of us will take today is not in any sense to renounce this enterprise: it is, however, to turn away from its self-imposed limitations, its exclusivity, its attempts sometimes to discredit the alternatives by suggesting that they aren't really worth doing, or that the time hasn't yet come to do them, and so forth. Loehr has always argued that history and other outside factors, even circumstances in the lives of the artists, were more or less irrelevant to the work of art. It will be no surprise if I say that on that issue I broke with him a long time back, while continuing to have the highest respect for his ideas and his contributions.

In one of several provocative lectures he delivered across China in the fall of 1986, he criticized the "decline" of artistic quality in some work of even such famous artists as Shitao and Qi Baishi when the paintings become sloppy in the name of the "sketching ideas" (*xieyi*); the lectures were later published as an essay titled "*Hsieh-i* as a Cause of Decline in Later Chinese Painting History," the afterword to *Three Alternative Histories of Chinese Painting* based on his Franklin D. Murphy Lectures delivered at the University of Kansas.[122] Furthermore, in his Murphy Lectures, he advocates that, in addition to style-history and documentary modes of study, we consider these questions: "For whom were the paintings done? How were they commissioned or purchased? When they were used as gifts, who gave them, and to whom, and on what occasion? And, more importantly, how do all these circumstances affect, and help to explain, the artist's choices of subjects and styles?"[123]

Over the years, as Fong focused much of his attention on building the collections of Chinese paintings at The Metropolitan Museum of Art and Princeton, he increasingly accepted the traditional authorship or dating of Chinese painting, as one can see in some of the works published in *Image of the Mind,* while Cahill has raised doubts about some of Fong's acquisitions. As Roderick Whitfield, who studied with Fong in the 1960s, has recently recalled: "It was almost shocking, later, when Fong became adviser to the Metropolitan, to discover from him that there were other authentic paintings by Ni Zan (1301–1374) than the *Rongxi Studio* of 1372, then a cornerstone of our study of the Four Masters of late Yuan."[124] Nevertheless, both Cahill and Fong are still committed to the enterprise of making sure that we have a large body of authentic Chinese paintings to write a history of Chinese painting. For instance, in a lecture in 2006, "Chinese Art History and the Modern Universal Museum: On the Benefits of Belatedness,"[125] Fong began by quoting approvingly Cahill's 2005 article on the "History and Post-History" of Chinese Painting:

> Our generation [of Chinese painting historians] . . . can be charged with having collectively failed to build on the achievements of the pioneers sufficiently to construct a history as solid and detailed as has been done (over a much longer period, to be sure) for European painting. Scholars in the generation after ours are on the whole disinclined to take part in such a project, or even are methodologically opposed to it. And so the great work of putting together such a history, which should be the basis upon which further studies of early Chinese painting can be undertaken, has been discredited before it has been accomplished. It is as though we had abandoned the practice of architecture before we had built our city.[126]

As Fong himself says, "When I say that all my writings are telling the same story with different pictures, I mean simply that as a working art historian I am compelled by the need to develop a narrative—a 'story,' if you will—for Chinese art history."[127] Thus, we can see that, in the end, both Fong and Cahill have been working to establish a grand narrative for the history of Chinese painting, even if the shape of that narrative is bound to be different.

While Cahill has not given up on issues of connoisseurship, he has since the 1980s focused on social, economic, and gender-related issues in Chinese painting. This is exemplified by his 1991 Bampton Lectures at Columbia University, which appeared in 1994 as *The Painter's Practice: How Artists Lived and Worked in Traditional China.* Other art-related topics in the Bampton Lectures series were given by such luminaries as Lewis Mumford, Lionello Venturi, Anthony Blunt, and John Summerson. The book covers a time span from the Six Dynasties to the late nineteenth century and focuses on the socioeconomic aspects of the context in which Chinese painting was created and consumed. His main goal in this book is, like many of his other controversial writings, to look for "a more real-world China behind the partial or deceptive vision," which, he believes, had been created by the Chinese literati and perpetuated by many sinologists and historians of Chinese art who tended to accept unquestioningly what they read. Perhaps so as not to offend too many of his colleagues, he adopted a cautious tone: his use of Western art historical parallels to Chinese practice are drawn without "any intention of presenting this book as a comparative study"; he wants only to "make the Chinese case less strange."[128] He makes selective use of insights from scholars working in the European tradition of art history and cultural history, for example Svetlana Alpers, Michael Baxandall, Pierre Bourdieu, Norman Bryson, Michel Foucault, and others, but he remains clearly aware of the pitfalls in his approach and carefully qualifies what he wants to accomplish: "Without undervaluing the self-revelatory capacity of art, one can play against other, more earth-bound and socially conditioned functions, and try to understand how the one impinged on the other. Without slipping into a reductive approach, one can aim at a more clear-eyed recognition of the true situation, sometimes the predicament, of the artist behind the work, the kind of recognition I will attempt to arrive at in these pages."[129] From *The Compelling Image* to his latest book project, *Pictures for Use and Pleasure: Vernacular Painting in High Qing China*,[130] it is evident that he is very much open to multiple approaches to Chinese painting studies.[131]

One can certainly appreciate Cahill's intellectual honesty and willingness to change his mind in *The Painter's Practice*: "I was myself, for my sins, one of the pioneering foreign exponents of the literati-amateur painting ideal as a key to understanding certain kinds of Chinese painting. Now, forty years later, I return to the same set of problems, but from a very different perspective, arguing instead that what seems remarkable now is the degree to which this ideal has been permitted to pervade our own interpretation of Chinese painting."[132] Cahill, however, does not blindly embrace all the latest trends or fashions in the field of Chinese painting in particular and art history in general. Thus, in his remarks on methodology at the Conference on the History of Painting in East Asia held in 2002 in Taipei, he cautioned us: "To move from some older methodological position into a new one, however intellectually dazzling the new one may appear, should not be thought of as any kind of progress, except insofar as it entails also a move into somewhat better scholarship—better informed, wider ranging, deeper probing, more precise, more enlightening. . . . It is . . . methodological presumptuousness more than methodological backwardness, that makes me uneasy about the future of our field."[133]

For his part, Fong has admitted that even his own "ideas of stylistic analysis necessarily evolved and changed" and that in his "life-long endeavor to authenticate and date ancient Chinese paintings," both his "successes" and "mistakes" in connoisseurship "depended on the questions" he asked.[134] It is humbling to hear Fong recount his evolving and changing understanding of the history of Chinese painting, exemplified by his study of the work of Qian Xuan.[135] In the end he sees himself as an art historian pursuing the discovery of "meaning," acting in his relationship to a work of art in the same way as so many Chinese artists and poets. As he puts it, "I think that meaning is inherent in the creative act and that critical response (*shenhui*, or 'spiritual response') is a re-creative act, successful only when the right questions, or problems, are posed. This process of re-experiencing the meaning of an art object has guided all my work as an art historian."[136] In his latest book, *On Writing Chinese Art History: Calligraphy and Painting as One*,[137] he will return to one of his favorite themes.

The body of writings Cahill and Fong have authored over the past fifty years suggests that their different approaches are directly related to their training and backgrounds. My goal in this essay has been to reflect on how these differences embody the history of our field. As we reflect on the tremendous contributions they have made to our common pursuit, let us not forget what Panofsky wrote more than fifty years ago: "We are chiefly affected by that which we allow to affect us; and just as natural science involuntarily selects what it calls the phenomena, the humanities involuntarily select what they call the historical facts" (1940); and, "Even when dealing with the remote past, the historian cannot be entirely objective" (1950).[138] Cahill and Fong have shaped, each in his own way, the field of Chinese painting studies in Postwar America. Each has his share of followers and critics.[139] In the historiography of Chinese painting in Postwar America, as exemplified by the writings of Cahill and Fong, we can reflect on the institutional power of knowledge and the ways in which knowledge was framed, spoken, and transmitted; it can also help us explore the extent to which discourse is contingent and never disinterested while often presenting itself as intact and objective.[140]

One of the most interesting formats in Chinese painting is undoubtedly the handscroll. It consists normally of a title sheet or frontispiece, the painting itself, and an inscription and colophon panel for the artist and others to write their comments either at the time of the completion of the painting or anytime afterward; often the comments written by later viewers can be added to the scroll, as often as needed, on the space either already provided by the existing scroll or additional space provided by remounting the scroll. Thus, a handscroll can contain comments written over several centuries; in each generation, the viewers will have the opportunity to read all the comments made by previous viewers of the same handscroll over the centuries before adding their own comments. The typical Chinese handscroll thus is not fixed and is constantly modified. My sketch of the work of Cahill and Fong in this essay perhaps should also be regarded as merely one of the comments added at the end of an imaginary long handscroll occupied by their many-faceted work for the past fifty years. I hope that others will join me in writing more comments, not only on Cahill and Fong but also on other scholars on Chinese painting in Postwar America, from different perspectives. But perhaps the most appropriate ending of this essay would be for me to quote from a poem ("Written on the Wall of the Xilin Temple") by the great poet-calligrapher-painter Su Shi: "How can we recognize the real face of Mt. Lu/When we are so deep in the mountains?"

Notes

An earlier version of this essay was presented at the panel "The Middle Path? Style and Cultural History in Chinese Painting Scholarship" organized by Kathleen Ryor and Jennifer Purtle for the annual conference of the College Art Association in February 2007 in New York City. I am especially indebted to the following previous studies on the historiography of Chinese art in general and Chinese painting studies in particular: John A. Pope, "Sinology or Art History: Notes on Method in the Study of Chinese Art," *Harvard Journal of Asiatic Studies* 10, nos. 3–4 (December 1947): 388–417; Wen C. Fong, "The Study of Chinese Painting in the West," *National Palace Museum Research Quarterly* 4, no. 2 (Winter 1986): 1–16; Jerome Silbergeld, "Chinese Painting Studies in the West: A State-of-the-Field Article," *Journal of Asian Studies* 46, no. 4 (1987): 849–97; James Cahill, "Five Notable Figures in the Early Period of Chinese Painting Studies," paper for the annual conference of the College Art Association, February 1991, Washington, D.C.; Xue Yongnian, *Shuhua shilun conggao* (Chengdu: Sichuan jiaoyu chubanshe, 1992), 455–97; Hong Zaixin, ed., *Haiwai Zhongguo hua yanjiu wenxuan* (Shanghai: Renmin meishu chubanshe, 1992); Warren I. Cohen, *East Asian Art and American Culture* (New York: Columbia University Press, 1992); Hong Zaixin, "The Verbal/Visual Controversy in Contemporary Chinese Academia: A Chinese Scholar's Perspective," paper for the conference "Stones from Other Mountains: Chinese Painting Studies in Postwar America," November 2005, University of Maryland, College Park.

1 James Cahill, "Wen Fong and Me," paper for "A Bridge to Heaven: A Symposium on East Asian Art in Honor of Professor Wen C. Fong," Princeton University, April 1–2, 2006, 1. The paper can be found on Cahill's website, www.jamescahill.info, where it is listed as CLP 155.

2 Wen C. Fong, *Reflections on Chinese Art History* (Princeton: P. Y. and Kinmay W. Tang Center for East Asian Art, Princeton University, 2006), 17.

3 For obvious reasons, this essay will not touch directly on sensational topics, such as the controversy about *Riverbank* (a hanging scroll at The Metropolitan Museum of Art), which Fong attributed to Dong Yuan (active 930s–960s); Cahill, on the other hand, has maintained that it is "a modern fabrication produced by the painter and collector-dealer Zhang Daqian." See two articles in Judith G. Smith and Wen C. Fong, eds., *Issues of Authenticity in Chinese Painting* (New York: The Metropolitan Museum of Art, 1999): James Cahill, "The Case Against *Riverbank*: An Indictment in Fourteen Counts," 13–63, and Wen C. Fong, "*Riverbank:* From Connoisseurship to Art History," 259–91. For Cahill's public discussions with others, see, for example, Richard Barnhart, James Cahill, and Howard Rogers, *The Barnhart-Cahill-Rogers Correspondence, 1981* (Berkeley:

Institute of East Asian Studies, University of California, 1982) and Richard Barnhart, James Cahill, Maxwell Hearn, and Stephen Little, "The Tu Chin Correspondence, 1994–95," *Kaikodo Journal* 5 (Autumn 1997): 8–62. Cf. Jason Kuo, ed., *Perspectives on Connoisseurship of Chinese Painting* (Washington, D.C.: New Academia Publishing, 2008).

4 (New York: Columbia University Press, 1994).

5 For example, see Linda Brodkey, *Academic Writing as Social Practice* (Philadelphia: Temple University Press, 1987); Walter Nash, ed., *The Writing Scholar: Studies in Academic Discourse* (Newbury Park, Calif.: Sage, 1990). For examples of this genre of writing, see Mark Rollins, ed., *Danto and His Critics* (Oxford: Blackwell, 1993) and Daniel Herwitz and Michael Kelly, eds., *Action, Art, History: Engagements with Arthur C. Danto* (New York: Columbia University Press, 2007).

6 For the contested meaning of the "West," see Martin Powers, "Reexamining the 'West'," in *Chinese Painting in the Twentieth-Century: Creativity in the Aftermath of Tradition*, ed. CaoYiqiang and Fan Jingzhong (Hangzhou: Zhejiang renmin meishu chubanshe, 1997), 465–96.

7 Presenters included James Cahill, Hung Wu, and Jonathan Hay, and the discussant was Anne Clapp.

8 (Dubuque: Kendall/Hunt Publishing, 2000). Participants included Richard Edwards, James Cahill, Jerome Silbergeld, Martin Powers, Julia Andrews, and Julia Murray.

9 Jason C. Kuo, ed., *Discovering Chinese Painting: Dialogues with Art Historians* (Dubuque: Kendall/Hunt Publishing, 2006); participants included Richard Edwards, James Cahill, Michael Sullivan, Jerome Silbergeld, Martin Powers, Julia Andrews, Julia Murray, Craig Clunas, and James Elkins. Subsequent references to *Discovering Chinese Painting* are from this second and expanded edition.

10 Unfortunately, several eminent scholars of Chinese painting (such as Nelson I. Wu and Wai-kam Ho) have passed away and with them, their stories.

11 *CAA 2007 Call for Participation* (New York: College Art Association, 2006), 18.

12 The contributions by several generations of scholars to the field can be seen in Silbergeld, "State-of-the-Field" (above, unnumbered n.); Xue Yongnian, *Shuhua shilun conggao* (Chengdu: Sichuan jiaoyu chubanshe, 1992), 455–97; Kuo, *Discovering Chinese Painting*.

13 See, for example, National Palace Museum, *Proceedings of the International Symposium on Chinese Painting* (Taipei: National Palace Museum, 1970); Anhui sheng wenxue yishu yanjiusuo, ed., *Lun Huangshen zhu huapai wenji* (Shanghai: Shanghai renmin meishu chubanshe, 1987); Wai-kam Ho, ed., *The Century of Tung Ch'i-ch'ang, 1555–1636*, 2 vols. (Kansas

City, Mo.: The Nelson-Atkins Museum of Art, 1992); Graduate Institute of Art History, National Taiwan University, *Taiwan 2002 Conference on the History of Painting in East Asia* (Taipei: Graduate Institute of Art History, National Taiwan University, 2002); Alfreda Murck and Wen C. Fong, eds., *Words and Image: Chinese Poetry, Calligraphy, and Painting* (New York: The Metropolitan Museum of Art; Princeton: Princeton University Press, 1991); Smith and Fong, *Issues* (above, n. 3).

14 For a discussion of some of these people, see David B. Honey, *Incense at the Altar: Pioneering Sinologists and the Development of Classical Chinese Philology* (New Haven: American Oriental Society, 2001). See also Martin Kern, "The Emigration of German Sinologists, 1933–1945: Notes on the History and Historiography of Chinese Studies," *Journal of the American Oriental Society* 118 (1998): 507–29.

15 Loehr studied with Ludwig Bachhofer (1894–1976); Bachhofer studied with Heinrich Wölfflin (1864–1945).

16 (London: Lund Humphries, 1956–58).

17 For additional information on Cahill's biography, see "James Cahill" in Kuo, *Discovering Chinese Painting*, 35–95; and four articles in *Orientations* 37, no. 1 (January/February 2006): "A Song of Experience: James Cahill by Himself," 41; Howard Rogers, "Jim Cahill at Eighty,"42–54; Julia F. Andrews, "The Lure of Cahill's California," 54–55; Arnold Chang, et al., "James Cahill: Scholar, Teacher and Friend," 56–57.

18 (New York and Tokyo: Weatherhill, 1976, 1978, 1982).

19 *The Spirit of Man in Asian Art: Being the Charles Eliot Norton Lectures Delivered in Harvard University, 1933–34* (Cambridge, Mass.: Harvard University Press, 1936).

20 See, for example, Susan E. Nelson's review in *Journal of Asian History* 16, no. 2 (1982); 154–55; Wen C. Fong's review in *The Art Bulletin* 68, no. 3 (September 1982): 504–8; Zheng Peikai's review in *Jiuzhou xuekan* [*Chinese Culture Quarterly*] 1, no. 1 (Autumn 1986): 75–98.

21 In *The Mozartian Historian: Essays on the Works of Joseph R. Levenson*, ed. Maurice Meisner and Rhoads Murphy (Berkeley: University of California Press, 1976): 137–65. "Influence" is a very loaded term and must be defined when used; see, for example, the extensive discussion in Göran Hermeren, *Influences in Art and Literature* (Princeton: Princeton University Press, 1975). As Michael Baxandall, one of Cahill's favorite art historians, puts it, "'Influence' is a curse of art criticism primarily because of its wrong-headed grammatical prejudice about who is the agent and who the patient"; see his *Patterns of Intension: On the Historical Explanation of Pictures* (New Haven: Yale University Press, 1985), 58–62.

22 Benjamin Schwartz, "The Intellectual History of China; Preliminary Reflections," in John K. Fairbank, ed., *Chinese Thought and Institutions* (Chicago: University of Chicago, 1957), 15–30.

23 John Beldon Scott, Larry Silver, and Suzanne Preston Blier, "Distinguished Lifetime Achievement Award for Writing on Art," *CAA News* 32, no. 2 (March 2007): 9.

24 Additional biographical information can be seen in Roderick Whitfield, "Streams and Mountains without End: The Far Vision of Wen Fong," *Orientations* 37, no. 2 (March 2006): 117–23; Maxell K. Hearn, "Wen C. Fong and Asian Art at the Metropolitan Museum," *Orientations* 37, no. 2 (March 2006): 124–31.

25 Yang Renkai, *Guobao chenfou lu: Gugong sanyi shuhua jianwen kaolue* (Shanghai: Renmin meishu chubanshe, 1991), 245; Fang Wen [Wen C. Fong], Preface to *Xinyin* (Chinese translation of *Images of the Mind: Selections from the Edward L. Elliott Family and John B. Elliott Collections of Chinese Calligraphy and Painting at The Art Museum, Princeton University* [1984]), trans. Li Wekun (Xi'an: Shaanxi renmin meishu chubanshe, 2004), 1. A pair of Fong's calligraphy couplet, probably from the 1940s, is in the Princeton University Art Museum (2006-32 a-b); stylistically, it resembles Li Jian's calligraphy couplet in Wang Chaobin, ed., *Minguo shufa* (Zhengzhou: Henan meishu chubanshe, 1989), 152. For a recent study on Wang Juchang's calligraphy, see Tang Shengtian and Xiao Hua, *Wang Juchang shufa yishu jiexi* (Nanjing: Jiangsu meishu chubanshe, 2001).

26 Fong, *Reflections* (above, n. 2), 16.

27 For example, see Wen C. Fong, *Between Two Cultures: Late-Nineteenth- and Twentieth-Century Chinese Paintings from the Robert H. Ellsworth Collection in the Metropolitan Museum of Art* (New York: The Metropolitan Museum of Art; New Haven and London: Yale University Press, 2001), 178–99.

28 In addition to *Between Two Cultures*, his major books and catalogues include *Sung and Yuan Painting* (1973); *Summer Mountains: The Timeless Landscape* (1975); *Returning Home: Tao-chi's Album of Landscapes and Flowers* (1976); *Images of the Mind: Selections from the Edward L. Elliott Family and John B. Elliott Collections of Chinese Calligraphy and Painting at The Art Museum, Princeton University* (1984); *Beyond Representation: Chinese Painting and Calligraphy, 8th–14th Century* (1992); and, with James C. Y. Watt and others, *Possessing the Past: Treasures from the National Palace Museum, Taipei* (1996). For an updated bibliography, see "Bibliography of Wen C. Fong," in Fong, *Reflections* (above, n. 2), 75–87.

29 *Harvard Magazine* 110, no. 6 (July–August 2008), 48.

30 Kuo, *Discovering Chinese Painting* (above, n. 9), 51–53.

31 Chu-tsing Li, "The Five Senses in Art: An Analysis of Its Development in Northern Europe" (PhD dissertation, University of Iowa, 1955);

Sherman E. Lee, "A Critical Survey of American Watercolor Painting" (PhD dissertation, Case Western Reserve University, 1941). Li did his postdoctoral in Chinese art work at Harvard and Princeton and Lee was trained in part by James Plumber, an expert in Chinese ceramics, at the University of Michigan; Lee's first full-time job was as Assistant Curator of Oriental and Italian Renaissance Art at the Detroit Institute of Art in 1941. For Li, see "Selected Bibliography of Chu-tsing Li," in *Tradition and Transformation: Studies in Chinese Art in Honor of Chu-tsing Li*, ed. Judith G. Smith (Lawrence, Kans.: Spencer Museum of Art, the University of Kansas, 2005), 16–23; Chu-tsing Li, "A Search for Chinese Art History," *Orientations* 37, no. 1 (2006): 58–60; Robert D. Mowry, "Notes from Conversations with Chu-tsing Li," in *A Tradition Redefined: Modern and Contemporary Chinese Paintings from the Chu-tsing Li Collection, 1950–2000*, ed. Robert D. Mowry (Cambridge, Mass.: Harvard University Art Museums, 2007), 60–71. For Lee, see Mary Stokrocki, "The Making of a Curator: An Interview with Sherman Lee," *Art Education* 36, no. 3 (May 1983): 24–25.

32 Chang's *Existence of Intangible Content* (Princeton: Princeton University Press, 1956) was based on his "An Investigation on Intangible Content in Architectonic Form Based upon the Practicality of Laotzu's Philosophy" (PhD dissertation, Princeton University, 1951). Fong's review, not included in the bibliography of his publications in *Reflections* (above, n. 2), was published in *Journal of Asian Studies* 16, no. 3 (May 1957): 421–23; Wing-tsit Chan's review was published in *Philosophy East and West* 6, no. 2 (July 1956): 169–70.

33 Mai-mai Sze, *The Tao of Painting*, 2 vols. (New York: Pantheon Books, 1956). Cahill's reviews were published in *Ars Orientalis* 3 (1959): 232–41 and as an article titled "A Clouded View of Chinese Painting," *Virginia Quarterly Review* (Summer 1957): 476–80. Compare Cahill's reviews with those by Alexander Soper, in *Artibus Asiae* 20, nos. 2–3 (1957): 191–95, and Nelson I. Wu, in *The Journal of Aesthetics and Art Criticism* 16, no. 2 (December 1957): 279–81.

34 *Ars Orientalis* 3 (1959): 233.

35 James Cahill Papers (in the Freer and Sackler Galleries), box 5, folder 48.

36 *Ars Orientalis* 3 (1959): 241.

37 Cahill, *Chinese Painting* (Geneva: Editions d'Art Albert Skira, 1960), 5–6.

38 Wen C. Fong, "On Hsieh Ho's 'Liu-fa'," *Oriental Art*, n.s., 9, no. 2 (Summer 1963): 73–78; "Ch'i-yun sheng-tung: 'Vitality, Harmonious Manner and Aliveness'," *Oriental Art*, n.s., 12, no. 3 (Autumn 1966): 159–64; "The First Principle of Hsieh Ho," *National Palace Museum Quarterly* 1, no. 3 (1966): 7–18.

39 James Cahill, "Confucian Elements in the Theory of Painting," in *The Confucian Persuasion*, ed. Arthur F. Wright (Stanford: Stanford University Press, 1960), 115–40; "The Six Laws and How to Read Them," *Ars Orientalis* 4 (1961): 372–81. See also his book review of *Some T'ang and Pre-T'ang Texts on Chinese Painting* by William Acker in *Ars Orientalis* 4 (1961): 440–44.

40 Arthur F. Wright, "Preface," in *Confucian Persuasion*, v.

41 See Susan Bush, *The Chinese Literati on Painting: Su Shih (1037–1101) to Tung Ch'i-ch'ang (1555–1636)*, 2nd ed. (Cambridge, Mass.: Harvard University Press, 1978) and John Steadman, *The Myth of Asia* (New York: Simon Schuster, 1969), 233, 236–38.

42 Sherman E. Lee and Wen C. Fong, *Streams and Mountains without End: A Northern Sung Handscroll and Its Significance in the History of Early Chinese Painting*, Artibus Asiae Suppl. 14 (Ascona: Artibus Asiae, 1955). The second edition appeared in 1967. See Susan Bush, "Yet Again 'Steams and Mountains without End'," *Artibus Asiae* 48, nos. 3–4 (1987): 197–223.

43 Wen C. Fong, *The Lohans and a Bridge to Heaven*, Freer Gallery of Art Occasional Paper, vol. 3, no. 1 (Washington, D.C.: Freer Gallery of Art, 1958).

44 Kuo, *Discovering Chinese Painting* (above, n. 9), 60.

45 Ibid., 62.

46 Richard Barnhart, *Painters of the Great Ming: The Imperial Court and the Zhe School*, with essays by Mary Ann Rogers and Richard Stanley-Maker (Dallas: Dallas Museum of Art, 1993), 6.

47 Ibid., 9.

48 James Cahill, "Wang Chi-ch'ien (1907–2003)," *Archives of Asian Art* 54 (2004): 95–96.

49 Kuo, *Discovering Chinese Painting*, 60.

50 Ibid.

51 James Cahill, "Foreword," in "A Definition of Brushwork-Oriented Criteria in Chinese Literati Painting," by Joan Stanley-Baker, unpublished manuscript; I am grateful to Stanley-Baker for making this manuscript available.

52 Wen C. Fong, "Asian Art for the Metropolitan Museum," in *The Chase and the Capture: Collecting at the Metropolitan*, Thomas Hoving et al. (New York: The Metropolitan Museum of Art, 1975), 131–48, at 135.

53 Fong, *Reflections* (above, n. 2), 27.

54 *Artibus Asiae* 25, nos. 2–3 (1962): 95–140.

55 The proceedings of that conference were later published in Doanda Randall, ed., *The Collectors of Asian Art and Archaeology: Problems of Assembly, Maintenance, and Study* (New York: Asian Conservation Laboratory, 1966); Fong's comment appears at 112.

56 In ibid., 111.

57 Cohen, *East Asian Art* (above, unnumbered n.), 230, n. 52.

58 Earl Morse, "On Collecting Chinese Painting," *The Metropolitan Museum of Art Bulletin* 29, no. 3 (November 1970): 156–62 (at 157).

59 James Cahill, letter dated February 15, 1963 in the James Cahill Papers at the Freer and Sackler Galleries.

60 Sirén, *Chinese Painting* (above, n. 16).

61 James Cahill, *An Index of Early Chinese Painters and Paintings: T'ang, Sung, and Yuan* (Berkeley: University of California Press, 1980). See Guo Jisheng [Jason C. Kuo], *Yishushi yu yishu piping* (Taipei: Shulin chuban, 1990), 306–10.

62 See the special issue on his collection (the Ching Yuan Chai Collection) in *Yiyuan Douying* 41 (June 1990).

63 *Oriental Art*, n.s., 9 (1963): 77–78.

64 *Proceedings of the American Philosophical Society* 115, no. 4 (August 1971): 282.

65 Ibid., 292.

66 Frederick W. Mote, "Preface: Calligraphy and Books—Their Evolving Relationship Through Chinese History," in *Calligraphy and the East Asian Book*, Frederick W. Mote and Hung-lam Chu, ed. by Howard L. Goodman (Boston: Shambhala, 1989), 3–16, at 5.

67 Cahill, "Style as Idea in Ming–Ch'ing Painting," in *The Mozartian Historian: Essays on the Works of Joseph R. Levenson*, ed. Maurice Meisner and Rhoads Murphy (Berkeley: University of California Press, 1976), 137–56; Richard M. Barnhart, "Wei Fu-jen's *Pi-chen T'u* and the Early Texts on Calligraphy," *Archives of the Chinese Art Society of America* 18 (1964): 13–25.

68 See, for example, Michael Sullivan, *The Three Perfections: Chinese Painting, Poetry and Calligraphy* (New York: George Braziller, 1980).

69 Cahill's opening remarks made at the workshop "New Directions in Chinese Art History" at the annual conference of the College Art Association on February 25, 1985 in Los Angeles.

70 "Types of Text-Object Relationships in Chinese Art," keynote address for the 31st International Congress of Human Sciences in Asia and North Africa, September 1, 1983, Tokyo.

71 Qian Zhongshu, "Zhongguo shi yu Zhongguo hua," in *Kaiming shudian ershi zhounian jinian wenji* (Shanghai: Kaiming shudian, 1946), 153–72; reprinted in Qian Zhongshu, *Juwen sipian* (Shanghai: Guji chubanshe, 1979), 1–25.

72 For instance, Murck and Fong, *Words and Image* (above, n. 13).

73 Tseng Yu-ho Ecke, *Chinese Calligraphy* (Philadelphia: Philadelphia Museum of Art, 1971); Shen C. Y. Fu, et al., *Traces of the Brush: Studies in Chinese Calligraphy* (New Haven: Yale University Art Gallery, 1977); Robert

E. Harrist, Jr. and Wen C. Fong, *The Embodied Image: Chinese Calligraphy from the John B. Elliot Collection* (Princeton: The Art Museum, Princeton University, 1999); Robert, E. Harrist, Jr., *The Landscape of Words: Stone Inscriptions from Early and Medieval China* (Seattle: University of Washington Press, 2008).

74 See, for example, Shen C. Y. Fu, "Huang T'ing-chien's Calligraphy and His *Scroll for Chang Ta-t'ung*" (PhD dissertation, Princeton University, 1976); Marilyn Wong Fu (M. W. Gleysteen), "Hsien-yu Shu's Calligraphy and His 'Admonitions' Scroll of 1299" (PhD dissertation, Princeton University, 1983); Hui-liang Chu, "The Chung Yu (A.D. 151–230) Tradition: A Pivotal Development in Sung Calligraphy" (PhD dissertation, Princeton University, 1990); Richard M. Barnhart, *"Pi-chen T'u"* (n. 67 above); John Hay, "The Human Body as a Microcosmic Source of Macrocosmic Values in Calligraphy," in *Theories of the Arts in China,* ed. Susan Bush and Christian F. Murck (Princeton: Princeton University Press, 1983), 74–102.

75 Wen C. Fong, *Images of the Mind* (above, n. 28), 3.

76 Fong, "Method" (above, n. 63).

77 *Artibus Asiae* 53, nos. 1–2 (1993): 303.

78 Fong, in Wen C. Fong and James C. Y. Watt, eds., *Possessing the Past: Treasures from the National Palace Museum* (New York: The Metropolitan Museum of Art, 1996), 28.

79 Fong, "Creating a Synthesis," in Fong and Watt, *Possessing the Past,* 424.

80 James Cahill, "Go Shōseki to Sai Hakuseki no geijutsu," in *Go Shōseki, Sai Hakuseki,* Bunjenga Suihen: Chugokū 10 (Tokyo: Chūōkōronsha, 1977). Cahill's much longer original text in English can be found on his website, www.jamescahill.info, where it appears as CLP 65. The title of the essay is somewhat misleading, as three other painters (Wang Yiting, Fu Baoshi, and Huang Binhong) are also discussed. In a letter dated March 31, 1977 that accompanied the English text, Cahill writes, "This essay was written to accompany a book that is primarily a collection of plates, and should not be thought of as an attempt at a serious study of the subject."

81 For Sullivan, see Shelagh Vainker, "Interview with Michael Sullivan," *Orientations* 32:9 (November 2001): 55–59; for Li, see Smith, *Tradition and Transformations* (above, n. 31), 16–23.

82 For example, see James Cahill, "The Shanghai School in Later Chinese Painting," in Mayching Kao, ed., *Twentieth-Century Chinese Painting* (Hong Kong: Oxford University Press, 1988), 54–77; "Ren Xiong and His Self-Portrait," *Ars Orientalis* 25 (1995): 119–32; "A 'Late Period' for C. C. Wang," in *C. C. Wang* (San Francisco: Asian Art Museum, 1996), 4–5.

83 P. 1.

84 Cahill was referring to these two exhibitions: Claudia Brown and Ju-hsi Chou, *The Elegant Brush: Chinese Painting under the Qianlong Emperor, 1935–1975* (Phoenix, Ariz.: Phoenix Art Museum, 1985) and *Transcending Turmoil: Painting at the Close of China's Empire, 1796–1911* (Phoenix, Ariz.: Phoenix Art Museum, 1992).

85 Cahill, *Distant Mountains* (above, n. 18), 205.

86 Personal communication, August 12, 2005.

87 P. 303.

88 Yingxing [Feng Zikai], "Zhongguo meishu zai xiandai yishu shang de shengli," *Dongfang zazi* 27, no. 1 (1930), 1–18; reprinted in He Huaishuo, ed., *Jindai Zhangguo meishu lunji*, 6 vols. (Taipei: Yishujia, 1991), 4:81–103.

89 In his "Postscript, 1978," Greenberg tried to clarify his position: "Many readers, though by no means all, seem to have taken the 'rationale' of Modernist art outlined here as representing a position adopted by the writer himself; that is, that what he describes he also advocates." See Clement Greenberg, "Modernist Painting," in *Postmodern Perspectives: Issues in Contemporary Art*, ed. Howard Risatti, 2nd ed. (Upper Saddle River, N.J.: Prentice Hall, 1998), 19.

90 Wen C. Fong, "Reflections on Chinese Art History," *Proceedings of the American Philosophical Society* 142, no. 1 (March 1998): 47–59; at 58.

91 Wen C. Fong, "The 'Han-Tang Miracle': Making Chinese Sculpture Art History," *Georges-Block-Jahrbuch, Special Edition: Festschrift in Honor of Professor Helmut Brinker's Retirement* (Zurich: Kunsthistorische Institut, forthcoming); I am grateful to Fong for sending me a copy of his manuscript.

92 *The Art Bulletin* 85, no. 2 (2003): 258–80.

93 Ibid., 268.

94 Fong, in Fong and Watt, *Possessing the Past* (above, n. 78), 572, note 5.

95 Jean Pierre Dubosc and Laurence Sickman, *Great Chinese Painters of the Ming and Ch'ing Dynasties* (New York: Wildenstein, 1949); Sherman E. Lee, *Chinese Landscape Painting* (Cleveland: Cleveland Museum of Art, 1954).

96 Cahill, *Chinese Painting* (above, n. 37), 167. Although Jean Pierre Dubosc is mentioned, there is no footnote. In the bibliography, however, Cahill cited Dubsoc's article, "A New Approach to Chinese Painting," *Oriental Art*, n.s., 3 (1950): 50–57. Dubosc, who once served in the French embassy in China, began to collect and promote Ming and Qing painting long before American scholars paid any serious attention to it. See Jean Pierre Dubosc, *Pao Hui Chi: Twelve Chinese Paintings in the Collection of J. P. Dubosc* (Peking: privately published, 1937); *Exposition de peintures chinoises de la collection J. P. Dubosc* (Paris: Bibliothèque Nationale, 1937); *Mostra di pitture cinesi delle dinastie Ming e Ch'ing* (Rome: Is. M. E. O., 1950).

97 Sherman Lee, *Chinese Landscape Painting,* revised edition (New York: Harper & Row, n.d.), 125.

98 James Cahill, *Fantastics and Eccentrics in Chinese Painting* (New York: Asia House Gallery, 1967), 105.

99 Wen C. Fong, "Song Mimesis and Beyond," in Smith, *Tradition and Transformation* (above, n. 31), 84–109, at 103; Fong quotes from Foucault, *The Order of Things: An Archaeology of the Human Sciences* (New York: Vintage Books, 1973), xxiii, 293.

100 Erwin Panofsky, "The History of Art as a Humanistic Discipline," *Meaning in the Visual Arts: Papers in and on Art History* (Garden City, N.Y.: Doubleday Anchor Books, 1955), 20; the essay was first published in T. M. Greene, ed., *The Meaning of the Humanities* (Princeton: Princeton University Press, 1940), 89–118.

101 Ibid.

102 Linda Seidel, "On Telling Tales," *The Art Bulletin* 76, no. 4 (December 1994): 581–83; at 583.

103 All part of a section on "A Range of Critical Perspectives: Writing (and) the History of Art" in *The Art Bulletin* 78, no. 3 (September 1996): Paul Barolsky, "Writing Art History," 398–400; David Carrier, "Artcriticism-writing, Arthistory-writing, and Artwriting," 401–3; Ivan Gaskell, "Writing (and) Art History: Against Writing," 403–6;

104 David Summers, "The 'Visual Arts' and the Problem of At Historical Description," *Art Journal* 42, no. 4 (1982): 301–10; "This Is Not a Sign: Some Remarks on Art and Semiotics," *Art Criticism* 3, no. 1 (1986): 30–45.

105 Kuo, *Discovering Chinese Painting* (above, n. 9), 35–36.

106 See the newsletter of the Department of the History of Art, University of Michigan, spring 2008, 2.

107 Cahill, *Chinese Painting* (above, n. 37), 82.

108 Kuo, *Discovering Chinese Painting,* 36.

109 James Cahill, *Hills Beyond a River* (above, n. 18), 80.

110 Fong, *Beyond Representation* (above, n. 28), 83.

111 Ibid., 83.

112 Cahill, *Chinese Painting,* 34.

113 Ibid.

114 Ibid., 35.

115 Fong, *Beyond Representation,* 93.

116 Wen C. Fong, *Sung and Yuan Painting,* with catalogue by Marilyn Fu (New York: The Metropolitan Museum of Art, 1973), 22.

117 Fong, *Beyond Representation,* 472.

118 Fong, *Sung and Yuan Painting,* 120.

119 Ibid., 121.

120 Cahill, *Hills Beyond a River* (above, n. 109), 128.

121 Kuo, *Discovering Chinese Painting*, 53.

122 (Lawrence, Kans.: The Spencer Museum of Art, University of Kansas, 1988), 100–110, 112 (endnotes).

123 Ibid., 10.

124 Whitfield, "Streams and Mountains" (above, n. 24), 119; for Fong's earlier position, see, for example, Fong, "Method" (above, n. 63).

125 Unpublished manuscript dated July 30, 2006; I am grateful to Fong for sharing a copy of his paper with me.

126 Quoting James Cahill, "Some Thoughts on the History and Post-History of Chinese Painting," *Archives of Asian Art* 55 (2005): 20; this essay should be read in conjunction with two accompanying commentaries: Jerome Silbergeld, "The Evolution of a 'Revolution': Unsettled Reflections on the Chinese Art-Historical Mission," *Archives* 55 (2005): 39–52, and Robert E. Harrist, Jr., "A Response to Professor Cahill's 'Some Thoughts on the History and Post-History of Chinese Painting'," *Archives* 55 (2005): 35–37.

127 Fong, *Reflections* (above, n. 2), 30.

128 Cahill, *Painter's Practice* (above, n. 4).

129 Ibid., 11.

130 Forthcoming from the University of California Press.

131 For example, his Getty Lectures, given at the University of Southern California in 1994, focused on the representations of women in later Chinese painting.

132 Cahill, *Painter's Practice*, 10.

133 James Cahill, "Discussant Paper on Methodology," in *Taiwan 2002 Conference* (above, n. 13), 398–413, at 411–12.

134 Fong, *Reflections*, 30.

135 Ibid., 31–32.

136 Ibid., 30.

137 Forthcoming from Yale University Press.

138 Erwin Panofsky, "The History of Art as a Humanistic Discipline" and "Three Decades of Art History in the United States: Impressions of a Transplanted European," both in *Meaning* (above, n. 100), 321.

139 See, for example, Xue Yongnian, *Shuhua shilun conggao* (above, n. 12), 455–97; Jonathan Hay, "Toward a Disjunctive Diachronics of Chinese Art History," *Res* 40 (Autumn 2001): 101–11. Hay characterizes the approach of both Cahill and Fong as a "rejuvenation of formalism by the cognitive model" (104); in response, Fong maintains: "I cling . . . to a 'universal approach to the history of art' that says that the true value of Chinese painting lies in its own special visual language and its unique form of expressivity." (Fong, "Why" [above, n. 92], 259.) See also Jerome Silbergeld, "Evolution," and Harrist, "Response," 35–37 (both above, n. 126).

140 See, for example, Michel Foucault, *The Archaeology of Knowledge*, trans. A. Sheridan Smith (New York: Routledge, 1989), 21–39.

Afterword
Chinese Art, European Art, Art

David Carrier

When Jason Kuo invited me to contribute to this collection of essays, I was both flattered and alarmed. Flattered because of my admiration for the writers and for Kuo himself. But also alarmed because I was not sure what I could add to their stimulating exchanges. My recently completed *World Art History and Its Objects* says what I have to say about the relationship between art's history in Europe and China.[1] But then when I reread his materials, I realized that I do have something to add.

Trained as a philosopher, I came into art history in the 1980s when I wrote a sequence of essays on methodological questions, material that I then turned into *Principles of Art History Writing*.[2] The 1980s were a good time to study the methodology of art history, for many American and English art historians were rethinking fundamental issues. Increasingly dissatisfied with the older inherited methodologies, these writers were fascinated by feminism, Marxist theories of art, and French post-Structuralist philosophy. They wanted to find new ways to write about visual art. And so there was interest also in my claims. My book, still in print, has sold four thousand copies, which means that it is used as a textbook.

The starting point for *Principles* was the chapters on Caravaggio and Manet. They were inspired by two large shows at The Metropolitan Museum of Art in New York, "Manet" (1983) and "The Age of Caravaggio" (1985). These exhibitions assembled a large group of paintings by these two canonical figures and resulted in excellent catalogues with full bibliographies. According to older interpretations, Edouard Manet (1832–1883) is a straightforward, perhaps even sometimes an inept painter. But a number of recent commentators have shown that his art frequently makes reference to earlier paintings and have argued that he often subtly comments on contemporary political events. Since Manet is usually identified as the first modernist painter, the view we take of his achievement has a large effect on how the entire history of twentieth-century art is written. In his own time, Michelangelo Merisi da Caravaggio (1571–1610) was famous for the dramatic realism of his painting. Then a reaction set in and, for a long time, he was much reviled and little understood. More recently, in a surprising reversal of critical fortunes, he has become one of the most admired painters. The newer accounts discuss his religious symbolism, the erotic power of his images, and the political implications of his art. Like Manet, Caravaggio has been reinterpreted in ways that show him to be a highly complex painter.

I was puzzled by the contrast between the older and more recent interpretations of Manet and Caravaggio. Soon, then, I found other art historical examples that pose similar problems. And so other chapters of my book are devoted to the development of art writing about Piero della Francesca and Jacques-Louis David, and the uses of allegory in Flemish painting. And my chapter contrasting ekphrasis—word-painting, as it is sometimes called—and interpretation in modern art history offers one way of understanding the evolution of art history. Earlier commentators describe what is depicted in paintings, while more recent historians explain the meaning of these works of art. The chapter on Johann Joachim Winckelmann and Walter Pater provides another perspective on the history of art history. By comparing and contrasting these two different writers, I show how thinking about visual art changed in the nineteenth century.

Given that styles of interpretation have changed dramatically, how it is possible to achieve objectivity in art history writing? That question turns out to be surprisingly difficult to answer. My "Conclusion" draws an analogy between the development of art history and the development of art itself. According to Ernst Gombrich the history of European art is the story of increasing perfection of naturalism. Analogously, so I suggest, the history of art history can be understood as progressive improvement of styles of interpretation. Even otherwise sympathetic readers were dissatisfied with this argument. My suggestion that art history progresses was found unsatisfying.

In 1976 my mentor Mark Roskill published an introductory survey *What Is Art History?*[3] In that book he said that "art history is a science, with definite principles and techniques." But the field was changing rapidly, and so in the second edition, published in 1989, Roskill noted how problematic this claim had become. He liked to joke that the book now should be called, *What Else Is Art History?* Gombrich believed in progress, but most of his successors do not. And after the Holocaust, postmodernists claimed that this belief in progress was naïve. Strictly speaking, their conclusion was not entirely logical. We might have progress in some domains but not others. That the political history of the twentieth century was disastrous, why does that show that progress in art historical interpretation was not possible? After all, during Hitler's time, science and technology certainly progressed. But most art historians resist the claim that their discipline progresses like science. Gombrich had a very problematic analysis of modernism. In truth, he was not in sympathy with the great movements of the first half of the twentieth century—Cubism, Surrealism, or Abstract Expressionism. When we look at this art, or more recent developments, the idea that art progresses seems highly problematic.

Apart from these concerns, which reflected larger changes in how art historians thought of their research, it soon became apparent that even on its own terms my analysis was problematic. Giorgio Vasari's *Lives of the Painters, Sculptors, and Architects*, first published in 1550, is a highly sophisticated commentary. And so, as Paul Barolsky has emphasized, it is implausible to think that present-day art historians have progressed beyond Vasari. But since styles of art history writing have changed, we need some way of comprehending that development. I came to think that the best approach is to examine the changing functions of such writing. Vasari was a court painter who wrote entertaining lives of artists. In his time, there was a sharp distinction between the relatively small, educated elite—who appreciated art—and the illiterate masses. Our culture is very different. Today most art historians are scholars who teach. They prepare students to appreciate the collections of our public art museums. And so it is unsurprising that these present-day art historians write in a style very unlike Vasari's. To understand present-day art writing you need to look at the institutions that were invented in the nineteenth century.

Looking back, what seems most surprising is that although *Principles of Art History Writing* claims to present the history of art history, it discusses only Western European painting from the Renaissance through the twentieth century, and in the chapter on Winckelmann's writings on Greek and Roman sculpture. It never occurred to me to look to art or art history from outside Europe. But here of course my choice of topics reflects practical realities. Most American art historians study Western art and most of the large exhibitions at The Metropolitan and elsewhere in this country are devoted to American and European art. In Gombrich's survey text *The Story of Art*,[4] the art of China, India, and the Islamic world is discussed in just one chapter. To what extent can my analysis apply also to Chinese art?

It seems obvious that all of my concerns in my books mentioned above are parochial, and apply only to Western art history. Who, we should ask, are the Chinese artists equivalent to Manet, Caravaggio, Piero della Francesca, and Jacques-Louis David? And who are the writers in Chinese to be set alongside Winckelmann, Pater, and Vasari? Once we see how difficult it is to answer these questions, then it seems obvious that my book really should be called *Principles of Western Art History Writing*. When it was translated into Chinese, one of my translators asked me to explicate the word "ekphrasis" or "word painting." Once you learn how difficult it is to find a real Chinese equivalent for this term, which is so important to Western historians, then the problems involved in applying my analysis outside of European art become apparent.

Here we can gain perspective by looking from art history to history proper. A number of scholars have compared the histories of China and Western countries. In *China Transformed: Historical Change and the Limits of European Experience*,[5] for example, R. Bin Wong notes the problems posed by taking for granted models of change based entirely upon Western cultures. He has a great deal to say about the problems involved in making comparisons. The role of the state, the place of religion, and the position of the military differ in China and in the West. And many historians ask why China did not industrialize and, notwithstanding its generally superior science and technology, why Western nations, and not China, became the successful imperialist power.

China and Europe have very different histories. China usually was unified, and the dangerous invaders, before the era of European imperialism, came from the north. After the end of the Roman Empire, Europe was never unified, but always endured internal strife. The history of philosophy, technology, and science is very different in these cultures. And yet, few scholars doubt that it is possible to write a history of China using the same basic intellectual tools that are employed in histories of Europe. We can explain why power in China tended to be centralized; why that country had advanced science, but no industrial revolution; and why China was weak enough to invaded by the West, but then learned successfully to resist by modernizing. And we can understand how Maoism was an adaptation of Marxism to a country very unlike any in Europe discussed in Marx's writings. There are many good histories of China, and also many comparative studies of China and Europe. The laws of historical explanation can be applied to all cultures.

With art history, however, the situation is clearly different. As I have noted, there is no obvious Chinese equivalent to the development from the early Renaissance to modernism. In his history, Gombrich leads us from Giotto to Constable. Progressive improvement in techniques of representation and detachment of painting in secular modernism from its function in Catholic Italy (i.e., the presentation of sacred narratives) serve to motivate this development. Gombrich's account has been much criticized, but however we redescribe these paintings, we need some way of placing them on a timeline. Giotto influences Masaccio, who influences Raphael: such is the story of European art. The difficulty for a world art history, then, arises when we try to envisage an equivalent story about Chinese art.

Gombrich's analysis claims to be based upon psychology of perception, and so it should be universal. Suppose that the development of naturalism takes place earlier in China. We would need to identify a Chinese Giotto, Masaccio, Raphael, and finally Constable. Doubtlessly that way of proceeding applies too literally a European model to China. But how then should we proceed? The older accounts of art in China assume that this history can be modeled on accounts of Western art. Perhaps that is mistaken. The Chinese have a very different concept of aesthetics. We can, of course, study indigenous aesthetic theories. But judging just by the translations, it is not obvious how these interesting materials provide the basis for a history.

What is most unsatisfactory about *Principles of Art History Writing* is its treatment of interpretation without reference to the institutions that support this practice. So the next development in my thinking involved looking at the art museum. I discussed Manet and Caravaggio because there were large exhibitions with full catalogues. But you cannot explain the practice of art history without asking why this esoteric intellectual exercise is supported by the larger culture. Perhaps the development of philosophy proceeds without close reliance upon some support structure, but to understand the history of art history we need to ask what goals this debate about interpretation serves. At that point, then, I turned my attention to one key institution supporting the development of modern art history, the art museum.

In the mid-seventeenth century, some European rulers opened their art collections to the public. On August 10, 1793, during the French Revolution, the French king's collection became the core of a new public museum, the Louvre. When Napoleon came to power, he looted Italy, Germany, Spain, and Holland, and took that art to his new public art museum in Paris. And in the 1820s, when Hegel was lecturing on art history in Berlin, a new museum was being established there. By the late nineteenth century, art museums were found in most large European cities. At that time art history was established as an academic discipline in Germany, and a little later it took root in the United States, England, and other countries. The development of art history and that of the art museum thus are closely linked.

My volume *Museum Skepticism: A History of the Display of Art in Public Galleries* tells this history.[6] After discussing conceptual issues, I present case studies: Isabella Stewart Gardner's Old Master collection in Boston; Ernest Fenellosa's introduction of Asian art to the Boston Museum of Fine Arts;

Albert Barnes's pioneering museum of modernist art outside Philadelphia; the Getty, with its highly unusual building in Los Angeles; and the Cleveland Museum of Art, which has an important role in the history of American art education. When I started writing *Museum Skepticism* in 2000, I was a scholar in residence at the research institute attached to the J. Paul Getty Museum in Los Angeles. And so it was natural for me to devote one chapter to that museum. The book discusses only the museums I had visited in America and Europe. And just one chapter is devoted to the reception of art from Asia; in chapter seven I explain how Ernest Fenellosa used Hegelian ideas to promote the reception of art from China and Japan in Boston. Thanks in large part to Fenellosa's pioneering efforts, during the twentieth century important collections of art from Asia were assembled by American museums. China and India have very old, extremely sophisticated artistic traditions. So too does the Islamic world. But these cultures did not develop art museums until they came in contact with the West. In Asian countries, the museum is a Western import.

Since my book does not take up this story, its subtitle should really be *A History of the Display of Art in Western Public Galleries*. Here again, as with the development of art history, there is no equivalent story to be told about museums in China. When I visited Hangzhou, Shanghai, and Beijing and, a little later, briefly stayed in Mumbai and New Delhi, I was extremely interested in the art museums in these cities. Thanks to imperialism, the British created India's museums. And after independence, the Indian government continued to support these collections. And China, too, is developing ambitious public collections. Nowadays almost every country has its own museums. Western art museums are the products of a very distinctive political and social history. And so when public art collections appear in other cultures, inevitably they are organized very differently.

In Europe the French Revolution and the development of political democracy opened the grand private collections of the old regime to the public. Western museums tended to focus initially on Renaissance and Baroque art, and the sculpture of Greco-Roman antiquity. Then in the later nineteenth century these institutions extended their collections to include medieval European art, and the arts of all other cultures. Sculpture from New Zealand, carpets from the Islamic world, and artifacts from Africa were added to Western museums. Ultimately the ambition of grand Western museums like The Metropolitan is to be museums of world art history. Like capitalism, another Western institution with which it has always been closely associated, the museum thus expanded. This development of Western museums depended upon colonialism and economic imperialism. For reasons discussed in *Museum Skepticism*, there are major collections of African art in London and Paris, and important European paintings and sculptures in America because England, France, and the United States became economically and politically powerful. In response to this development, nowadays almost all countries prohibit export of major works of art.

And there are attempts to undo the results of this looting. The Greeks are demanding the return of the Elgin Marbles from the British Museum, and Italy seeks the return of smuggled antiquities. Soon after Fenellosa drew attention to the significance of traditional Japanese art, the government there prohibited any further export of masterpieces. When China was weak in the early twentieth century, many significant works of art were exported to Western museums. But today newly rediscovered art is displayed in that country's museums or loaned to America in exchange for exhibits of Western art.

Since China has a history very different from that of the West, its museums are inevitably different. When Europeans learned about silk and papermaking from China, or when

Chinese cuisine became popular in America, these distinctively Asian technologies and forms of life were transformed. The same surely happens with the art museum. Because the museum is too distinctively a Western European creation, it is transformed when transported to other cultures. Today it is too late to assemble a strong collection of Old Master European art. Even the Getty, with all its enormous financial resources, has gathered only a relatively modest group of paintings and sculptures. However prosperous China becomes, it will never be able to create a world art museum like The Metropolitan. The artifacts required will never be removed from Western museums. But China is likely to host a great variety of important loan exhibitions of Western art. American and European museums are happy to loan their collections in return for loans of newly rediscovered Chinese art.

Museum Skepticism focuses on a particular problem—how can Old Master art remain accessible to the public? When modernism was born in the mid-nineteenth century, ambitious painters and sculptors wanted to show their art in museums. This was a new development—Manet painted for the museum, but Caravaggio did not. And so Western historians are very concerned about understanding the relationship of this modernist art to Old Master art. In China, art has a very different history. There is no exact equivalent to the French and American development of modernism, although starting early in the twentieth century many Chinese artists visited the West or adopted Western styles. And so collections of Chinese art inevitably have a very different structure than do displays of European and American painting. Recently, it is true, there have been many exhibits in America of contemporary Chinese art. But most of these installations, performances, and videos heavily exhibit Western ways of thinking. And so it is too soon to tell whether contemporary Chinese art will deserve a place in the history of art.

The art museum became and has remained an important institution because it has proven to be extremely adaptable, capable of thriving in changing circumstances. Consider how many different goals it has. Museums are nationalistic showplaces, displaying the power of the collecting culture. They educate us about exotic cultures, allowing us to learn about temporally and geographically remote places. They provide us with democratically accessible aesthetic pleasure. And nowadays they often are fun palaces, public spaces for entertainment. Because great works of art are very expensive, museums have consistently attracted critics who note that these are essentially paternalistic institutions. Compared with mass culture—film, pop music, television—museum art remains difficult for the larger public to access. And so, for some decades, artists and scholars have critiqued museums and the ways of thinking associated with the Old Master art they display. Museums have generally responded favorably to these critics. They exhibit politically critical art and publish catalogue essays by leftist commentators. And they work hard to make art more accessible. It seems reasonable to hope that museums in China will be equally adaptable.

However good the permanent display, large numbers of museum visitors come to see only temporary shows, particularly blockbuster exhibits. Impressionist painting is especially attractive. These issues arise because American museums need large audiences. Most museums charge for admission, but even those that don't, feel that only high attendance figures show that they are truly serving the public. Often, then, the result is a vicious cycle in which the building and temporary exhibitions become increasingly expensive, and so there is a need to accommodate ever-larger audiences. For example, one of our most prominent museums, The Museum of Modern Art, New York (MOMA), has been rebuilt twice in the past thirty years. When I first visited it, there were usually few studying its masterpieces. Now admission is much more expensive, the hanging of the art in the newest building is not on the whole convincing, and it is always crowded.

But here, of course, a historical perspective is essential. It would be absurd to complain about these crowds, which show how successful we scholars have been in persuading the public that modernist and contemporary art matters. Thanks to the classes run by art historians, our students and their families come to MOMA. In America, conservative commentators tend to be nostalgic, preferring the old days when museums felt no need to create blockbuster exhibitions, highly publicized loan shows that often require special tickets. But while some of these new large shows are bad, many of them are extremely instructive. In the old days, as I note in *Museum Skepticism,* museums often were very paternalistic. Now, surely it is a good thing that they welcome the larger public. Recently there has also been much critical discussion about the bookstores, gift shops, and restaurants in our museums. Some people feel that these institutions, like the lavish architecture, take us away from the primary goal of the museum, displaying art.

Here again, however, it is hard to balance practical financial concerns against such complaints. In a democratic society, museums have to account to the public, if only by being popular enough to balance the budget. As a visitor, I am sometimes also nostalgic for the old days when museums were less crowded. But often I enjoy the new buildings, purchase books in the shop, and dine in the restaurant. On the whole, present-day American museums are amazingly good at making accessible a great variety of art and organizing exhibitions, including the blockbusters, which are enjoyable. As I say at the end of *Museum Skepticism,* at this time when the world is changing rapidly, nostalgia is unproductive. I know too little about China to imagine how much of this analysis applies to museums in that country. But thanks to the generous support of Professor Ding Ning of Peking University in Beijing, I do know a little about the teaching of art history in China. And so I offer a comparison, which may be suggestive.

In the West, the way that art history is taught in America and elsewhere derives from the practice of late nineteenth-century German universities. And so, as this Western literature is translated into Chinese, and as China develops graduate programs, then it is natural that this educational system will be modified. When, thanks to Hitler, the leading art historians from the German-speaking world moved to England and America in the 1930s, the style of art history was changed. The migration of Western art history to China is a much more drastic move, and so we can expect that again the interpretation of visual art will change dramatically. China has its own distinguished tradition of art writing, and its own grand visual art tradition. And so it will be extremely interesting to see how Western styles of thinking are modified there. Chinese scholars will interpret Western art in novel ways that we cannot yet imagine. And they will describe their own paintings and sculptures in ways equally unpredictable. Something similar is likely to happen, I suggest, when the art museum migrates to China. This Western institution is being and will be radically transformed. I hope that I live long enough to witness that process develop fully.

In looking to other cultures, it is important to acknowledge their diversity but also note the very real parallels. Consider again our analogy between history and art history. The media of China are distinct, its social history is different, and its indigenous religions are exotic to Westerners. But these are relatively parochial differences, like the differences between our languages, which are mutually translatable. The cultural differences are small in the end because we have common ancestors and so are biologically related. In an important book, *Neuroarthistory: From Aristotle and Pliny to Baxandall and Zeki*,[7] John Onians argues that neuroscience provides the ultimate basis for art history. Since we all have the same neurology, we should be able to understand one another's art. The difficulty, of course, is moving from a very general analysis of mental activity to discussing something so culturally specific as visual art. A lot of work must be done by future art historians. But there is no good reason, so Onians implies, to doubt that this project will ultimately succeed. Imagine intelligent aliens from another solar system who make artlike artifacts. Suppose that they have tentacles, not arms, and three sexes, and that they perceive wavelengths of light inaccessible to us. Their brains are not much like ours. So no doubt their cultures, religions, and wars are very unlike ours. We would have difficulty seeing their equivalent to our works of art. And so interpreting their art may be difficult, even impossible. This little thought experiment shows that the differences between China and the West are relatively parochial.

Why then do scholars resist creating a world art history? Some obvious difficulties are practical. When it is hard enough to master the literature devoted to any small subdivision of the history of art in China or the West, no one knows enough to write such a book. This is why the *Atlas of World Art* edited by Onians is the creation of a large team of specialists.[8] The other problem is political. Present-day Western scholars are very sensitive to the dangers of Eurocentricism. Knowing how often racism and sheer ignorance marred the scholarship of our ancestors, we fear that it is impossible for us truly to understand exotic art. This worry is supported by the very influential writings of Michel Foucault, who argued that scholarly objectivity is an impossible ideal. Ultimately, so this argument runs, study of other cultures always becomes an exercise in imperialism that seeks to control these cultures.

We are right to be cautious, but in my opinion none of these arguments are decisive. Any adequate history of art must deal with the art of all cultures. And so we need to find ways to bring specialists together, to build upon their results. Right now, when there are increasingly frequent exchanges between museums in China and the West, who could be satisfied by the refusal of art historians to compare and contrast these artifacts? As for the political worries, cultural imperialism is the natural result of strong societies imposing their ways of thinking. But now, as China becomes a major industrial power, it is increasingly in a position not just to borrow intellectually from the West but to develop its own distinctive ways of thinking. Just as Chinese manufacturers compete with those in the West, so too soon enough their professors will challenge ours. The Cultural Revolution ended just a little over thirty years ago. Seeing how dramatically China has changed since then gives reason, in my judgment, for optimism. The world now really is one. And so it is time for art history to reflect that political reality.

Bibliography

On Chinese art my essential sources are James Cahill, *Chinese Painting* (Geneva: Editions d'Art Albert Skira, 1960), a traditional history, and *The Compelling Image: Nature and Style in Seventeenth-Century Chinese Painting* (Cambridge, Mass.: Harvard University Press, 1982) and *The Painter's Practice: How Artists Lived and Worked in Traditional China* (New York: Columbia University Press, 1994). I owe a large debt to Craig Clunas, *Superfluous Things: Material Culture and Social Status in Early Modern China* (Urbana: University of Illinois Press, 1991) and his more recent *Art in China* (Oxford: Oxford University Press, 1997) and *Pictures and Visuality in Early Modern China* (Princeton: Princeton University Press, 1997), which make important methodological claims. Wen C. Fong, *Beyond Representation: Chinese Painting and Calligraphy, 8th–14th Century* (New York: Metropolitan Museum of Art, 1992) presents the paintings in that important collection. Zhang Hongxing, "Rereading Inscriptions in Chinese Scroll Painting: The Eleventh to the Fourteenth Centuries," *Art History* 28, no. 5 (2005): 606–25, deals with an important specialist concern. Wu Hung, *The Double Screen: Medium and Representation in Chinese Painting* (Chicago: University of Chicago Press, 1996) is a very original methodological analysis, while his *Remaking Beijing: Tiananmen Square and the Creation of a Political Space* (Chicago: University of Chicago Press, 2005) deals with political issues. Sherman E. Lee, *Chinese Landscape Painting* (Cleveland:

Cleveland Museum of Art, 1954), Lawrence Sickman and Alexander Soper, *The Art and Architecture of China* (Harmondsworth: Penguin, 1971), and Michael Sullivan, *The Arts of China*, 5th ed. (Berkeley: University of California Press, 2008) are good survey histories. Jerome Silbergeld, "Chinese Painting Studies in the West: A State-of-the-Field Article," *The Journal of Asian Studies* 46, no. 4 (1987): 849–97, helpfully summarizes the literature. Michael Sullivan, *The Birth of Landscape Painting in China* (Berkeley: University of California Press, 1962), William Watson, *The Arts of China to AD 900* (New Haven: Yale University Press, 1995), and Yang Xin and others, *Three Thousand Years of Chinese Painting* (New Haven: Yale University Press; Beijing: Foreign Languages Press, 1997) represent traditional scholarship. Two books on Chinese aesthetics are essential: Susan Bush, *The Chinese Literati on Painting: Su Shih (1037–1011) to Tung Ch'i-ch'ang (1555–1636)* (Cambridge, Mass.: Harvard University Press, 1971) and *Early Chinese Texts on Painting*, edited by Susan Bush and Hsio-yen Shih (Cambridge, Mass.: Harvard University Press, 1985). As its title implies, Jason C. Kuo, ed., *Discovering Chinese Painting: Dialogues with Art Historians*, 2nd ed. (Dubuque: Kendall/Hunt Publishing Company, 2006), presents essential background material.

Notes

1 (University Park, Pa.: Penn State Press, 2008).
2 (University Park, Pa.: Penn State Press, 1991).
3 (London: Thames and Hudson, 1976).
4 See above, Introduction, n. 7.
5 (Ithaca, N.Y.: Cornell University Press, 1997).
6 (Durham, N.C.: Duke University Press, 2006).
7 (New Haven: Yale University Press, 2007).
8 (Oxford and New York: Oxford University Press, 2004).

About the Editor

Jason C. Kuo is Professor of Art History and Archaeology at the University of Maryland and has taught at the National Taiwan University, Williams College, and Yale University. He is the author of *Wang Yuanqi de shanshuihua yishu* [*Wang Yuanqi's Art of Landscape Painting*] (Taipei: National Palace Museum, 1981), *Long tiandi yu xingnei* [*Trapping Heaven and Earth in the Cage of Form*] (Taipei: Shibao wenhua, 1986), *The Austere Landscape: The Paintings of Hung-jen* (Taiwan and New York: SMC Publishing in cooperation with University of Washington Press, Seattle and London, 1992), *Zhuang Zhe, 1991–92* (Taipei: Longmen hualang, 1992), *Cuo wanwu yu biduan* [*Embodying Myriad of Things as the Tip of Brush*] (Taipei: Dongda tushu, 1994), *Word as Image: The Art of Chinese Seal Engraving* (New York: China House Gallery, China Institute in America; distributed by University of Washington Press, Seattle and London, 1992), *Chen Qikuan* (Taipei: Jinxiu chuban shiye, 1995), *Yishushi yu yishu piping de tansuo* [*Rethinking Art History and Art Criticism*] (Taipei: National Museum of History, 1996), *Yishushi yu yishu piping de shijian* [*Practicing Art History and Art Criticism*] (Taipei: National Museum of History, 2002), and *Transforming Traditions in Modern Chinese Painting: Huang Pin-hung's Late Work* (Berlin and New York: Peter Lang Publishing, 2004). He is the editor of several books and exhibition catalogs, including *Heirs to a Great Tradition: Modern Chinese Painting from the Tsien-hsiang-chai Collection* (College Park, Md.: Department of Art History and Archaeology; distributed by University of Washington Press, Seattle and London, 1993), *Discovering Chinese Painting: Dialogues with American Art Historians* (Dubuque: Kendall/Hunt Publishing, 2000), *Understanding Asian Art* (Dubuque: Kendall/Hunt

Publishing, 2001), *Discovering Chinese Painting: Dialogues with Art Historians* (Dubuque: Kendall/Hunt Publishing, 2006), *Visual Culture in Shanghai, 1850s–1930s* (Washington, D.C.: New Academia Publishing, 2007), and *Perspectives on Connoisseurship of Chinese Painting* (Washington, D.C.: New Academia Publishing, 2008). His writings have appeared in a broad spectrum of publications, including *Art Journal, Asian Culture Quarterly, Chinese Culture Quarterly, Chinese Studies, National Palace Museum Bulletin, National Palace Museum Research Quarterly, Orientations, China Quarterly, China Review International, Journal of Asian Studies, Journal of Asian and African Studies,* and *Ars Orientalis*. He is a contributor to *The Dictionary of Art* edited by Jane Turner (New York: Grove, 1996) as well as *Oxford Art Online* published by Oxford University Press and *Allgemeines Künstlerlexikon: Die bildenden Künstler aller Zeiten und Völker* edited by Günter Meissner (München and Leipzig: K. G. Saur, 1992-).

He has received an Andrew W. Mellon Foundation Fellowship, a grant from the National Endowment for the Humanities, two Stoddard Fellowships in Asian Art at the Detroit Institute of Arts, two fellowships from the J. D. Rockefeller III Fund, and many other scholastic honors. In 1991–1992, he received the Lilly Fellowship for teaching excellence at the University of Maryland. In 1992–1993 he organized and directed a National Endowment for the Humanities Summer Institute for College Teachers on "The Art of Imperial China." From 1993 to 1998, he undertook the study of the nineteenth- and twentieth-century art of Shanghai, a research project funded by the Henry Luce Foundation that combined the work of six scholars from China and six from the United States. He directed the Summer Institute of Connoisseurship in Chinese Calligraphy and Painting from 2001 to 2003, also funded by the Luce Foundation. He was a Fulbright Scholar in Taipei in 2001–2002.

About the Authors

James Cahill

In the field of Chinese painting, James Cahill (Professor Emeritus of the History of Art, University of California at Berkeley) is generally regarded in the United States as its most important art historian, even though his stature is not unchallenged or unrivaled. In 1978–1979, he delivered the Charles Eliot Norton Lectures at Harvard University; since its establishment in 1925, the Charles Eliot Norton Professorship of Poetry has become one of the nation's most illustrious guest lectureships, with past incumbents such as Luciano Berio, Leonard Bernstein, Harold Bloom, Jorge Luis Borges, John Cage, Carlos Chávez, Aaron Copland, e. e. cummings, Umberto Eco, T. S. Eliot, Robert Frost, Dame Helen Gardner, Paul Hindemith, Roger Sessions, Leo Steinberg, Frank Stella, Igor Stravinsky, Lionel Trilling, and Thornton Wilder. Cahill's lectures were published in 1982 as *The Compelling Image: Nature and Style in Seventeenth-Century Chinese Painting* (Cambridge, Mass.: Harvard University Press, 1982). The book was awarded the College Art Association's Morey Prize for the best art history book of 1982. The College Art Association, recognizing that this is "a time of great methodological shifts in the field" and that the profession must foster a "dialogue within and among the different generations of art historians," saluted him as the Distinguished Scholar at its annual convention in 2004. In 2007, he received the Distinguished Lifetime Achievement Award for Writing on Art from the College Art Association.

His 1991 Bampton Lectures at Columbia University appeared in 1994 as *The Painter's Practice: How Artists Lived and Worked in Traditional China* (New York: Columbia University

Press, 1994). He gave the Reischauer Lectures at Harvard University in 1993; these lectures appeared as a book in 1996 under the title *The Lyric Journey: Poetic Panting in China and Japan* (Cambridge, Mass.: Harvard University Press, 1996). Another book, *Pictures for Use and Pleasure: Vernacular Painting in High Qing China,* is forthcoming from the University of California Press. A study of paintings done for women in the Ming–Qing period, given as a lecture at several places, is being prepared for publication.

His other publications include *An Index of Early Chinese Painters and Painting: T'ang, Sung, Yuan* (Berkeley: University of California Press, 1980), *Hills Beyond a River: Chinese Painting of the Yuan Dynasty, 1279–1368* (New York: Weatherhill, 1976), *Parting at the Shore: Chinese Painting of the Early and Middle Ming Dynasty, 1368–1580* (New York: Weatherhill, 1978), *The Distant Mountains: Chinese Painting of the Late Ming Dynasty, 1570–1644* (New York: Weatherhill, 1978), and *Three Alternative Histories of Chinese Painting* (Lawrence, Kans.: Spencer Museum of Art, University of Kansas, 1988).

Before his appointment at Berkeley, he was Curator of Chinese Art at the Freer Gallery of Art in Washington, D.C. Among United States–resident art historians of Chinese painting, Professor Cahill is perhaps the best known in China, in part because several of his books have been translated into Chinese, in part because he frequently traveled to and lectured at institutions of higher learning in China. In 1977 he was Chair of the Chinese Painting Delegation to China. His writings on Chinese painting have generated much enthusiasm, as well as opposition and anger, among Chinese scholars, exactly because they differ from the standard versions of Chinese painting history, raise new issues, and make challenging arguments. An anthology of his essential writings will be published in Chinese soon.

David Carrier

David Carrier received his PhD from Columbia University in 1972 and taught at the Carnegie-Mellon University from 1973 to 2000. In 2001, he was appointed the Champney Family Professor at Case Western Reserve University and the Cleveland Institute of Art. He has been Lecturer in the Council of the Humanities and Class of 1932 Fellow in Philosophy at Princeton University, and in 1999–2000 he was a Getty Scholar. He has been a visitor in the Department of Art History (University of Auckland, New Zealand) and a visiting lecturer at the National Academy of Art (Hangzhou, China).

David Carrier's books include *Artwriting* (Amherst: University of Massachusetts Press, 1987); *Principles of Art History Writing* (University Park and London: Penn State University Press, 1991); *Poussin's Paintings: A Study in Art-Historical Methodology* (University Park and London: Penn State University Press, 1993); *The Aesthete in the City: The Philosophy and Practice of American Abstract Painting in the 1980s* (University Park and London: Penn State University Press, 1994); *High Art: Charles Baudelaire and the Origins of Modernism* (University Park and London: Penn State University Press, 1996); *The Aesthetics of the Comic Strip* (University Park and London: Penn State University Press, 2000); *Rosalind Krauss and American Philosophical Art Criticism: From Formalism to beyond Postmodernism* (Westport: Greenwood/Praeger, 2002); *Writing about Visual Art* (New York: Allworth Press, 2003); *Sean Scully* (London: Thames and Hudson, 2003); *Museum Skepticism: A History of the Display of Art in Public Galleries* (Durham: Duke University Press, 2006). He is the editor of *Nicolas Poussin: Lettere sull'arte* (Cernusco: Hestia edizione, 1995) and *England and Its Aesthetes: Biography and Taste* (Amsterdam: Gordon and Breach, 1997). His book *Principles of Art History Writing* has been translated into Chinese and published in China (Beijing: China People's University Press, 2004). His book *World*

Art History and Its Objects was published by the Penn State University Press in 2008.

David Carrier has given more than ninety lectures since 1976 at philosophy, art, and art history departments, and at art history and philosophy conventions in the United States, Canada, Europe, New Zealand, and China. And he has curated exhibitions in New York City and Pittsburgh. Since 1975 he has published more than 180 book reviews in art journals and philosophy journals, and more than 120 art reviews. He has published art criticism in such journals as *Arts Magazine, Art in America, Artforum, ArtInternational, The Burlington Magazine, Kunstchronik, Leonardo, Modern Painters,* and *Tema Celeste.* He has also published numerous exhibition catalogues for museums and commercial galleries. He is a Fulbright scholar at Tsinghua University in Beijing in 2009.

James Elkins

Since 1989, James Elkins has been teaching at the School of the Art Institute of Chicago where he is currently E. C. Chadbourne Chair and Professor in the Department of Art History, Theory, and Criticism. He also teaches in the Department of Visual and Critical Studies at the School of the Art Institute of Chicago, and was Head of History of Art at the University College Cork, Ireland.

Professor Elkins grew up in Ithaca, New York, separated from Cornell University by a quarter-mile of woods once owned by the naturalist Laurence Palmer. He stayed in Ithaca long enough to get his BA degree (in English and Art History), taking summer hitchhiking trips to Alaska, Mexico, Guatemala, the Caribbean, and Columbia. For the last twenty-five years he has lived in Chicago, where he earned a graduate degree in painting, then switched to art history, got another graduate degree, and went on to earn a PhD in art history, which he finished in 1989 (all from the University of Chicago).

His writing focuses on the history and theory of images in art, science, and nature. Some of his books are exclusively on fine art (*The Poetics of Perspectives* [Ithaca: Cornell University Press, 1994], *What Painting Is: How to Think about Oil Painting, Using the Language of Alchemy* [New York: Routledge, 1998], *Why Are Our Pictures Puzzles? On the Modern Origins of Pictorial Complexity* [New York: Routledge, 1999]). Others include scientific and non-art images and archaeology (*The Domain of Images* [Ithaca: Cornell University Press, 1999], *On Pictures and the Words That Fail Them* [Cambridge: Cambridge University Press, 1998]), and some include natural history as well (*How to Use Your Eyes* [New York: Routledge, 1999]) His *Stories of Art* (New York: Routledge, 2002) has been described by Keith Moxey (author of *The Practice of Persuasion: Paradox and Power in Art History*) as "a much needed, thoughtful, and intelligent reflection on the disciplinary status and cultural function of the history of art." Moxey adds: "*Stories of Art* is an invaluable aid in articulating the hidden agenda that informs art history as it is currently constituted, and an indispensable addition to our increasingly self-aware art historical enterprise." He is also the editor of *Master Narratives and Their Discontents* (New York: Routledge, 2005), *Photography Theory* (New York: Routledge, 2006), *Is Art History Global?* (New York: Routledge, 2007), and *Visual Literacy* (New York: Routledge, 2007).

Harold Mok

Harold Mok was educated at the University of Hong Kong, and later received his D.Phil. at the University of Oxford in 1993. He has taught Chinese art history, particularly Chinese painting and calligraphy, in the Department of Fine Arts, The Chinese University of Hong Kong, since 1989, and is at present Professor in the department and Head of the Division of Fine Arts. He received best teacher awards in 1995–1996 and 2001–2002, a D. H. Chen Foundation Fellowship from the Asian Cultural Council in 1995, and a Certificate of Commendation by the Hong Kong Government in 2005 on his contributions to the development of local art and culture.

Dr. Mok is the editor of the annual *Hong Kong Visual Arts Yearbook,* sponsored by the Hong Kong Arts Development Council, as well as several books of art history, including volume 2 of *Double Beauty: Qing Couplets from the Lechangzai Xuan Collection, Shuhai Guanlan: Collected Essays from the International Conference of Chinese Calligraphy, Xuedao Yangchen: Collected Essays of Chinese Art History,* and *Bimo Lunbian: Collected Essays on Modern Chinese Painting*. His dozens of papers cover Chinese painting, Chinese ceramics, Hong Kong art and art education, while most of them concern Chinese calligraphy from the Song to the Qing dynasty as well as Hong Kong calligraphy. He has carried out several research projects sponsored by the Competitive Earmarked Grants, the most recent ones being "A Study of the Devolution and Impact of the *Chunhua ge tie,*" "A Comprehensive Study of Song Rubbings of the *Chunhua ge tie,*" and "A Study of Calligraphy in Twentieth-Century Hong Kong."

Richard Vinograd

Richard Vinograd is Christensen Professor in Asian Art in the Department of Art & Art History at Stanford University, where he has taught since 1989. His research interests include Chinese portraiture, landscape painting and cultural geography, urban cultural spaces, painting aesthetics and theory, and media studies.

Professor Vinograd earned his PhD at the University of California at Berkeley in 1979. He taught at Columbia University and the University of Southern California, where he twice served as Chair of the Department of Art History. At Stanford, he was Chair of the Department of Art and Art History from 1995 to 2002.

He teaches a broad range of Chinese art history courses, from introductory surveys to advanced graduate seminars and colloquia. Specialized topics that intersect with his own and his students' research interests have included: Gendered Narratives in Later Chinese Pictorial Arts; Cultural Spaces in Late Ming China; Contemporary Chinese Art; Across Cultures: Encounters of Eastern and Western Art; Landscapes, Geographies, Ideologies: Inter-Cultural Perspectives; Cultural Sensibilities in Ming Dynasty China; Nineteenth-Century Painting in Shanghai; Topics in Song Period Painting; Liao Painting and Representations of Gender and Technology; Late Ming Woodblock Illustrated Books; and Chinese Cultures of Collecting.

His current teaching and research interests circulate around issues of cultural space and media studies in late imperial China. He is interested in exploring the emergence of cultural arenas as substantially independent and active components of social life in and after late Ming Dynasty China, set comparatively against the experience of early modern Europe. The role of woodblock printed pictures and publishing in the formation of public spheres of cultural production, and the emergence of urban centers as environments for pictorial art are other aspects of this large problematic.

He is the author of *Boundaries of the Self: Chinese Portraits, 1600–1900* (Cambridge: Cambridge University Press, 1992), the co-editor of *New Understandings of Ming and Qing Painting*, catalogue of a special exhibition held at the Central Academy of Fine Arts in Beijing, China (Shanghai: Shanghai Calligraphy Painting Publishing House, 1994), and the co-author of *Chinese Art & Culture* (New York: Prentice Hall and Harry N. Abrams, 2001). He has also written numerous journal articles, anthology essays, conference papers, and catalogue essays on topics ranging from tenth-century landscape to contemporary transnational arts.

Select Bibliography

African Art Studies: The State of the Discipline. Washington, D.C.: National Museum of African Art, 1990.

Asiatic Art in the Museum of Fine Arts, Boston. Boston: Museum of Fine Arts, 1982.

Bakewell, Elizabeth, William O. Beeman, and Carol McMichael Reese. *Object, Image, Inquiry: The Art Historian at Work*. Santa Monica, Calif.: The Getty Art History Information Program, 1988.

Barnhart, Richard. *Wintry Forests, Old Trees: Some Landscape Themes in Chinese Painting*. New York: China House Gallery, China Institute in America, 1972.

Barnhart, Richard, James Cahill, and Howard Rogers. *The Barnhart-Cahill-Rogers Correspondence, 1981*. Berkeley: Institute of East Asian Studies, University of California, 1982.

Barnhart, Richard, with Mary Ann Rogers and Richard Stanley-Baker. *Painters of the Great Ming: The Imperial Court and the Zhe School*. Dallas: Dallas Museum of Art, 1993.

Barnhart, Richard, and others. *Three Thousand Years of Chinese Painting*. New Haven: Yale University Press; Beijing: Foreign Languages Press, 1997.

Boone, Elizabeth Hill, ed. *Collecting the Pre-Columbian Past*. Washington, D.C.: Dumbarton Oaks Research Library and Collection, 1993.

Brown, Claudia, and Ju-hsi Chou. *Transcending Turmoil: Painting at the Close of China's Empire, 1796–1911*. Phoenix: Phoenix Art Museum, 1992.

Bush, Susan, and Hsio-yen Shih, eds. *Early Chinese Texts on Painting*. Cambridge, Mass.: Harvard University Press, 1985.

Cahill, James. *Chinese Painting*. Geneva: Editions d'Art Albert Skira, 1960.

_____. *Chinese Paintings, XI–XIV Centuries*. New York: Crown Publishers, 1962.

_____. *Fantastics and Eccentrics in Chinese Painting*. New York: The Asia Society, 1967; distributed by Harry N. Abrams, New York.

_____, ed. *The Restless Landscape: Chinese Painting of the Late Ming Period*. Berkeley: University Art Museum, 1971.

_____. *Hills beyond a River: Chinese Painting of the Yüan Dynasty, 1279–1368*. New York and Tokyo: Weatherhill, 1976.

_____. *Parting at the Shore: Chinese Painting of the Early and Middle Ming Dynasty, 1368–1580.* New York and Tokyo: Weatherhill, 1978.

_____. *An Index of Early Chinese Painters and Painting: T'ang, Sung, and Yüan.* Berkeley and Los Angeles: University of California Press, 1980.

_____, ed. *Shadows of Mt. Huang: Chinese Painting and Printing of the Anhui School.* Berkeley: University Art Museum, 1981.

_____. *The Distant Mountains: Chinese Painting of the Late Ming Dynasty, 1570–1644.* New York and Tokyo: Weatherhill, 1982.

_____. *The Compelling Image: Nature and Style in Seventeenth-Century Chinese Painting.* Cambridge, Mass.: Harvard University Press, 1982.

_____. *Three Alternative Histories of Chinese Painting.* Lawrence, Kans.: Spencer Museum of Art, The University of Kansas, 1988.

_____. *The Painter's Practice: How Artists Lived and Worked in Traditional China.* New York: Columbia University Press, 1994.

_____. *The Lyric Journey: Poetic Painting in China and Japan.* Cambridge, Mass.: Harvard University Press, 1996.

_____. "Some Thoughts on the History and Post-History of Chinese Painting." *Archives of Asian Art* 55 (2005): 17–33.

_____. "Response" to section IV, "Art Historical Methodology." In *The History of Painting in East Asia: Essays on Scholarly Method,* edited by Naomi Noble Richard and Donald E. Brix, 487–96. Taipei: Rock Publishing International, 2008.

Carrier, David. *Museum Skepticism: A History of the Display of Art in Public Galleries.* Durham, N.C.: Duke University Press, 2006.

Chang, Joseph, with Stephen D. Allee and Qianshen Bai. *In Pursuit of Heavenly Harmony: Paintings and Calligraphy by Bada Shanren from the Estate of Wang Fangyu and Sum Wai.* Washington, D.C.: The Freer Gallery of Art and The Arthur M. Sackler Gallery of Art, 2003.

Chou, Ju-hsi, ed. *Art at the Close of China's Empire.* Tempe: Arizona State University, 1998.

Clapp, Anne de Courcey. *The Painting of T'ang Yin.* Chicago: University of Chicago Press, 1991.

Clunas, Craig. *Superfluous Things: Material Culture and Social Status in Early Modern China.* Cambridge: Polity, 1991.

_____. "Oriental Antiquities/Far Eastern Art." *Positions: East Asian Cultures Critiques* 2, no. 2 (Fall 1994): 318–57

_____. *Fruitful Sites: Garden Culture in Ming Dynasty China.* Durham, N.C.: Duke University Press, 1996.

_____. *Pictures and Visuality in Early Modern China.* Princeton: Princeton University Press, 1997.

_____. "What about Chinese Art?" In *Views of Difference, Different Views of Art*, edited by Catherine King, 121–41. New Haven: Yale University Press, 1999.

_____. "Social Art History." In *Critical Terms for Art History*, second edition, edited by Robert S. Nelson and Richard Shiff, 465–77. Chicago: University of Chicago Press, 2003.

_____. "The *Admonitions* Scroll in the Eighteenth, Nineteenth and Twentieth Centuries: Discussant's Remarks." In *Gu Kaizhi and the* Admonitions *Scroll*, edited by Shane McCausland, 295–98. London: British Museum Press in association with Percival David Foundation of Chinese Art, 2003.

_____. *Elegant Debts: The Social Art of Wen Zhengming, 1470–1559*. Honolulu: University of Hawaii Press, 2004.

Cohen, Paul A. *China Unbound: Evolving Perspectives on the Chinese Past*. London and New York: RoutledgeCurzon, 2003.

Cohen, Warren I. *East Asian Art and American Culture: A Study in International Relations*. New York: Columbia University Press, 1992.

Culler, Jonathan. *Literary Theory: A Very Short Introduction*. Oxford: Oxford University Press, 1997.

Easton, David, and Corrinne S. Schelling, eds. *Divided Knowledge: Across Disciplines, Across Cultures*. London: SAGE Publications, in cooperation with the American Academy of Arts and Sciences, 1991.

Edwards, Richard. *The Field of Stones: A Study of the Art of Shen Chou (1427–1509)*. Washington, D.C.: Freer Gallery of Art, 1962.

_____. *Li Ti*. Washington, D.C.: Freer Gallery of Art, 1967.

_____. *The World around the Chinese Artist: Aspects of Realism in Chinese Painting*. Ann Arbor: University of Michigan Press, 1989.

Edwards, Richard, and others. *The Painting of Tao-chi*. Ann Arbor: The University of Michigan Museum of Art, 1967.

_____ and others. *The Art of Wen Cheng-ming (1470–1559)*. Ann Arbor: The University of Michigan Museum of Art, 1976.

Edwards, Steve, ed. *Art and Its Histories*. New Haven and London: Yale University Press, 1999.

Fong, Wen C. *The Lohans and a Bridge to Heaven*. Washington, D.C.: The Freer Gallery of Art, 1958.

_____. *Beyond Representation: Early Chinese Painting and Calligraphy, 8th to 14th Centuries*. New York: The Metropolitan Museum of Art, 1992.

_____. *Between Two Cultures: Late-Nineteenth- and Twentieth-Century Chinese Paintings from the Robert H. Ellsworth Collection in the Metropolitan Museum of Art*. New York: The Metropolitan Museum of Art, 2001.

Fong, Wen C., and Judith G. Smith, eds. *Issues of Authenticity in Chinese Painting*. New York: Department of Asian Art, The Metropolitan Museum of Art, 1999.

Fong, Wen C., and James Watt, with contributions by Richard M. Barnhart and others. *Possessing the Past: Treasures from the National Palace Museum, Taipei*. New York: The Metropolitan Museum of Art, 1996.

Fong, Wen C., et al. *Chinese Calligraphy*. New Haven: Yale University Press; Beijing: Foreign Languages Press, 2008.

Harrist, Robert E. *Painting and Private Life in Eleventh-Century China:* Mountain Villa *by Li Gonglin*. Princeton: Princeton University Press, 1998.

_____. "A Response to Professor Cahill's 'Some Thoughts on the History and Post-History of Chinese Painting.'" *Archives of Asian Art* 55 (2005): 35–37.

Harrist, Robert E., and Wen C. Fong, with contributions by Bai Qianshen and others. *The Embodied Image: Chinese Calligraphy from the John B. Elliott Collection*. Princeton: Art Museum, Princeton University in association with Harry N. Abrams, 1999.

Hearn, Maxwell K. *How to Read Chinese Painting*. New York: The Metropolitan Museum of Art, 2008.

_____, ed. *Landscapes Clear and Radiant: The Art of Wang Hui (1632–1717)*. New York: The Metropolitan Museum of Art, 2008.

Hearn, Maxwell K., and Wen C. Fong. *Along the Riverbank: Chinese Painting from the C. C. Wang Family Collection*. New York: The Metropolitan Museum of Art, 1999; distributed by Harry N. Abrams, New York.

Ho, Wai-kam, ed. *The Century of Tung Ch'i-ch'ang, 1555–1636*. Kansas City, Mo.: The Nelson-Atkins Museum of Art in association with University of Washington Press, Seattle and London, 1992.

Jiang Zhaoshen. *Gugong canghua jieti*. Taipei: National Palace Museum, 1968.

_____. *Wupaihua jiushinian zhan*. Taipei: National Palace Museum, 1975.

Kuo, Jason C. [Guo Jisheng]. *Wang Yuanqi de shanshuihua yishu*. Taipei: National Palace Museum, 1981.

_____, ed. *Meigan yu zaoxing*. Taipei: Lianjing chuban, 1982.

_____. *Long tiandi yu xingnei*. Taipei: Shibao wenhua, 1986.

_____. *The Austere Landscape: The Paintings of Hung-jen*. Taipei and New York: SMC Publishing in cooperation with University of Washington Press, Seattle and London, 1990.

_____, ed. *Luo Qing huaji*. Taipei: Dongda tushu, 1990.

_____, ed. *Dangdai Taiwan huihua wenxuan, 1945–1990*. Taipei: Xiongshi tushu, 1991.

_____. *Word as Image: The Art of Chinese Seal Engraving.* New York: China House Gallery, China Institute in America; distributed by University of Washington Press, Seattle and London, 1992.

_____. *Zhuang Zhe, 1991–92.* Taipei: Longmen hualang, 1992.

_____, ed. *Heirs to a Great Tradition: Modern Chinese Painting from the Tsien-hsiang-chai Collection.* College Park, Md.: Department of Art History and Archaeology, University of Maryland; distributed by University of Washington Press, Seattle and London, 1993.

_____. *Cuo wanwu yu biduan.* Taipei: Dongda tushu, 1994.

_____. *Chen Qikuan.* Taipei: Jinxiu chuban shiye, 1995.

_____, ed. *Taiwan shijue wenhua, 1975–1995.* Taipei: Yishujia chubanshe, 1995.

_____. *Yishushi yu yishu piping de tansuo.* Taipei: National Museum of History, 1996.

_____. *Art and Cultural Politics in Postwar Taiwan.* Bethesda, Md.: CDL Press; distributed by University of Washington Press, Seattle and London, 2000.

_____. *Yishushi yu yishu piping de shijian.* Taipei: National Museum of History, 2002.

_____. *Transforming Traditions in Modern Chinese Painting: Huang Pin-hung's Late Work.* Berlin and New York: Peter Lang Publishing, 2004.

_____, ed. *Discovering Chinese Painting: Dialogues with Art Historians.* Dubuque: Kendall/Hunt Publishing, 2006.

_____, ed. *Visual Culture in Shanghai, 1850s–1930s.* Washington, D.C.: New Academia Publishing, 2007.

_____, ed. *Perspectives on Connoisseurship of Chinese Painting.* Washington, D.C.: New Academia Publishing, 2008.

_____, ed. *Xiandai Zhongguo yuefenpai: Lishu, yishu, yu wenhua.* Taipei: SMC Publishing, forthcoming.

Kuo, Jason C. [Guo Jisheng], and Peter Sturman, eds. *Double Beauty: Qing Dynasty Couplets from the Lechangzai Xuan Collection.* Hong Kong: Art Museum, Chinese University of Hong Kong, 2003.

Laing, Ellen Johnston. *Chinese Paintings in Chinese Publications, 1956–1968: Annotated Bibliography and an Index to the Paintings.* Ann Arbor: Center for Chinese Studies, University of Michigan, 1968.

_____. *The Winking Owl: Art in the People's Republic of China.* Berkeley and Los Angeles: University of California Press, 1988.

_____. *An Index to Reproductions of Paintings by Twentieth-Century Chinese Artists*, rev. ed. Ann Arbor: Center for Chinese Studies, University of Michigan, 1998.

Li, Chu-tsing. *The Autumn Colors on the Ch'iao and Hua Mountains: A Landscape by Chao Meng-fu.* Ascona: Artibus Asiae, 1965.

Li, Chu-tsing, with James Cahill and Wai-kam Ho, eds. *Artists and Patrons: Some Social and Economic Aspects of Chinese Painting.* Lawrence, Kans.: The Kress Foundation Department of Art History, University of Kansas and The Nelson-Atkins Museum of Art, Kansas City, Mo., in association with University of Washington Press, Seattle and London, 1989.

Murray, Julia K. *A Decade of Discovery: Selected Acquisitions, 1970–1980.* Washington, D.C.: Freer Gallery of Art, 1979.

_____. *Last of the Mandarins: Chinese Calligraphy and Painting from the F. Y. Chang Collection.* Cambridge, Mass.: Arthur M. Sackler Museum, Harvard University Art Museums, 1987.

_____. *Ma Hezhi and the Illustration of the Book of Odes.* Cambridge: Cambridge University Press, 1993.

Powers, Martin J. *Art and Political Expression in Early China.* New Haven: Yale University Press, 1991.

_____. "Art and History: Exploring the Counterchange Condition." *The Art Bulletin* 77, no. 3 (September 1995): 382–86.

Preziosi, Donald, ed. *The Art of Art History: A Critical Anthology.* Oxford: Oxford University Press, 1998.

Saussy, Haun. *Great Walls of Discourse and Other Adventures in Cultural China.* Cambridge, Mass.: Harvard University Asia Center, 2001.

Silbergeld, Jerome. *Chinese Painting Style: Media, Methods, and Principles of Form.* Seattle and London: University of Washington Press, 1982.

_____. *Mind Landscape: The Paintings of C. C. Wang.* Seattle: Henry Art Gallery, University of Washington and University of Washington Press, Seattle and London, 1987.

_____. *China into Film: Frames of References in Contemporary Chinese Cinema.* London: Reaktion Books, 1999.

_____. *Hitchcock with a Chinese Face: Cinematic Doubles, Oedipal Triangles, and China's Moral Voice*. Seattle and London: University of Washington Press, 2004.

_____. "The Evolution of a 'Revolution': Unsettled Reflections on the Chinese Art-Historical Mission." *Archives of Asian Art* 55 (2005): 39–52.

_____. "Changing Views of Change: The Song-Yuan Transition in Chinese Painting Histories." In *Asian Art History in the Twenty-first Century,* edited by Vishaka N, Desai, 40–63. Williamstown, Mass.: Sterling and Francine Clark Art Institute, 2007.

Silbergeld, Jerome, with Gong Jisui. *Contradictions: Artistic Life, the Socialist State, and the Chinese Painter Li Huasheng*. Seattle and London: University of Washington Press, 1993.

Smith, Judith G., and Wen C. Fong, eds. *Issues of Authenticity in Chinese Painting.* New York: Department of Asian Art, The Metropolitan Museum of Art, 1999.

Smyth, Craig Hugh, and Peter M. Lukehart, eds. *The Early Years of Art History in the United States: Notes and Essays on Departments, Teaching, and Scholars.* Princeton: Department of Art and Archaeology, Princeton University, 1993.

Steadman, John M. *The Myth of Asia.* New York: Simon and Schuster, 1969.

Sullivan, Michael. *Chinese Art in the Twentieth Century.* With a Foreword by Herbert Read. London: Faber & Faber, 1959; Berkeley and Los Angeles: University of California Press, 1959.

_____. *The Birth of Landscape Painting in China.* London: Routledge & Kegan Paul, 1962.

_____. *Symbols of Eternity: The Art of Landscape Painting in China.* Stanford: Stanford University Press, 1978.

_____. *The Three Perfections: Chinese Painting, Poetry and Calligraphy.* New York: George Braziller, 1980.

_____. *Art and Artists of Twentieth-Century China.* Berkeley and Los Angeles: University of California Press, 1996.

_____. *The Arts of China.* Fifth ed. Berkeley and Los Angeles: University of California Press, 2008.

_____. *The Meeting of Eastern and Western Art.* Revised and expanded ed. Berkeley and Los Angeles: University of California Press, 1997.

_____. *The Three Perfections: Chinese Painting, Poetry, and Calligraphy.* Revised, second ed. New York: George Braziller, 1999.

_____. *The Night Entertainment of Han Xiza: A Scroll by Gu Hongzhong.* Berkeley and Los Angeles: University of California Press, 2008.

Vinograd, Richard. *Boundaries of the Self: Chinese Portraits, 1600–1900.* Cambridge: Cambridge University Press, 1992

_____. "Art Historical Topologies." *The Art Bulletin* 76, no. 3 (December 1994): 593–95.

Vinograd, Richard, James Cahill, and Xue Yongnian, eds. *New Interpretations of Ming and Qing Paintings.* Shanghai: Shanghai shuhua chubanshe, 1994.

Vinograd, Richard, and Robert Thorp. *Chinese Art & Culture.* New York: Harry N. Abrams, 2001.

Wang, Fangyu, and Richard Barnhart. *Master of the Lotus Garden: The Life and Art of Bada Shanren (1626–1705).* Edited by Judith G. Smith. New Haven: Yale University Art Gallery and Yale University Press, 1990.

Whitfield, Roderick. *In Pursuit of Antiquity: Chinese Paintings of the Ming and Ch'ing Dynasties from the Collection of Mr. and Mrs. Earl Morse.* Princeton: Art Museum, Princeton University, 1969.

Wu, Hung. *The Wu Liang Shrine: The Ideology of Early Chinese Pictorial Art.* Stanford: Stanford University Press, 1989.

_____. *Monumentality in Early Chinese Art and Architecture.* Stanford: Stanford University Press, 1995.

_____. *The Double Screen: Medium and Representation in Chinese Painting.* Chicago: University of Chicago Press, 1996.

_____. *Transience: Chinese Experience Art at the End of the Twentieth Century.* Chicago: The David and Alfred Smart Museum of Art, University of Chicago, 1999.

Ye Weilian [Wai-lim Yip]. *Yü dangdai yishujia de duihua: Zhongguo xiandaihua de shengcheng*. Taipei: Dongda tushu, 1987.

Index